A+ ALBUMS
The Stories Behind
50 Rock Classics (Vol. I)
1970-1982

A+ ALBUMS

The Stories Behind
50 Rock Classics (Vol. I)
1970-1982

By Greg Prato

Written by Greg Prato
Printed and distributed by Greg Prato Writer, Corp
Published by Greg Prato Writer, Corp
Front cover design by Mary Prato
Back cover photo by Bill O'Leary
Copyright © 2022, Greg Prato Writer, Corp. All rights reserved.
First Edition, October 2022

ISBN: 9798358320239

Intro

"What are the greatest rock albums of all-time?" Perhaps one of the more common questions examined between music-loving chums, that has led to many a good-natured debate. But if you really dig deeper into the question...is it from the standpoint of the album's importance in rock history? A classic release that proved significant to an artist's career? Or perhaps merely a personal favorite, that you just can't get enough of? While assembling the book you are now committed to, I took all three of these pointers into consideration while painstakingly trying to whittle it down to 50 entries that spanned 1970-1982 (in "Vol. I"), and an additional 50 that spanned 1982-2000 (in "Vol. II") of *A + Albums*.

Additionally, while attempting to cover all the expected classics, I have included a few surprises and/or uncommon albums by renowned artists that I felt were just as good as their better-known selections. And admittedly, a few big names are nowhere to be found (the Who, Lynyrd Skynyrd, Bruce Springsteen, Motörhead, the Clash, etc.), but again, space was limited. And besides, who knows...if these books become big hits, perhaps it will inspire me to assemble future volumes and cover *all* the bases!

The set-up is simple – set in chronological order vis-à-vis release date, each entry contains a brief artist history, where the album fits in their history, an analyzation of the material, and in most cases, quotes from either the artist or someone associated with the recording, and/or a renowned admirer (as well as chart placements and certifications, where applicable). Also, the vast majority of entries are newly-penned for this book, but a few are reprints of earlier articles I assembled for magazines or sites (but don't fret – I've listed where/when they originally appeared).

And while I still have your attention, a few additional points need to be made. Firstly, it's remarkable to see just how much rock music changed in this twelve-year span (if you were to gaze at the complete list of the albums in this book, which you can find in the handy "Contents" section). Secondly, if you are not familiar with an album included within, by all means, feel free to discover/inspect it – I have a hunch you'll enjoy it! And thirdly, just for the record, if there are quotes from others included in an entry, I'd estimate that there is a 90-95% chance that it was from an interview conducted by yours truly (from either an article I penned for a site/mag, or from one of my books).

Lastly (and I admit, the following is a semi-shameless plug), if you find yourself getting a kick out of *Vol. I* or *Vol. II*, I have two earlier books that would serve as solid follow-up reads/listens – *Facts on Tracks: Stories Behind 100 Rock Classics* and *Overlooked/Underappreciated: 354 Recordings That Demand Your Attention.*

So now that we've gotten all that pre-emptive chatter out of the way, it's time to discover, learn more about, or become reacquainted with some of the very best rock recordings of all-time…with Greg Prato as your guide!

Catch the spirit/catch the spit,
Greg Prato

p.s. Questions? Comments? Feel free to email me at gregprato@yahoo.com

Contents

Black Sabbath
(Black Sabbath, 1970)

Satanic imagery. Doomsday lyrics. Detuned riffs. Plodding tempos. *Pure metal magic*. It's not a common occurrence to be able to single out one album that may be responsible for launching an entire genre of music. But Black Sabbath's self-titled debut just may be one of the chosen few – as it was arguably the first rock album that could truly be classified as "heavy metal."

Flower power and lyrics about peace, love, and understanding permeated throughout society around the dawn of the 1970s. So looking back, there was a void that needed to be filled – for a hard rock band to tackle much darker subject matter. And four lads from Birmingham, England were just the right men for the job – equipped with doomsday lyrics, detuned riffs, and plodding tempos.

Comprised of Ozzy Osbourne (vocals), Tony Iommi (guitar), Geezer Butler (bass), and Bill Ward (drums), Black Sabbath originally formed in 1968. After going through a few names (including Earth), and Iommi briefly serving as a member of Jethro Tull (check out Tull's performance on the Rolling Stones' *Rock and Roll Circus* to spot Iommi), the band settled on the now world-renowned Black Sabbath moniker – nicking it from the title of a horror flick from 1963, starring Boris Karloff.

The band attracted the attention of Vertigo Records, who signed Sabbath in 1969 and sent them off to Regent Sound Studios in London to record what would be their debut album – with producer Rodger Bain overseeing the sessions. Since the songs had been performed in front of audiences and already fine-tuned, the album was recorded live (rather than one instrument at time) and quite rapidly.

"*Black Sabbath*, we recorded in 12 hours, believe it or not," Ozzy said in an interview from 1981 on the *After Hours* TV show. "The whole thing was done in 12 hours – on an eight-track machine in a little backstreet studio in London. It cost like…10 bucks to make or something." Released on February 13th, 1970 in the UK (June 1st in the United States), the tracklist on the North American version did not exactly mirror the one that Europeans had received

– which will be discussed in a bit. For now, we'll stick with discussing the North American version.

Kicking things off was the song "Black Sabbath." If you were to try and pinpoint a single song that may have birthed heavy metal, then "Black Sabbath" would be a wise pick. Beginning with the sound of a thunderstorm and the ominous tolling of a bell, one of Iommi's great guitar riffs is soon unveiled before the song dials down the volume to focus on its lyrics, which paint the picture of what doomsday would probably be like (including the now-classic line, "*Oh no, no, please God help me!*"). But three-quarters of the way through, all the plodding gives way to a speedier tempo, plus another killer guitar riff and a guitar solo.

Up next, we are greeted by an instrument that would never be featured (to the best of my knowledge) again on a Sabbath recording – harmonica – which kicks off another classic, "The Wizard." And now would be a perfect time to discuss another element that made Sabbath stick out from the rest of the pack – they were one of the first rock bands to include Satanic imagery in both their lyrics and album packaging ("Satan's coming 'round the bend" is sung in the title tune, while "The Wizard," can be construed about being about black magic, as well as the record label deciding to feature an upside down cross design when the LP's gatefold sleeve was opened).

You know you have a classic on your hands when even the lesser-known tunes would top most of the competition's best efforts, and that is the case here with the largely-forgotten/overlooked "Behind the Wall of Sleep" (which contains the decidedly anti-hippie dippie lyric, "Sleeping wall of remorse/Turns your body to a corpse"). But another bona fide metal classic is lurking right around the corner, with "N.I.B."

Some have taken guesses at what the mysterious initials stand for, but it turns out that it was a goof on Ward's goatee (which resembled a "nib" – or the pointy part – of a pen). Featuring another one of Iommi's best guitar riffs, the lyrics also include mention of ol' Beelzebub, to boot ("Look into my eyes, you'll see who I am/My name is Lucifer, please take my hand"). Additionally, the song featured an intro of sorts, titled "Bassically," which was one of the first-ever unaccompanied bass solos on a metal album (Butler's bouncy bass would serve as an influence on countless subsequent metal bassists – especially the late, great Cliff Burton).

Admittedly, it appears as though the Sabs front-loaded their debut with all their best tunes, as the second side features a pair of tunes that focus more on the band's penchant for jamming rather than ripping your scalp off with behemoth riffs. First up was the tune "Wicked World," which admittedly does contain a mighty riff, but not on par with the likes of "Black Sabbath" or "N.I.B."

Closing things is the album's longest tune – the nearly 15-minute long "A Bit of Finger/Sleeping Village/Warning," which sounds at times like its main purpose was to serve as a space-filler – especially when the song stops dead in its tracks about 10 minutes in, and Iommi begins an unaccompanied solo (which lasts for nearly three minutes!). Lastly, for reasons unknown, Europe was treated to an extra tune (a cover of Crow's "Evil Woman," which kicked off Side B), that would not be included on Stateside pressings.

And the cherry on top of the Satanic sundae was the album's front cover – a mysteriously, shadowy, witchy figure standing amongst leaves and trees, in front of a watermill (to be precise, it is Mapledurham Watermill, located in Oxfordshire, England), which has gone on to become one of the most iconic album cover images in all of metal history.

Straight away, *Black Sabbath* was a hit – cracking the top-10 in the UK (peaking at #8), while eventually reaching a respectable #23 in the States, and being certified gold and platinum in the respected aforementioned regions…and setting the stage for Sabbath to become one of the top metal bands of the '70s. However, Iommi recounted in his 2011 book, *Iron Man*, that the debut – nor the band – was beloved early on.

"The press hated us, and we got slagged left, right, and center. You obviously got concerned, but it's not like we thought, oh, we're going to change the music then. The album was selling, so obviously we'd done something right. We believed in what we did and we loved it, so there was nothing else we could do apart from carry on what we were doing. Only when grunge became popular, and all those musicians said that Black Sabbath was a great influence, did we become flavor of the month, or the flavor of the time."

But looking back on the album a half century later, there is no denying its influence – name just about every major metal band, and there is an element of early Sabbath that can be detected. Heck, this era of the band would also later spawn at least two sub-genres – doom metal and stoner metal (and possibly a third, as Iommi just stated…grunge). And that my friends, is why *Black Sabbath* remains an all-time metal classic.

Let It Be
(The Beatles, 1970)

It's easy to be fooled into believing that *Let It Be* was the last studio album ever recorded by the Beatles – especially after viewing the film of the same name, and later, the epic *Get Back* documentary, which seems to be detailing the band's split up amidst tension and general unhappiness. But as many well-versed fans of the Fab Four know, while this was apparently a rough patch for John, Paul, George, and Ringo, it was *not* the end of the Beatles. It turns out that the sessions for *Let It Be* wrapped in January 1969, while the recording of *Abbey Road* would take place from February through August of '69. But…*Abbey Road* would hit the shops almost a full year before *Let It Be* arrived.

Originally titled *Get Back,* the album was to be a return to the group's earlier, more straight-forward direction – without all the extra/added production bits. "They were going to get back to their roots," explained Beatles expert Brian Kehew in the book *John Winston Ono Lennon.* "They got tired of all the flanging and overdubs. 'We are a rock band. We used to play in the Cavern. Let's get back to that style.' So, the *Get Back* project later turned into *Let It Be* – with overdubs. But the concept was to strip it back to their early days."

The initial idea was to film the band in rehearsal at Twickenham Film Studios in London, during January 1969 (for a planned live performance by the band – which would have been their first since August 29, 1966 at Candlestick Park in San Francisco). But as seen in the footage that would eventually comprise the *Let It Be* and *Get Back* films…it floundered, as it appeared as though the members were simply not enjoying each other's company much anymore. "I think Yoko Ono has unfairly become the scapegoat for the Beatles breaking up," added original Dream Theater drummer Mike Portnoy in the same *John Winston Ono Lennon* book. "But realistically, the Beatles didn't break up until after *Abbey Road.* People see a lot of the stuff in the *Let It Be* movie – Yoko hanging around the studio. I don't think she ever asked for that – I think it was John including her."

"So, if anything, you have to put a lot of that stuff on John. If you have resentment over Yoko being there, I don't know if it's necessarily fair to aim it at her. I think it was John that wanted her included, and John was looking for a new partner at that point in his life, because the Beatles were so fragmented. But again, if you watch *Let It Be,* yes, Yoko's presence there is a little strange, but you can really see that the band was falling apart for its own reason. Ringo left during *The White Album* and George left the band during the making of *Let It Be...*or *Get Back.* So, it was already falling apart – regardless of Yoko being there. And at that point, you have to remember that Linda was also newly wed to Paul, as well. I think it's unfair to point any of the blame at her, specifically."

A wise decision was made for the band to relocate to Apple Studio (located at 3 Savile Row in London) – with keyboardist Billy Preston joining in on the fun, and producer George Martin and engineer Glyn Johns overseeing the sessions – and the dark cloud that seemingly hung over the band at Twickenham dissipated. Recording sessions took place inside the studio, and famously, *on top of it.* "It was in January or February of '69 that I got sent down by Apple to do the *Let It Be* sessions," recalled engineer Alan Parsons (yes, *the same* Alan Parsons from the Alan Parsons Project) in a *Songfacts* interview from 2019. "It was pretty intimidating. I walk into a control room, and there's all four Beatles, George Martin, Glyn Johns, and Yoko Ono. I walk in and say, 'Hello! I've come to help!' They were all a bit long faced, but thank goodness, it all improved a bit when the 'rooftop day' came and we recorded them on the roof. It made an enormous difference to the enthusiasm that they had for the songs."

Ah yes, the now-legendary "rooftop performance." Instead of playing a one-off show at a stadium or in a television studio, the lads opted to perform atop Apple Studio on January 30th, with a film crew documenting the performance and professionally recording the audio. "It was brilliant," remembers Parsons, who also found himself atop the roof. "It was a great day, but there was an undertone of disappointment because I thought it would probably be the last time they'd play together as a band, in front of an audience. But it was a great day. A very cold day."

The majority of the eventual *Let It Be* album would be comprised of Lennon-McCartney compositions, and started with a rather breezy, barebones number, "Two of Us," which starts with Lennon exclaiming the mysterious phrase, "'I Dig a Pygmy' by Charles Hawtrey and the Deaf-Aids! Phase one, in which Doris gets her oats!" But it wasn't until the second number, "Dig a Pony," in which it truly sounds like the Beatles stripped down *and* rocking – and was one of the few tunes on the album that was utilized from the rooftop performance. And seemingly from out of nowhere, the "psychedelic Beatles" magically reappear for "Across the Universe," and with good reason – the basic track was recorded all the way back in February of '68 (which even predates the sessions for *The White Album* by a few months).

The George Harrison-penned and sung "I Me Mine" sounds exactly like the melodic type of tune you'd expect from the guitarist from this era, and was one of two tunes on the album not to have been recorded either in or atop Apple in January of '69...but rather, via two different sessions in January and April 1970 (at EMI in London). A tune that sounds like it was written on the spot follows, "Dig It," and provides a bit of filler...before the album's best tune. Of course, I'm talking about the title track, which lyrically, mentions McCartney's late mother by first name ("Mary," as in Mary Patricia McCartney) and certainly serves as one of the Beatles' most moving and emotional compositions ever.

Another throwaway, the blink-and-it's-over "Maggie May" lasts for a mere 40 seconds, before the awesome rocker "I've Got a Feeling" follows – which sees McCartney and Lennon take turns singing, while Preston's organ adds a new element to the Beatles sound (also taken from the rooftop performance). And there's a reason why the next tune, "One After 909," sounds like an old-time rock n' roller – it was supposedly penned by Lennon way back when he was 17 (which would have been circa 1957) – with the "909" representing the number of a train, or, perhaps its arrival

time. And like "Dig a Pony" and "I've Got a Feeling," it was the live rooftop performance version that made the cut for the album.

The description "schmaltz" is not one you'd often associate with the Beatles, but "The Long and Winding Road" certainly fits in that category – due to the addition of a symphony and a female choir. But in the group's defense, the over-the-top production was not their decision, but rather, Phil Spector (more on him and how he got involved in the project in a bit). An additional fine Harrison tune follows, "For You Blue," before another one of the album's top standouts, "Get Back," closes the album – once more featuring great keyboard work from Preston.

So, while the majority of the material for *Let It Be* was recorded in January of 1969, it sat on a shelf for over a year, before Spector was invited to make sense of the project, and apparently took it upon himself to not credit Martin as producer (despite Sir George overseeing much of the material recorded before Spector entered the picture). As a result, it solely lists Spector as the album's producer. Finally seeing its release on May 8, 1970 (and with a cover that featured close-up photos of all four of the members' faces, in their own designated square), *Let It Be* was another worldwide smash hit for the band. The album would top the US and UK album charts, while "Get Back," "Let It Be," and "The Long and Winding Road" were issued as singles, and all hit #1 in the US.

The accompanying film, also titled *Let It Be*, would be issued on May 13, 1970, directed by Michael Lindsay-Hogg, before Peter Jackson was able to get a hold of all the January 1969 footage, and assembled a simple *behemoth* of a documentary, *Get Back*, which ran for nearly eight hours (!), and was premiered via Disney+ from November 25-27, 2021. "I am in the new movie," Parsons proudly told me during an interview for *BraveWords* in 2022. "I was not in the *Let It Be* version. I met Peter Jackson about a year ago and he showed me some clips – which I was delighted about. He not only played those clips in the movie, but he put my name on the screen and the credit as 'tape operator.' Fame at last on the Beatles!"

"There are some scenes when I'm in the basement with a tape machine, and other still shots when I'm on the roof [when the Beatles perform]. I think the new film is great. I think it's too long. We saw a screening that Peter Jackson had put together in Hollywood before the release, and I thought that was perfect – about an hour and a half and had all the highlights and the whole concert on the roof. It was perfect."

However, by the time the *Let It Be* LP and film were released, the Beatles were no more – on April 10, 1970, it was announced that the band had split up (via McCartney in an interview). Over the years, *Let It Be* would be issued as several different configurations – perhaps the most interesting one being 2003's *Let It Be...Naked*, which stripped away all of Spector's heavy-handed production (with three gents now earning production credits: Paul Hicks, Guy Massey, and Allan Rouse) and brings the material back to its original, true essence. And on October 15, 2021, an expanded box set of the album was released, *Let It Be: Special Edition*, which included the Phil Spector "original album," a Glyn Johns "1969 *Get Back* mix," and a brand new remix from Giles Martin (George's son), plus other assorted goodies.

Paranoid
(Black Sabbath, 1970)

The "sophomore slump" has spelt the beginning of the end for quite a few rock acts over the years. But looking back, one of the cases in which the exact opposite occurred was when Black Sabbath delivered one of the greatest metal albums of all time, *Paranoid*.

The Birmingham, UK-based band – singer Ozzy Osbourne, guitarist Tony Iommi, bassist Geezer Butler, and drummer Bill Ward – had already caught the attention of rock fans with their detuned and doomy self-titled debut (released in February 1970 in the UK, and June in the United States). And they wasted no time capitalizing on the buzz – issuing *Paranoid* in the UK in September of that year (it would arrive in the States in January 1971). While Sabbath amazingly knocked out the recording of their debut album in a single day, they would take a bit longer on the follow-up. No, we're not talking Def Leppard or Guns N' Roses lengths…this time, they took five days (June 16-21), utilizing the same recording studio (Regent Sound) and producer (Roger Bain) as its predecessor.

Although the debut is rightfully considered one of metal's all-time great debuts, Sabbath really upped their ante on their second LP – offering up an all-killer-no-filler effort. Few rock or metal albums have featured such a stellar side one as *Paranoid* did, kicking things off with "War Pigs." The nearly eight-minute-long track remains one of the most venomous anti-war songs in rock history (perhaps only matched by "Fortunate Son" by Creedence Clearwater Revival) – with lyrics that merge the politics of war along with Satanic shout-outs (particularly "Generals gathered in their masses/Just like witches at black masses" and "On their knees the war pigs crawling/Begging mercies for their sins/Satan laughing, spreads his wings").

Speaking to *Heavy Consequence*, former Queens of the Stone Age/Screaming Trees singer Mark Lanegan explained the significance of hearing "War Pigs" for the first time. "I first heard Black Sabbath as a teenager. There was a kid in my high school who had his own apartment – he was from another town, had to leave. It was odd that this kid lived on his own. But he played 'War Pigs' for me, and I made him play it five hours straight. It just blew my mind. I was completely floored."

"War Pigs" is followed by the album's iconic title track, a last minute addition to the album. The song's speedy power chords, fuzzed-out guitar solo, and succinct length (clocking in at a mere 2:48) stand out from the rest of the LP, offering a proto-punk vibe. "Paranoid" has gone on to become one of Sabbath's most popular tunes – serving as their first true hit single (climbing within the top-5 on the singles charts of seven countries). And it turns out that another gent that knows a thing or two about composing metal classics, Iron Maiden bassist Steve Harris, was inspired by the song way back when. "I remember playing the song 'Paranoid' itself, and I remember really struggling with it, and throwing the guitar down," Harris recalled to *Heavy Consequence*. "I threw it on the bed – I didn't throw it on the floor, because if I broke it, I couldn't afford to buy another one. I just learned from that thing that I've got to go back, take it as it comes, and just play when I feel like it, and not force it. And then, the riffs just came fine – after that, I was alright. But I distinctly remember that riff."

On just about every Sabbath album, a space was reserved for at least one trippy slow-paced tune, and on *Paranoid*, that is the hauntingly bare-boned "Planet Caravan," which years later would receive a closer re-inspection when Pantera surprisingly covered it on *Far Beyond Driven*. Closing the first half of the album is a tune that boasts one of metal's instantly recognizable guitar riffs – "Iron Man." The tune has gone on to influence countless musicians, including the man responsible for laying down some of the funkiest and heaviest guitar riffs ever, Tom Morello. "The first Sabbath song that I think I got turned onto was probably 'Iron Man'," the Rage Against the Machine guitarist told *Heavy Consequence*. "That was my intro. Then I bought the *Paranoid* record and lost my mind. I thought, 'There's never been music like that and that's so great.' It began my life-long love of riffs."

Kicking off side two was the oft-overlooked "Electric Funeral" – which contains a killer wah-wah'd Iommi guitar riff, and lyrics you'll never find on a Hallmark card: "Buildings crashing down to a cracking ground/Rivers turn to wood, ice melting to flood/Earth lies in death bed, clouds cry water dead/Tearing life away, here's the burning pain." "Electric Funeral" (along with the next tune) can be pinpointed to the birth of what later became known as the metal subgenre "doom metal." Because just when you thought Sabbath couldn't get darker lyrically, they manage to out-do themselves on another one of their more overlooked songs, "Hand of Doom," which lyrically contains references to both Vietnam and drug addiction. Next, Ozzy gets to take-five while the others offer up a rockin' instrumental, the curiously culinary-titled "Rat Salad" (a phrase that supposedly Eddie Van Halen considered nicking for the name of his band, early on), before *Paranoid* wraps up on a high-note, with another gloriously-titled rocker, "Fairies Wear Boots."

The album was originally titled *War Pigs*, but changed to *Paranoid* at the request of record execs who felt "Paranoid" was the more marketable single – hence, the puzzling cover artwork. The LP's release date is listed as September 18th, 1970, which is coincidentally and sadly the same day Jimi Hendrix died. *Paranoid*, which has been certified quadruple platinum in the United States, has undoubtedly inspired countless musicians over the years. There's no doubt there is a youngster someplace at this very moment who has just become spellbound by this masterful metal opus. 50 years later, *Paranoid* sounds as heavy and brilliant as ever.

The Cry of Love
(Jimi Hendrix, 1971)

Between May 1967 and October 1968, Jimi Hendrix issued a whopping three studio albums – *Are You Experienced*, *Axis: Bold as Love*, and *Electric Ladyland* (the latter of which was a double-LP!). But for the remainder of his life (he tragically passed on September 18, 1970, at the age of 27), Hendrix would not issue another studio recording. But that's not to say he was just sitting around doing diddly. Turns out he was quite hard at work – forming two bands, Gypsy Sun and Rainbows *and* Band of Gypsys (the latter of which issued a self-titled live recording in 1970), touring, overseeing the construction of a recording studio (Electric Lady in NYC), and continuing to write/record new material.

The plan was to issue a new 2-LP studio effort in either late 1970 or early 1971, to be titled *First Rays of the New Rising Sun*, and featuring the trio of Hendrix on vocals/guitar, Billy Cox on bass, and Mitch Mitchell on drums (along with many a special guest). And the style of music was quite unlike what was heard on his previous studio efforts, as all the psychedelia and production trickery had been completely wiped away – replaced with a more straight-ahead sound and approach, with an unmistakable funk/R&B flair added.

"In the earlier times, when he was with Noel [Redding] and Mitch, the songs were very simple songs – 'Foxy Lady' [hums riff], 'Purple Haze' [hums riff]," Cox explained in the book *Avatar of the Electric Guitar: The Genius of Jimi Hendrix*. "The songs were very simple in their formation and in their production. And then, he was growing musically, and all artists do grow. The body grows – new cells come every day. So all artists continue to grow in some way, form, or fashion – whether they're a painter, a musician, whatever. So he was growing. The simplicity of the 'Foxy Ladys' and the 'Purple Hazes' now went into some pretty intricate things, like 'Jam Back at the House' and then later the 'Freedoms,' the 'Dolly Daggers,' and 'In from the Storm.' And you don't have the time to do a lot of pyrotechnics; you've got to play."

To back up a bit, Hendrix (born on November 27, 1942, in Seattle, Washington) honed his craft backing various artists during

the early to mid '60s – including Little Richard and the Isley Brothers, among others. But it wasn't until he was discovered by Animals bassist Chas Chandler and brought over to the UK that he soon became one of the top rock artists – as the leader of the Jimi Hendrix Experience. But most importantly, he completely revolutionized rock guitar (via his use of distortion and feedback, and such gimmicks as playing the guitar with his teeth and/or behind his back…while manning a right-handed guitar turned upside down). All three of his aforementioned albums were worldwide hits, and he became one of the top concert draws (highlighted by a now-classic performance at Woodstock, in 1969).

However, towards the end of his life, there have been conflicting reports about Hendrix's state of mind and health. As the Who's Pete Townshend reminisced in the 2001 DVD, *30 Years of Maximum R&B Live* – "What made me work so hard was seeing the condition that Jimi Hendrix was in [at a performance at the Isle of Wight Festival, on August 31, 1970]. He was in such tragically bad condition physically. And I remember thanking God as I walked on the stage that I was healthy." Additionally, eventual Television guitarist (and then-acquaintance of Jimi's) Richard Lloyd recalled in the same *Avatar of the Electric Guitar* book a conversation he had with him at a NYC nightclub during the last year of his life.

"He was like, *really* downtrodden. Super-sad. He was talking about, 'I'm not long for the world.' And 'I'm being made to be like a clown. I'm in the circus and I can't get out.' Finally, I broke my silence, and said, 'Jimi, you should be able to do whatever you want to do. People really love you and what you do.' And I guess he took that part and parcel of the bullshit he was hearing, because he called it, 'Mickey Mouse' – which apparently is a term used in the army for 'bullshit.' Like what the sergeant says or the drill sergeant."

But then there have been reports to the contrary about the guitarist – he being particularly pleased with the progress of how the construction of his cherished recording studio, Electric Lady, was coming along. "He was really, really happy with that studio," said Jimi's engineer Eddie Kramer, in an article for *Experience Hendrix* in 1998. "When he finally came down to work in the studio, he was just completely knocked out and didn't want to leave. He was there every day and every night for like four months, from May to August. He was there literally as much as he could be'." And judging from the last conversation Cox ever had with Jimi (just a few days before his passing), he was looking forward to finishing off the *First Rays* material – "Hey man, we're going back in the studio Friday, OK? *Be there.*"

Shortly after Hendrix's death, it was decided that selections planned for the double LP would be whittled down to just a single LP, entitled *The Cry of Love* (after the title of what was Hendrix's last-ever tour) – with Kramer working alongside Mitch Mitchell in a production capacity, and with Hendrix also being posthumously listed as a producer. The album-opener, "Freedom," is the perfect intro to the "new Jimi" – a funky rocker with backing vocals provided by a pair of chaps known simply as "The Ghetto Fighters" (aka Albert and Arthur Allen, who were interviewed at length for the 1972 film, *Jimi Hendrix*). And speaking of vocals, Hendrix was supposedly never entirely comfortable with his singing abilities. But judging from "Freedom," it sounds like he may have finally found a newfound confidence in his vocals.

The beautiful ballad "Drifting" is perfectly named, as the clean guitar sounds filtered through a Leslie speaker (as well as a bit of backwards guitar – one of the few instances of Jimi revisiting an old studio trick) expertly creates the feeling of…*drifting.* "Ezy Ryder" (a title obviously nicked from the classic 1969 film, *Easy Rider*, starring Peter Fonda, Dennis Hopper, and Jack Nicholson) is next, and proves to be one of the album's hardest rockers – featuring great guitar work throughout. "Night Bird Flying" turns out to be a surprisingly melodic tune, while "My Friend" perfectly recreates the vibe of inside a blues bar (thanks to the presence of harmonica and background chatter/clanging glasses). Two more rockers then rock side by side, "Straight Ahead" and "Astro Man" (the latter of which begins with a tribute to the *Mighty Mouse* theme song), before what is probably the album's best tune, the ballad "Angel."

Supposedly written for his late mother (Lucille Jeter, who died in 1958 at the age of 33, when Jimi was just 16), the lyrics to "Angel" are some of Jimi's best, and sadly, prove eerily prophetic since by the time the song appeared on *The Cry of Love*, he would be deceased, as well. The song would also reach a pop audience a year later, when Rod Stewart covered it for his album, *Never a Dull Moment*, and scored a #4 UK hit single. The slightly Zeppelin-ish rocker "In from the Storm" follows, before one of the album's more oddly-titled tunes, "Belly Button Window" (its title and lyrics supposedly reflect the view that a baby has, peeking through its mommy's tummy) closes things out.

Released on March 5, 1971 (and featuring a pencil and charcoal drawing of Hendrix's face atop a blue sky on its front cover), *The Cry of Love* was expectedly, a hit – peaking at #3 in the US and #2 in the UK. Years later, an attempt was made to try and assemble a lengthier tracklist reflecting how the guitarist originally envisioned the 2-LP version. The result was the release of an album in 1997 that included all the tunes from *TCoL* along with several newly added ones, entitled…*First Rays of the New Rising Sun*.

Despite *The Cry of Love* not containing a tune as universally known as say, "Purple Haze," "Hey Joe," or "All Along the Watchtower," it remains a strong – if underappreciated – album. And it was this album that just happened to leave an impression on future King's X singer/bassist Doug Pinnick, and served as his gateway to one of his favorite artists. "I was on the road with a show group that did choreography and stuff, and that's when I started reading rock magazines, and that's when I read that Jimi Hendrix had died. I was sad about it. I remember driving in the van – going to Arizona, or something – and I stopped at this music store and bought a cassette of *Cry of Love*, because I wanted to get into it, and to see, 'Well, what did I miss'?"

"I played *Cry of Love*, and I'm going, 'Wow...I like this record!' I wasn't crazy about it, but I was digging it. And then, I listened to *Band of Gypsys*, and I go, "Alright. *This is exactly what*

I've been looking for all my life." Buddy Miles was one of my favorite singers and drummers at the time, and I had been listening to Buddy Miles. So, when he got together with him and Billy Cox, and it was a three-piece, all-black rock band, it was something that I really related to."

Maggot Brain
(Funkadelic, 1971)

As with seemingly many Caucasian, teenaged metalheads of the late '80s/early '90s, I was introduced to funk music via the Red Hot Chili Peppers' breakthrough 1989 release, *Mother's Milk*. And as a result, found myself reading quite a few interviews done by the band in publications. One such interview with their bassist, Flea, was in a guitar mag (either *Guitar Player* or *Guitar World*, I'm not 100% certain anymore), and I read a quote that stuck with me, that went something along the lines of – but is not a direct quote – "All you metalheads out there who think Black Sabbath is heavy, you should check out Funkadelic's *Maggot Brain*." I certainly stored that tidbit in my memory bank, and I put in a special request with Old Saint Nick for Christmas 1990 to deliver the *Maggot Brain* CD. He obeyed my request and upon listening to it...I was absolutely floored.

But enough about me, let's talk the Funkadelic backstory leading up to *Maggot Brain* for a bit, shall we? The group can be traced back to the Parliaments – a multi-membered, all-black soul group based in Plainfield, New Jersey, who originally formed back in the '50s, before scoring a crossover hit in 1967 with "(I Wanna) Testify." Members would come and go, but the one who assumed the leadership role (and remained a constant member through it all) was singer/songwriter George Clinton. However, the backing group for the Parliaments would eventually split off on their own in 1968 – going by the name of Funkadelic. And contained within the band were some exceptional musicians, including guitarists Eddie Hazel and Tawl Ross, bassist Billy "Bass" Nelson, keyboardist Bernie Worrell, and drummer Tiki Fulwood (with a variety of vocalists vocalizing).

Obviously inspired by a certain left-handed Stratocaster player who specialized in psychedelic-funk-rock, Funkadelic followed in a similar stylistic path on their first two albums, 1970's self-titled debut and 1971's *Free Your Mind...and Your Ass Will Follow*. But it was on 1972's *Maggot Brain*, that it all coalesced into Funkadelic's first true masterpiece. With Clinton serving as producer, sessions for Funkadelic's third release overall took place from late 1970 through early 1971, at United Sound Systems in Detroit (the same town that the group's label, Westbound, called home). With Jimi Hendrix having tragically passed shortly before the recording sessions were to take place, a void was certainly left for six-string guitar heroes. And while he never received the same adulation as Jimi, Funkadelic's Hazel was an exceptional guitarist in his own right, and played in a style similar to Jimi's – as heard on the album's epic album-opening title track.

After a mysterious opening spoken part ("Mother Earth is pregnant for the third time, For y'all have knocked her up, I have tasted the maggots in the mind of the universe, I was not offended, For I knew I had to rise above it all, Or drown in my own shit"), Hazel simply pours his heart and soul out through the strings of his instrument...*for nearly nine minutes straight*. In Clinton's 2014 autobiography, *Brothas Be, Yo Like George, Ain't That Funkin' Kinda Hard on You?*, Funkadelic's leader recalled the song's recording. "Eddie and I were in the studio, tripping like crazy but also trying to focus our emotions. I told him to play like his mother had died, to picture that day, what he would feel, how he would make sense of his life, how he would take a measure of everything that was inside him and let it out through his guitar. I knew immediately that he understood what I meant. I could see the guitar notes stretching out like a silver web. When he played the solo back, I knew that it was good beyond good, not only a virtuoso display of musicianship but also an almost unprecedented moment of emotion in pop music."

Up next, "Can You Get to That," is a more straight-ahead soul tune. And while funk music is not usually associated with acoustic guitar, Ross was seemingly one of the few funk guitarists of the era that preferred playing "unplugged" – as heard throughout the tune. "Hit It and Quit It" features a great Jimi-esque guitar riff, before another one of the album's true highlights, the soulful gem "You and Your Folks, Me and My Folks," which lyrically seems to focus on the "we should all learn to live in harmony" message that proved popular in rock and pop tunes at the time (i.e., Sly's

"Everyday People"). With Nelson handling lead vocals on the tune, it should be noted that Funkadelic rotated who sang lead.

And wouldn't ya know it, *another* of the album's undisputed highlights follows immediately thereafter, with the fierce rocker, "Super Stupid," which again, features some simply outstanding Jimi-like six-string work from Hazel. The last song on the album to feature *sung* lyrics arrives next, "Back in Our Minds," which is probably one of the only rock songs to begin with what sounds like the clanging of warped bells or glasses of water. And the last tune on the album turns out to be another extended jam-fest, "Wars of Armageddon," which unlike the title track, features the entire band rocking together (and various dialogue and sound effects carefully placed throughout – including an unexpected blast of flatulence at one point).

When I had the opportunity to interview Clinton in 2018 for *Songfacts*, I asked which P-Funk (short for Parliament-Funkadelic) tune had the best guitar work. He replied, "I'll have to go with 'Maggot Brain'." But when I countered with "It seems like people tend to overlook another track with great guitar work – 'Wars of Armageddon'," he shared an interesting tidbit concerning the track. "You know who didn't overlook that? Miles Davis. He actually came and hired our drummer [Tiki Fulwood] after we did that record. Listen to his record, *On the Corner*, and then listen to 'Wars of Armageddon.' When we did 'Free Your Mind,' 'Wars of Armageddon,' and 'Maggot Brain,' that sound, Miles said he thought that was the brand new thing."

Released on July 12, 1971, *Maggot Brain* reached an impressive #14 on *Billboard's* "black album" chart, but peaked at only #108 on the "pop album" chart. Which proves befuddling, as it rocked just as hard as most rock albums released that year, and should have reached a much wider audience. But time has been kind to *Maggot Brain*, as it *has* received its rightfully deserved kudos – including Dr. Dre sporting a *Maggot Brain* shirt in his classic video for "Dre Day," renowned guitarists listing it as an inspiration (John Frusciante, Vernon Reid, Dean Ween, etc.), as well as *Rolling Stone* placing it at as the #136 "greatest album of all-time" in 2020.

Lastly, in the same chat I had with Clinton for *Songfacts*, I asked one more *M. Brain*-related question I'd like to share with you – "Circa the early '70s, how much of a role did drugs play in the creation of albums like *Maggot Brain*?" He replied, "And *Free Your Mind...And Your Ass Will Follow*. The trendy chemical substance at the time was LSD. Right up until like, '72 or '73 was when we stopped doing that. But that was the era. To me, it seemed like some sort of spirit just took over everybody between '68 and '72. To get rid of that Vietnam War, it wasn't just acid or just hippies. That peace and love had to come from someplace special. It didn't make sense as far as where I'd come from – it was about 'watch your back.' But for that period of time, it just seemed like that was real. And it still is, to me."

"But it was very real during that period. That war had to end some kind of way, and it seemed like that's what it took – that frame of mind. Because it didn't even work after that – you'd take all the acid you'd want, and you did nothing but stay up all night and speed, and couldn't go to sleep. It wasn't trips or sights – all that was over. Once Woodstock was over, from then on, it seemed like it started going downhill. Hippies became the bad guys, the long-haired freaks, that whole Manson trip. It's like it poisoned everybody with long hair or hippie clothes. The whole thing changed after that."

Led Zeppelin IV
(Led Zeppelin, 1971)

I think we can all agree that Led Zeppelin's fourth offering (although officially untitled, often goes by the name of *Led Zeppelin IV*) is truly one of the greatest rock albums of all-time. After all, it has the sales (as of 2021, it has sold 24 million copies in the US alone), the material ("Stairway to Heaven" is on it, for goodness sake!), and the influence (the hefty amount of "Zep clone" bands in the '80s who mimicked the sound of "Black Dog" and "When the Levee Breaks," as well as hip-hop artists sampling the latter tune).

By the time that Zeppelin – singer Robert Plant, guitarist Jimmy Page, bassist/keyboardist John Paul Jones, and drummer John Bonham – began work on their fourth LP in December of 1970, it was decided that they would record once again in the same location as their previous album, *Led Zeppelin III*, at Headley Grange. Headley who? Let me explain. Headley Grange was a former "workhouse" located in Headley, Hampshire, England, which was a large building in which those who did not have the means to support themselves financially were offered to live and work. And once again, Zep borrowed the Rolling Stones Mobile Studio to capture their tunes on tape. Also, Island Studios in London was utilized, as well (with sessions wrapping up in February 1971, and mixing taking place in July).

Also what would set the ensuing album apart from the rest of the pack was its awesome sonics – particularly heard in the spacious drum sound – courtesy of Jimmy Page pulling double duty once more, and serving as the LP's producer. "Jimmy Page of course overlaid tracks for guitars, but it was the bass and drums, and he had plenty of room for the guitars and vocals," explained original Alice Cooper drummer Neal Smith in the book, *Bonzo: 30 Rock Drummers Remember the Legendary John Bonham.* "And had plenty of room to get that big bass drum sound – that nobody had ever heard before. *That was Jimmy Page.* Talk about a team player – Jimmy Page was already pretty famous by then. He was producing the album and could have put the guitar way up – but he was listening to the whole sound of the band. And I think as good as John Bonham was...Jimmy Page's production was equal to that. And I think that's what makes him such an amazing musician. And I think that years later, they still sound great."

Also in the same *Bonzo* book, Stone Temple Pilots drummer Eric Kretz explained how Zep's straightforward approach on albums such as *IV* makes it sound not dated one iota. "This whole formula with bass, drums, guitar, and vocals, for me, it's the most pleasing of sounds live. I get frustrated when I see three guitar players and a keyboard player. I just go, '*Why?*' Unless everybody is doing something different – like in a prog rock form – it's so much better to hear each instrument and to have each musician contribute to the sonic balance that has to happen on stage. And you look back at what Led Zeppelin did – all the live stuff and how they recorded in the studio. Even though Jimmy had a lot of overdubs going on, the sound of the bass drum and the focus of the guitar in the midrange...it just makes me want to high-five the world every time I hear a good Zeppelin song on the radio in my car!"

Kicking things off would be a tune titled after a certain unnamed canine that also utilized the grounds of Headley Grange during the recording of *IV* – "Black Dog." Plant's "sex god" persona is on display throughout the tune ("Ah ah, ah ah, ah ah, ah ah, ah ah, ah ah, ahhh"), while there is a repeating call and response between the vocals and the music in the verses. Additionally, Page once again proves why he and Black Sabbath's Tony Iommi are probably the two greatest riff meisters in the 'istory of 'eavy rock. Original Dream Theater drummer Mike Portnoy once admitted to me that he still remains in awe of Page's "B. Dog" riff. "You don't realize how complicated that riff is, until you actually try and figure out what the hell the drums are doing."

Next would be an ode to the old time music that all four members of Zep grew up on...the appropriately-titled "Rock and Roll." But according to Bonham's son, Jason, it is "the hardest song to play correctly. It's 16th notes and the hi-hat, which is a little bit like a Texas shuffle, but it's also like Little Richard's 'Keep A-Knockin' (But You Can't Come In)'." A throwback to the sublime folky second side of *III* follows, "The Battle of Evermore," which sees (hears?) Jones strumming a mandolin in place of his bass, and Page manning an acoustic guitar, while Plant duets with Fairport Convention's Sandy Denny (the first time since Viram Jasani provided tabla on *Led Zeppelin I* that an outsider was allowed to guest on a Zep record). Lyrically, the tune includes references to *The Lord of the Rings* (Ringwraiths!), and funny enough, there is no drumming on the tune...despite it containing the lyric "The drums will shake the castle wall."

And then closing side one, the tune that is undoubtedly one of the best known (and admittedly, overplayed on rock radio) tunes, "Stairway to Heaven." Composed by Page and Plant, the tune's first four minutes and seventeen seconds once again are drum-less, as it slowly builds bit by bit/instrument by instrument – acoustic guitar, recorder, vocals, electric guitar, electric 12-string guitar, electric piano, before...BONHAM.

There has been much said over the years about what the song's lyrical meaning is – particularly such seemingly nonsensical lines as "If there's a bustle in your hedgerow don't be alarmed now, It's just a spring clean [or is it 'sprinkling'?] for the May queen." And it seems like Mr. Plant isn't planning on giving a frank explanation any time soon – as I recall when the singer was asked what that the line meant during an interview on *The Howard Stern Show* in the late '80s, he replied, "A hedgerow might be a cluster of old Mercury Monarchs all in a row."

Also, a misconception over the years is that Page utilized his trademark Gibson EDS-1275 double neck guitar for the song's recording. But as Brad Tolinski explained to me in the book *Iconic Guitar Gear*, this was simply not the case. "All of his electric 12 stuff in the studio was done on a Fender 12, and then he would just use other guitars for the 6-string work. So, the double neck [a 1971 model], he brought that out because the Led Zeppelin songs often needed a 12-string, and for him to switch quickly to 6-string on live performances. But it was a stage guitar."

Lastly concerning "Stairway" was the controversy it has caused over the years. First, during the '80s when people with obviously far too much time on their hands claimed that there were very dangerous/demonic messages contained in it if you played your *IV* vinyl backwards. Second, when a copyright infringement suit was filed against Zep – concerning a claim that parts of "Stairway" were just too darn similar to an obscure instrumental, "Taurus," from the rock band Spirit. Listening to both tunes side by side, there is a slight resemblance, but nothing that sounds like a blatant rip – which resulted in the copyright dispute ruling in favor of Zeppelin in 2020.

Side two proved to be exceptionally consistent, starting with the electric piano-led "Misty Mountain Hop" (whose title was another nod to the author of *Lord of the Rings*, JRR Tolkien – this time, his book series *The Hobbit*), while "Four Sticks" once again showcased the nifty riffs of Page (with its title coming from the fact that Bonham opted to play the tune while holding two drum sticks per hand). Bonham takes five once more for another *III*-like folk tune, "Going to California" (which may or may not be about Joni Mitchell…but at the very least, it is very Joni-like musically), before the album's swan song, "When the Levee Breaks."

Lyrically based on a tune of the same name by blues singer/guitarist Memphis Minnie (real name: Lizzie Douglas), musically, "Levee" sounds nothing like the original – featuring slide guitar work and simply one of the greatest drum sounds ever captured in a studio recording. When talking Bonham for the *Bonzo* book, drummer Gregg Bissonette was willing to spill the beans concerning what Zep engineer, Andy Johns, once told him about how Bonham created his now-legendary "Levee" sound.

"I recorded a lot with a very good friend of mine who passed away a few years ago, and when we did Joe Satriani's *The Extremist*, he was hired to engineer and produce – Andy Johns. He said, 'What do you want your drums to sound like, mate?' And I said, 'How about any of those drum sounds you got with John Bonham?' He said, 'First of all, don't put anything inside your kick.' He took a Sennheiser 421 and dangled it inside a little hole, soldered it, and that 421 was dangling inside there. He close-mic'd the drums, but he mic'd the drums so much from far away. He ran the drums through a PA system."

"He said when he walked in the room and heard Zeppelin play 'When the Levee Breaks,' he walked up to the top of the stairwell of this castle that they were rehearsing in, and he heard that [sings opening drum part] and he captured that. If you listen to a song called 'Friends' on Joe Satriani's *Extremist,* you'll hear Joe, my brother Matt, and I playing, and Andy Johns recorded all that – he kind of got that sound. Nobody's ever going to really sound like John Bonham, but if you listen to some of that drum track...Andy had a lot to do with that. One time, Andy told me he ran into John a year later and said, 'How about that sound we got on 'Levee Breaks'?' And he said, '*We*?! That's *my* drums and *me* playing it'!" And as mentioned earlier, the drums on "Levee" have proven quite popular over the years within the hip-hop community, as two of the genre's most renowned artists, the Beastie Boys and Eminem, nicked bits of Bonzo's beat for their own creations ("Rhymin' & Stealin'" and "Kim," respectively).

Released on November 8, 1971, the cover of the vinyl version folded out to be a gatefold – with the front image showing a framed photo (affixed to a wall of a poorly-kept house) of a hunched over old chap, with a bustle of sticks tied to his back. And when you gaze at the back cover, you discover that the house is partially torn down, and in the distance is more modern-looking (at least for the early '70s) housing. When you opened the gatefold and took a peek inside, you'd find an illustration of another elderly man atop a tall mountain looking down – while holding a cane and a lantern. Additionally, the LP's dust jacket listed the lyrics to one song and one song only – "Stairway to Heaven" – on one side, and on the other, a listing of the album's eight tunes, as well as four mysterious symbols. Later, it would become known that these four symbols would represent each member of Zep: Zoso/Page, triquetra/Jones, circles/Bonham, and feather/Plant (and it should be noted the resemblance between Bonham's design and an upside down Ballantine Beer symbol).

27 A+ ALBUMS (Vol. I)

As with all the Zep albums issued during the '70s, *IV* was a blockbuster – topping the charts in several countries (including the US and UK). However, only two singles would be issued from the album – "Black Dog" and "Rock and Roll" (peaking at #15 and #47 respectively in the US), with the song that would have probably been a worldwide #1 smash, "Stairway to Heaven," shockingly never issued as a single. Which just may have been a genius move on the band's part – as it forced people to purchase and listen to *the entire album.*

Blue Öyster Cult
(Blue Öyster Cult, 1972)

Think "heavy metal," and for many, distorted/mammoth riffs and screaming amps immediately come to mind. However, this was not the case on Blue Öyster Cult's self-titled debut. Despite not offering up many crank-yer-amp-to-ten tunes here, BÖC still managed to give off a seriously creepy vibe on an album that includes precious few tunes that the casual fan of the band – or of rock/metal in general – would be familiar with. Yet still, from a consistency standpoint, may just be BÖC's best.

Originally formed way back in 1967 on Long Island, New York, and going by several different names (tops being Soft White Underbelly) before settling on their now-famous moniker in '71, BÖC's line-up consisted of a pair of singer/guitarists, Buck Dharma (real name: Donald Roeser) and Eric Bloom, plus guitarist/keyboardist Allen Lanier, bassist Joe Bouchard, and drummer Albert Bouchard. And when it came to songwriting (and in particular, lyric-penning), the band welcomed their manager, Sandy Pearlman, plus rock critic, Richard Meltzer, to lend a hand – which resulted in sometimes odd titles (especially when compared to your average rock song titles of the day), and lyrics that often embraced an unmistakable sci-fi, supernatural, and/or horror vibe.

Signed to Columbia Records, the band recorded what would be their self-titled debut in October 1971, with three gents credited as producer – Pearlman, Murray Krugman, and David Lucas. When I chatted with Joe Bouchard in 2022 for *BraveWords*, the topic of BÖC's debut came up, and he shared his memories of the sessions. "I was learning how records are made – this was at David Lucas' jingle studio in New York. On eight tracks. That's all you had – you had to do the whole album on eight tracks. But he would show us little magical ways of doubling things and doing live bounces. They'd be flipping the tape over backwards and he'd be making flanging using duplication of the part. So, he was all into what was happening with the Beatles and that production. And of course, Sandy Pearlman and Murray Krugman produced that record – so they kept us conceptually…instead of going way off track, they wanted to establish what was going to become Blue Öyster Cult. It had to have that vibe."

"We had 'band houses,' Bloom recalled in a 2016 interview with *Songfacts,* concerning how the band's songwriting process worked early on. "And in the band houses, we had a variety of ways of coming up with tunes. Around the early '70s, the 4-track tape recorder became commercially available, and once that happened, people started doing their own recording at home. When that happened, a lot of people started self-writing their material. People brought in finished songs. That did not always mean that the finished songs became their own – very often, someone would bring in a finished song, and someone would say, 'I like your music, but I think the lyrics need help,' and then there would be some co-writing. So there was still some collaboration. But songs would go into pre-production, and there would still be collaboration before songs ever hit vinyl."

As mentioned before, the subsequent songs on the debut are not a kin production nor sonic-wise to what you'd expect from a hard rocking record from 1972 (especially if you do a side-by-side taste-test with say, Alice Cooper's *School's Out*, Black Sabbath's *Vol. 4*, or Deep Purple's *Machine Head*). But there are a handful of exceptions, such as the album opener, "Transmaniacon MC," which lyrically touches upon Altamont (the notorious Rolling Stones' free concert in 1969, which featured Hells Angels as security and led to a fatal stabbing), with the "MC" in its title an abbreviation for "motorcycle club."

The first of the album's peculiar song titles comes next, the boogie rocker "I'm on the Lamb but I Ain't No Sheep," which contains lyrics that would later reappear in the future BÖC tune, "The Red and the Black." Then…the album's first true classic tune (and the first that Dharma sings lead on), the mid-paced "Then Came the Last Days of May." "That was a true story about some Long Island kids that were dealing pot in the early '70s," Dharma told me during a *Songfacts* interview in 2019. "In those days, for middle class/collegiate-type people to get involved in drug sales was pretty unusual. It was an awful story – they went out to Tucson,

Arizona, met up with some crooks, and got killed. The aspect of 'good kids gone bad' was a big part of that."

Further tunes with eccentric titles followed (which just happened to be two more standout tracks), including "Before the Kiss, a Redcap" and in particular, "She's as Beautiful as a Foot." Concerning the latter, the tune features almost Donovan-esque music, and when asked about the song's title (and such unusual lyrics as "Didn't believe it when he bit into her face, It tasted just like a fallen arch"), Dharma simply replied, "That was a Richard Meltzer lyric. I'm imagining its intent was to make sort of a snarky, goof of a song. But actually, a foot can be beautiful." Also included are tunes that while help tie the album together when listened to as a whole, admittedly aren't particular standouts ("Stairway to the Stars" and "Screams").

The hardest rocking tune of the entire album is undoubtedly "Cities on Flame with Rock and Roll," which contains a very Zep-like guitar riff. But when I asked Albert Bouchard if he was going for a Bonham-esque groove within the tune in the book *Bonzo: 30 Rock Drummers Remember the Legendary John Bonham*, he replied, "If it did it was completely subconscious, because there were other drummers that I was imitating on that song – like the James Gang's Jimmy Fox. I kind of was imitating him and I was also imitating Bill Ward. And I was also imitating the guy on the first King Crimson record [Michael Giles is the drummer on 1969's *In the Court of the Crimson King*]."

Then possibly the album's most underrated tune, "Workshop of the Telescopes," which again, gets its point across with a minimal amount of distortion on the guitars, and also, concludes with sound effects that sound like either a spaceship departing or landing. And perhaps fittingly, instead of finishing the album off with a bang, we receive another mid-paced tune that features some nifty guitar picking, "Redeemed."

Released on January 16, 1972, *Blue Öyster Cult* sported a spacey graphic on its cover (am I the only person who is reminded of when an X-wing Starfighter descends close to the Death Star in *Star Wars* when gazing at the image?), and provided an introduction to what would become the band's trademark icon – the astrology symbol of Kronos (Saturn). And while the album would register just a mere blip on the *Billboard 200* (peaking at #172), the band was able to successfully build upon it – within just a few short years, *BÖC* had become a major arena rock attraction and scored a major hit with "(Don't Fear) The Reaper."

However, Joe Bouchard was nonplussed concerning the initial album's sound. "When it came out, I was a little disappointed – I didn't like the vinyl pressing. But then maybe about 15 years later, they put it out on CD, and then all of a sudden, it brought me back to the studio. It was cleaner, and it was like sitting in the control room, listening to the playback of the mixes. I think we were all tremendously excited to be working on that record. And it sounds like it."

And when asked what his all-time favorite *Blue Öyster Cult* LP was, the bassist was able to overlook his initial sonic disappointment. "The first album. Because I had the most fun. I couldn't believe how much fun I was having. Every day I'd get up and we'd be going to the studio, and I'd be like, 'I can't believe we're going to a studio to make an album…a real album, on Columbia Records!' So, I was excited every day."

Harvest
(Neil Young, 1972)

Has there ever been a rock artist as unpredictable and fearless as Neil Young (OK, OK...*besides* David Bowie)? Probably not. Whether it be firing up proto-grunge (*Everybody Knows This Is Nowhere* with Crazy Horse), penning protest songs ("Ohio" with CSNY), going all electro-techno on us (*Trans*), revisiting rockabilly (*Everybody's Rockin'* with the Shocking Pinks), or serving as a one-man band (*Le Noise*), Neil Percival Young has always done what he has wants to do musically – with little consideration concerning what others (particularly his record company) want him to do.

But the style of music that he has enjoyed the most commercial success with is mellow country/folk – as evidenced by the sole chart-topping album of his entire career, *Harvest*. Arguably Canada's greatest rock artist of all-time (at least *singular* rock artist), Young first came to the attention of music fans as a member of psychedelic rockers Buffalo Springfield, before jumping ship and going solo (1968's self-titled debut), joining forces with Crazy Horse (1969's *Everybody Knows This Is Nowhere*), and then Crosby, Stills & Nash (who were then rechristened Crosby, Stills, Nash & Young for 1970's *Déjà Vu*).

For 1970's *After the Goldrush,* Young had begun adding clear elements of country into his sound (namely a cover of Don Gibson's "Oh Lonesome Me"), while also still offering up folk tunes ("Tell Me Why") and amp-crackling rockers ("Southern Man"). For his fourth solo offering, Young followed in the same direction as *AtG*. And since his last album was a top-10 hit, he already knew going into the sessions that there was a large audience primed and ready.

Although he had quite a bit of the material already penned (on his later-released *Live at Massey Hall 1971* recording, five of *Harvest*'s ten tracks were performed), Young suffered from a slipped disc back injury that resulted in having to don a back brace for the second half of the year. So, although the ten tunes that would comprise *Harvest* were recorded from January through September of that year, its release was delayed – resulting in it being the first year since Young's recording career began with Buffalo

Springfield's self-titled debut in 1966 that there was no new studio album released that featured Young in some capacity.

Forming a backing band dubbed the Stray Gators, the line-up would be comprised of Ben Keith (pedal steel, slide guitar, vocals), Jack Nitzsche (piano, vocals), Tim Drummond (bass), and Kenny Buttrey (drums), with Neil handling lead vocals, electric/acoustic guitars, piano, and harmonica, and others contributing, as well (including such big-named backing singers as James Taylor, Linda Ronstadt, David Crosby, Stephen Stills, and Graham Nash).

To describe the album's opener, "Out on the Weekend," as "laidback" would be an understatement – it sounds as if Neil and his cohorts are about to nod off at any second! But the sleepy pace and feel certainly adds to its charm, and also sets the stage for what is to follow on the album with its barebones accompaniment – with the focus on Neil's voice, acoustic guitar strumming, and harmonica blowing. The title track follows, which also continues the relaxed pace and folk-country approach of the opener, which tells the tale of a woman who appears quite unlucky in the romance department.

As hinted at by its title, "A Man Needs a Maid" is not exactly the most PC tune Neil ever composed (sample lyric – "I was thinking that maybe I'd get a maid, Find a place nearby for her to stay, Just someone to keep my house clean, Fix my meals and go away"). And musically, it served as a bit of a detour – Neil's acoustic guitar and backing band take-5, and in their place is just Neil's piano...and a bombastic symphony orchestra!

Up next is not only the best-known track on the entire album, but probably of Neil's entire career, the simply sublime "Heart of Gold," as it features the perfect blend of pedal steel guitar, acoustic guitar, and harmonica, plus some of Neil's most hopeful lyrics – with Linda Ronstadt's unmistakable backing vocals joining in at the end.

On the final tune of the album's first side (back in the vinyl days), "Are You Ready for the Country?" sees the first appearance of electric guitar...but is not exactly rockin'. True, the whole backing band is behind Neil, but remain quite restrained throughout

– not coming close to approaching the raw rock free-for-alls of say, "Cinnamon Girl," "Tonight's the Night," or "Hey, Hey, My, My" (Into the Black)."

And then…there is the song that if I were to personally pick as the best of the entire album, I could feel confident selecting – "Old Man." Certainly amongst the best lyrics Neil ever penned – which were inspired by a caretaker that looked after his ranch in Northern California (not about Neil's father, as some have assumed over the years) – the tune returns musically back to the country-folk approach of "Heart of Gold" (with James Taylor plucking along on banjo and singing backing vocals, and Ronstadt once more joining in on backing vocals, too).

"There's a World" turns out to be the album's second and last "symphony piece" (once again featuring Neil on vocals/piano, and the London Symphony Orchestra following along), which honestly, probably comes closest to a throwaway on the album. But all is forgiven with the album's first true rocker, "Alabama," which like "Southern Man," lyrically deals with racism in the US south.

I hate to keep repeating the same sentiment over and over again, but what follows is…*another* Neil classic! "The Needle and the Damage Done" has gone down as one of the top anti-drug songs ever – supposedly inspired by Neil witnessing what heroin was doing to original Crazy Horse singer/guitarist Danny Whitten (who sadly would die before the end of the year). Although one of Neil's most bare tracks instrumentally (featuring only his voice and acoustic guitar), it perfectly captures the frustration of witnessing hard drugs taking down a friend, and also features the classic line, "But every junkie's like a settin' sun."

Closing things is one of Neil's most overlooked tunes, the long-and-winding jamfest, "Words (Between the Lines of Age) – featuring 2/3's of CSNY on backing vox (Nash and Stills) – and also serving as the album's longest tune, by almost stretching to seven minutes in length.

Released on February 1, 1972, *Harvest* would sport a plain album cover (the album title and the artist's name in fancy font, atop a mostly tan backing and an orange circle smack dab in the middle) and would not only top the album charts in the US, UK, and Australia, but it would also go on to become the bloody #1 selling album of *the year* in the States. Additionally, "Heart of Gold" would also hit the #1 spot on the US singles charts on March 18, 1972 (and also hit the top spot in Canada, as well).

But instead of playing it safe in the wake of the album's massive success and delivering *Harvest* parts 2, 3, 4, etc., Young would instead completely reject this easy-to-digest direction throughout his next few solo efforts (resulting in what he would refer to as the "ditch trilogy," including some of the most raw – and exceptional – releases of his entire career...1973's *Time Fades Away*, 1974's *On the Beach*, and 1975's *Tonight's the Night*).

Thick as a Brick
(Jethro Tull, 1972)

The late '60s saw the birth of Blackpool's own Jethro Tull, who apart from the presence of a quirky front man who played flute while often balanced on one leg, initially didn't sound much different than the rest of the blues rock pack. But once the '70s got underway, Tull transformed into an entirely different beast, as explained by leader Ian Anderson. "At the very beginning of the '70s, we were – I suppose like many others, including the then-defunct Cream and the rampant Led Zeppelin – thought of primarily as a 'riff band.' Although there were obvious elements of folk, classical, jazz, and world music, in some of what we did. But a lot of it was riff-based – repeating motifs that were typical of that evolution, from pop and rock music to the 'thing' that became progressive rock music. But epitomized by bands like Cream, and developed in the more heavy metal sense by Black Sabbath and Led Zeppelin."

"Led Zeppelin was probably the biggest and most potent musical force at the time. We were, I suppose, in a similar vein, but not quite as grand or aggressive – or quite as 'sex, drugs, and rock n' roll' as Led Zeppelin were. We were a kind of slightly more esoteric band than perhaps the 'Zeppelins' were. American blues was the big moving force. That was what we were always looking for – a new riff, an exciting phrase. But as the '70s progressed, and particularly as bands like Yes, Genesis, and the early Emerson Lake and Palmer came to the fold, the bombastic and overblown side of rock music became known as progressive rock. And concept albums were the rage. We diverted in 1972, to the 'Spinal Tap version' of the concept album [*Thick as a Brick*] – a deliberate send-up, a spoof of that genre. Something that was meant to be larger than life, and a little surreal and ridiculous, in what was then the age of Monty Python. So that kind of overblown, slightly satirical side was where we fooled around for a couple of years, in '72 and '73."

As exemplified by selections from their first two albums (namely "A Song For Jeffrey" from 1968's *This Was* and "A New Day Yesterday" from 1969's *Stand Up*), Anderson is spot-on by describing Tull as an initial blues-based band. But soon after the dawn of the '70s, it seemed like Anderson and his ever-changing band mates – guitarist Martin Barre proved to be the only other constant member – made a conscious decision towards a more challenging and varied approach, especially on 1970's *Benefit* and 1971's *Aqualung*. Anderson is quick however to point out that this wasn't a deliberate move. "It wasn't an idea, it was just a natural development from longer songs into something more continuous. But the Moody Blues were one of the first bands to do something that was recognized as a 'concept album.' It was I think in the wake of the Moody Blues, that many of the more musically adventurous bands, like Yes and ELP, went down that road. But it was, from the beginning, that approach to music did have its critics. People did see it as overblown, overly ambitious, bombastic. So it was a fitting opportunity to fool around with it in a tongue in cheek way. And I think *Thick as a Brick* played it both ways."

Ask any '70s era prog rock fan what some of the landmark albums of the era were, and Jethro Tull's over-the-top 1972 tour de force, *Thick as a Brick* (and to a lesser degree, 1973's *A Passion Play*), is sure to be at the top of the list. But what many prog heads don't realize is that Ian Anderson and his Tull bandmates were actually poking fun at the genre. "We were being overtly spoof and satire oriented in the way that we did it. I guess we had it both ways – in as much as people enjoyed it for its adventurous, complex, and large-scale nature. I think we got lucky with that one – it worked both as a concept album and a piece of music – but its saving grace was that it was a piss take. And its performance on stage, and everything about the way we did it, seemed I thought pretty obvious. But looking back on it, 50% of the people didn't get the joke – they thought it was an entirely serious and grandiose work."

"But it was just a bit of fun, for the most part – as was evidenced in the lyrics and the album cover [which told the highly entertaining story of a young chap named Gerald Bostock, and claims that the lyrics contained on the album were a poem he wrote…but were really penned by Tull's leader], it was I think a pretty clear pointer that we were having a bit of fun with the concept album genre. It was taken seriously, and half-seriously, by the same people that like to *believe* in Spinal Tap. The same people that like to believe in Iron Maiden, Status Quo, Judas Priest, and Black Sabbath – believe in this stuff that is sort of real. As opposed to some pantomime rock creation designed to simply glorify the often inane and quite silly side of rock music. People go along with the joke. I say the joke – of course I'm not making necessarily references to Black Sabbath, Judas Priest or whoever just being a joke, but there's a sense of humor of what they do. And I know that – I'm not great pals with [them], but have been around some of those bands, and I know they have a sense of humor about what they do."

Recorded during December 1971 in Morgan Studios in London (with Anderson serving as producer and Terry Ellis as "executive producer"), the resulting *Thick as a Brick* album would be comprised of two extended tracks that took up a side each – "Thick as a Brick, Part I" and "Thick as a Brick, Part II." But while "II" is a mere throwaway and not at all memorable, "I" is the keeper here. Comprised of apparently nonsensical poetic phrases (including the legendary "Your sperm's in the gutter your love's in the sink"), the song goes through many twists and turns through its 22 minutes and 40 seconds – starting with the strum of acoustic guitar, introducing the full band (with a bang) at the 3:03 mark, and also presenting one of the most jolly and bouncy pieces of music a rock band has ever offered up at 12:32. Released on March 3, 1972, *Thick as a Brick* was a global smash – topping the charts in the US, Canada, and Australia (and peaking at #5 in Tull's homeland).

After their dalliance with the "concept album" on *Thick* and *Passion*, Tull returned (for the most part) back to basics for the rest of their '70s studio sets, with varying results – 1974's *War Child*, 1975's *Minstrel in the Gallery*, 1976's *Too Old to Rock N' Roll*, 1977's *Songs from the Wood*, 1978's *Heavy Horses*, and 1979's *Stormwatch*. Anderson recalls that this era "Developed for Jethro Tull in a variety of ways – the folk music side came into the music. Classical and folk music were influences that continued to bare upon our music in the mid to late '70s, and less of the American forms – jazz and blues. So I suppose we were more European in our affiliations in the latter part of the '70s, particularly."

Machine Head
(Deep Purple, 1972)

The inclusion in this book of Deep Purple's sixth studio album overall, *Machine Head*, can't be much of a surprise. After all, it included a tune that boasts the greatest – and most instantly-recognizable – rock guitar riff of all time..."Smoke on the Water." But it also just happens to be the group's greatest album as far as its consistency and quality from start to finish. And another reason why it just had to be included is because it catapulted Purple career-wise – where for a spell in the early-mid '70s, they were one of rock's top dogs (selling/drawing on par with such mega-acts as the Stones and Zeppelin).

Although Purple formed in 1968 (and even scored a sizeable hit the same year with a cover of Joe South's "Hush"), it was not until the band's "Mark II" line-up – singer Ian Gillan, guitarist Ritchie Blackmore, bassist Roger Glover, keyboardist Jon Lord, and drummer Ian Paice – fell into place that massive success occurred. And thanks to such albums as 1970's *In Rock* and 1971's *Fireball*, Purple helped contribute to the emergence of heavy metal, and also, found themselves on the cusp of worldwide stardom.

As with their previous three LP's, Deep Purple would also collectively serve as the producer of their next studio offering (with a then-largely unknown Martin Birch assisting as engineer). The original plan was for the quintet to record the album utilizing the Rolling Stones Mobile Studio at the Montreux Casino in Switzerland during December 1971. But as the famous story goes – during a performance by Frank Zappa and the Mothers of Invention on December 4th, an audience member had the bright idea of shooting a flare gun off mid-performance, which landed in the roof, and soon after, created a fire – which eventually, "burned the place to the ground" (fortunately, there were no fatalities).

With Purple's first choice for a recording site now up in smoke (no pun intended...well, maybe a little), they were able to quickly locate a replacement location – but as it turns out, not nearly as ideal – the Grand Hotel, also in Montreux. "We set the gear up in the hallways and the corridors of the hotel," recalled Gillan to *Songfacts*, in 2020. "And the Rolling Stones' mobile truck was out back with very long cables coming up through the windows. We tried to re-create an atmosphere in a technical sense the best we could." So from December 6 through 21, 1971, Purple got to work.

Comprised of only seven songs total, the selections can be split into three categories – tunes that became all-time classics ("Highway Star," "Smoke on the Water," "Space Truckin'"), tunes not well-known outside of their fanbase ("Maybe I'm a Leo," "Pictures of Home," "Never Before"), and a tune that would become a jam-heavy concert favorite ("Lazy"). Shockingly, it turns out that "Smoke on the Water" was an afterthought, that almost didn't make it onto the album.

"When we went to write the lyrics, because we were short on material, we thought it was an 'add-on track,' said Gillan in the same *Songfacts* Q&A. "It was just a last-minute panic. So, the riff and backing track had been recorded on the first day as a kind of soundcheck. There were no lyrics. The engineer told us on the last day, 'Man, we're several minutes short for an album.' So, we dug it out, and Roger and I wrote a biographical account of the making of the record: 'We all came out to Montreux…' etcetera, etcetera. That's how it ended up on the album."

Also in the same chat, Gillan shed light on what the phrase "a few red lights and a few old beds" meant in the tune. "We ended up at the Grand Hotel, and it was very bright, so we changed the light bulbs. We got some red light bulbs, and we used the bed mattresses as sound baffles." And concerning the song's now instantly-recognizable riff, Blackmore once explained the inspiration behind its creation to CNN, as "An interpretation of inversion. You turn it back and play it back and forth, it's actually Beethoven's "Fifth" [aka "Symphony No. 5"]. So, I owe him a lot of money."

Elsewhere, the Purples must have had a hankering for their automobiles, as two tunes here seem to focus on motorvatin' – "Highway Star" and "Space Truckin'," the latter of which contains some out of leftfield lyrics, such as the mysterious phrase "pony trekker." "It's not literal – nothing in that song is literal," explained the singer. "It's all a play on words, like, 'We'd move to the

Canaveral moonstop' and 'pony trekker' and 'Borealis.' It's all nonsense." And besides being a riff master, Blackmore was a solo specialist as well, most obviously with the classic lead breaks in all three of the aforementioned standout rockers. And the three album cuts, "Maybe I'm a Leo," "Pictures of Home," and "Never Before," would have probably been considered many other rock bands' a-material (particularly the riff-rocker "Pictures"), while "Lazy" showcases Lord's distorted organ.

Released on March 25, 1972, *Machine Head* (which featured the members' mugs on the cover slightly twisted, as if they were reflected in a carnival mirror) was a worldwide hit – topping the charts in the UK, Australia, Canada, France, Germany, Denmark, and the Netherlands, as well as peaking at #7 in the US. However, it was not until more than a year after the album's release (in May 1973) that "Smoke on the Water" was issued as a single.

"It never got played on the radio for a year because it was too long," reflects Gillan. "It was only when a guy from Warner Bros. came to see a show and saw the reaction of the crowd. He ran back to the studio and did an edit of three-and-a-half minutes, and it got played for the first time on the radio. That was a year after the album release. It would never have gotten played if we hadn't done the edit."

As a result, Purple were rewarded with one of the highest-charting singles of their entire career (#4 on the *Billboard Hot 100* – the same spot "Hush" claimed five years earlier). And at last count, the album had obtained double platinum certification in the US (in 1986) and gold in the UK (in 1974). Undoubtedly, if the sales were to be properly updated today, the certifications would increase (especially in the band's UK homeland, where they are apparently quite sluggish to update sales for classic albums).

And the album's success also solidified Blackmore's standing as one of rock's top guitarists (be sure to consult YouTube and look up the '72 "Highway Star" performance from Beat-Club for some additional visual/audio proof) – and as a result, inspired countless subsequent players. "Always, in my book, it is going to be Ritchie Blackmore," gushed Dio guitarist Craig Goldy. "He set his foundation before, in the 70s." And Diamond Head guitarist Brian Tatler also offered praise for the guitarist and for *Machine Head*. "The second album I ever bought was *Machine Head*, which was I think in probably late 1973. I really wanted to play the guitar solo in 'Highway Star,' so I practiced more. I probably didn't start practicing properly until about '75/'76. I also bought a Fender Strat in '76 because of Ritchie – that was what I thought would be the right sound. You often do that, don't you? If you've got a favorite player, you want to play a similar-looking/sounding guitar."

However, despite Purple now obtaining much-cherished "elite status" in the rock world, Blackmore had seemingly gained control of the band, and the same year that "Smoke" scaled the charts, Gillan and Glover were surprisingly excused from the band. And while Purple would enjoy further success upon filling the vacated positions with David Coverdale and Glenn Hughes, respectively, Blackmore would also leave the group later, in 1975 (and in 1976, the band would be finished all together). Luckily for us, *Machine Head* captured Purple at the peak of their powers…just in the nick of time.

Some Time in New York City
(John Lennon & Yoko Ono/Plastic Ono Band with Elephant's Memory, 1972)

Something that you will probably figure out about the listening tastes of yours truly after reading this book – while I do indeed fancy most of the obvious classic albums, I also have a soft spot for lesser-known and/or albums that for whatever reason, never received the proper props they deserved. For example, *The Cry of Love, Maggot Brain, Raw Power, Queen II*, and also, John Lennon's third album after splitting from the Beatles, the double-LP, *Some Time in New York City.*

Coming off of what is rightfully widely considered his two best solo efforts, 1970's *John Lennon/Plastic Ono Band* and 1971's *Imagine*, Lennon opted to take a sharp left turn away from what the mainstream expected of him, and delivered a rough, raw, and abrasive half studio/half live recording. And backing Lennon and Yoko Ono on the recording was the NYC-based band, Elephant's Memory, which included Gary Van Scyoc on bass – who I was able to interview for the book *John Winston Ono Lennon.*

"Rehearsing for *Some Time in New York City*...there were no rehearsals. It was a 7-7 deal at the Record Plant. For the first couple of days, Phil Spector was there...he just *hated* us. He really looked down his nose at us. He believed what a lot of people were writing – that Elephant's Memory was just a bunch of people off the street. Which couldn't be further from the truth – we were all studio players, and were playing with a lot of other stars. I was working with Paul Simon, [saxophonist] Stan Bronstein was doing some early Aerosmith records, [pianist] Adam Ippolito actually played on 'Celebration' by Kool and the Gang – one of the biggest singles *ever* in the music business. So, it wasn't like we were people off the street. I think they confused us with David Peel. They thought we were just a continuation of the David Peel thing [who Lennon name-checked in the tune 'New York City']."

"But anyway, he hated us – Phil Spector. It turns out John didn't appreciate him at all coming in and laying a big bag of cocaine on the mixing board, with a gun. He was just a weirdo, man. It turns out that Phil and John were not hitting it off *at all*. I think Phil was only there two nights, and then he went packing. Basically, John produced the record – even though he gave Phil credit for it. John stepped in and did the producing himself, really. With help from Roy Cicala, who was just a phenomenal engineer."

And according to the bassist, a few surprise special guests dropped by the sessions. "Rudolf Nureyev and Jackie Kennedy showed up. It was just a procession of stars and wildness. Secret Service Agents. It was crazy, man. And the pressure was really on us to shine. It was really difficult for us, and I think we did a pretty good job – considering the nature of the material. I think 'New York City' is a landmark track...but I don't want to start blowing my horn too much here." [Laughs]

Kicking things off was probably the most controversial composition Lennon ever issued as a solo artist – and quite possibly his entire career – a sax-led rocker entitled "Woman Is the Nigger of the World," which lyrically, focuses on the mistreatment of females in society. "I kind of saw the uproar coming," admitted Van Scyoc in the aforementioned book. "But you have to take care of business. When Elephant's Memory was in the studio, besides our normal partying, we were also very 'take care of business studio players.' So, we really had to get down to business – despite all that noise about the politics and stuff. It was music, so we had to get down to business and come up with our parts, because John didn't really give you a lot of ideas for your parts. He respected us, or he wouldn't have hired us in the beginning. And he knew about all the backgrounds of the studio players in town – he had done his homework. He gave us a lot of freedom."

"I just remember – personally – one of the things that stuck with me my whole life was at the end of 'Woman Is the Nigger of the World,' when it keeps saying, 'We make her paint her face and dance,' it gets into this weird time signature repetition in the end, on the way out. And I just remember we were playing that part, and looking across the room at John, and John and I made this eye contact, and we kept that through looking at each other, and playing almost to each other, through four or five times of the repetition of the outro of that song. It was kind of surreal. I was doing my part, but when you're looking at somebody and you get a vibe, it was running through my head, *'I'm standing here, playing with John Lennon from the Beatles...and we're recording what will probably be the single from the record.'* It was just awesome. I can close my eyes and see it now."

Elsewhere on the first two sides of *STiNYC*, quite a few politically-charged ditties are featured, including "Attica State" (about the Attica Prison riot that took place in September 1971), "Sunday Bloody Sunday" (which tackles the horrific Bloody Sunday massacre which occurred in January 1972 in North Ireland), and "John Sinclair" (concerning the manager of proto-punks the MC5, who was sentenced to ten years in prison for offering a pair of joints to an undercover female officer), among other tunes. Also contained is a healthy helping of Yoko on the first disc, including compositions that seemingly deal mostly with feminism and oppression, including the rockers "Sisters, O Sisters" and "We're All Water," and the more slow-paced/near-ballad "Born in a Prison."

The second album is recorded entirely live, with side three taped on December 15, 1969 (at the Lyceum Ballroom in London, England, for a UNICEF charity concert with George Harrison), and featuring just two tunes – "Cold Turkey" and "Don't Worry Kyoko." Meanwhile, side four is comprised of four tunes recorded on June 6, 1971 at the Fillmore East in New York City, with Frank Zappa and The Mothers of Invention. In an unedited interview with MTV in 1984, Zappa explained how his "collaboration" with John and Yoko came about.

"A journalist knocked on my door at a hotel called One Fifth Ave about 2:00 o'clock in the afternoon on the day of that show, and he was waiting there at the door – this man writes for *The Village Voice* – he was waiting there at the door with a tape recorder in his hand. And I just crawled out of bed my hair sticking out all over the place and my eyes were twirling like that [makes wild hand gesture]. 2:00 o'clock in the afternoon is very early to wake up if you played two shows in a night. And he says, 'Hi Frank. I'd like to introduce you to John Lennon.' He was sticking the mic at me like I'm gonna go, '*Eek!*' or something like that. So, I said, 'OK, come in'."

"The first thing he said to me is that 'You're not as ugly as I thought you'd be.' Which leads me to wonder about the strength of his glasses – because I'm as ugly as I ever was. Just as ugly now as I was then. And it's a great credit to Mr. Lennon that he wasn't shocked by all of this. So, he came in and we talked for a few minutes, and I asked him whether he wanted to play with us at the concert at the Fillmore East that night. And we just happened to have a recording truck there 'cause we were recording the shows for another purpose and the tapes were made."

"Now, *here's the bad part*. During the performance when Lennon was on stage with Yoko, we played one of my songs called 'King Kong.' And the deal that was made according to the usage of the tapes, was he got to use the tapes for his purpose and I got to use the tapes for my purpose. He released part of that performance on an album called *Some Time in New York City*, and changed the name of the song 'King Kong' to 'Jamrag,' and gave *himself and Yoko* writing and publishing credit on the song. Now obviously, this song has a melody and chord changes – somebody did write it, and it was not them. So…whoops!" When the same interviewer asked, "Did you ever do anything about it?" Zappa replied, "*Not yet.*"

Released on June 12, 1972, the album would go on to become the least commercially successful post-Beatles effort by Lennon (peaking at only #48 on the *Billboard 200*), with the album's lone single, "Woman Is the Nigger of the World," fairing even worse (#57 on the *Billboard Hot 100*). But despite its underwhelming chart performance, *Some Time in New York City* does have its moments, and perhaps offers the most definitive proof that Lennon was possibly the most fearless rock musician. *Ever.*

And it even left its mark on at least one notable rocker. "I had the John Lennon record, *Some Time in New York City*, when I was pretty young," recalled the Pixies' Frank Black. "I really love that record a lot. When John Lennon did more kind of arty, abrasive, dissonance – which you hear on some Plastic Ono records – I think it scared me a little bit. I didn't quite understand it." Neither did many others. And that's precisely what makes *Some Time in New York City* stand out so much from the rest of the Lennon discography.

The Rise and Fall of Ziggy Stardust
and the Spiders from Mars
(David Bowie, 1972)

The early '70s were chock full of flamboyant characters who were not afraid to dress the part. Case in point, Freddie Mercury, Elton John, Alice Cooper, Marc Bolan, and of course, David Bowie – particularly when the latter assumed an alter-ego, Ziggy Stardust, in time for the 1972 classic, *The Rise and Fall of Ziggy Stardust and the Spiders from Mars.*

But interestingly, Bowie was not always flashy – his early solo efforts were quite acoustic-y (especially such classic tunes as "Space Oddity" and "Changes"), and apart from very long hair and a penchant for wearing dresses, his fashion sense was not anything that was that much out of the ordinary. But once hooking up with guitarist Mick Ronson, Bowie's rockin' side certainly came to the surface – especially on the majority of 1970's *The Man Who Sold the World* (in particular the title track) and bits of 1971's *Hunky Dory* (the tune "Queen Bitch").

But with a solidified line-up that included a rhythm section of Trevor Bolder (bass) and Mick "Woody" Woodmansey (drums), Bowie was ready to take on his most ambitious work yet. Although some consider it to be a concept album, it does not truly tell a story from beginning to end like say, *Tommy* or *The Wall* did. But rather, each song tells its own little tale – with the seemingly doomed space alien rock star Ziggy Stardust letting his presence be felt throughout.

Recorded from November 8, 1971 through February 4, 1972 at Trident Studios in London, the sessions were co-produced by Bowie and Ken Scott (the same production team that had overseen *Hunky Dory*), *Ziggy Stardust* would be comprised of eleven tracks total. Although seemingly thought of as a hard rockin' recording, the album actually starts off quite mellow – with "Five Years" (which lyrically, sets the stage that Planet Earth only has five years left before an apocalypse) and "Soul Love," both of which wouldn't have sounded entirely out of place on *Hunky Dory*.

But by the third track, "Moonage Daydream," the rock finally begins to roll – with perhaps the most boldly nonsensical opening, when Bowie declares, "I'M AN ALLIGATOR!" The track also features one of Ronson's most wailing guitar solos at the end of the tune (which when performed live, would be extended even further). The next track, "Starman," would go on to become the album's highest-charting single in the UK (hitting #10), which shouldn't come as a surprise – it's the most melodic and "pop" offering of the bunch, before the first side comes to an end with the largely forgettable "It Ain't Easy" (a cover of a tune composed by US songwriter Ron Davies).

The second side begins with quite possibly the most underrated tune on the album, the sullen "Lady Stardust" (due to its memorable and melodic chorus), followed by another oft-overlooked tune, "Star" (which would finally get the attention it rightfully deserved years later when Bowie included it on his 1978 tour – and as heard on the concert recording *Stage*). And then…comes the final four, which puts *Ziggy* over the top.

"Hang on to Yourself" was such a keister-kicker that it rightfully served as the opening number for the subsequent tour in support of *Ziggy*, which is followed by the album's near-title track, "Ziggy Stardust." Truth be told, I would feel quite confident declaring this the album's top tune – due to a now-classic opening chord progression and a twistedly-anthemic chorus. And a bonus factoid about the tune – the phrase "leper messiah" is utilized…some fourteen years before thrashers Metallica recycled it as the title for a ditty on their classic *Master of Puppets* album.

And then the album's best-known tune – that unexplainably was not released at the time as an a-side single – "Suffragette City." If you were to name the #1 glam rock anthem of all time (and I'd like to stress glam rock of the early '70s – not the largely stinky glam metal movement of the mid-late '80s), it would probably be this rowdy n' rocking gem. Perhaps sensing that it would be bloody difficult to top that track's energy, *Ziggy* ends with a much more restrained and morose tune, "Rock n' Roll Suicide."

When *Ziggy* was released on June 16, 1972, it was an immediate success in the UK (where "Bowie mania" was sweeping the country) – peaking at #5. In the US it was a whole other story – while *Ziggy* only peaked at a measly #75, it continued to sell steadily, resulting in it being certified gold two years later (and it has never been re-certified since, which leads one to believe it may very well be multi-platinum by now).

And the album's artwork has gone on to become iconic – photographer Brian Ward snapped a shot of Bowie posing with a guitar on Heddon Street in London (although the cover was obviously touched up color-wise to make it look almost like a painting). And shortly afterwards, Bowie opted to undergo a major fashion makeover – shaving off his eyebrows, sporting a neon red mullet (quite possibly the first rocker to model this "short on the sides/long in the back" hairstyle), and wearing extravagant costumes designed by Kansai Yamamoto or Freddie Burretti.

Not only would the whole Ziggy era help launch glam rock globally, but would also be one of the contributing factors in the creation of punk rock (the spiky hairstyle of Sex Pistol Sid Vicious being a descendent of Ziggy's) and inspire other rockers over the years (Bauhaus would score a UK hit in 1982 with a cover of "Ziggy Stardust," Def Leppard mentioned Ziggy in their 1989 hit "Rocket," Marilyn Manson copying Bowie's eyebrow-less look decades later, etc.). But despite the success and buzz that the *Ziggy* album generated for Bowie, he opted to "break up the band" (to quote a line from the song "Ziggy Stardust") – announcing such onstage at the tour's final show on July 3, 1973 at the Hammersmith Odeon, and going solo soon after.

Lastly, just how "classic" is *The Rise and Fall of Ziggy Stardust and the Spiders from Mars*? How about *Library of Congress-level classic* – in 2017, it was selected for preservation in the National Recording Registry!

School's Out
(Alice Cooper, 1972)

By 1972, Alice Cooper (or should I say, "the original Alice Cooper *band*," just to be crystal clear) was already one of the leading hard rock/glam rock acts. But it was their fifth studio album overall that made them into one of *the world's* top leading hard rock/glam rock acts – and in particular, a certain tune.

Interestingly, when the Phoenix by way of LA by way of Detroit band – singer Alice Cooper (real name: Vincent Furnier), guitarists Glen Buxton and Michael Bruce, bassist Dennis Dunaway, and drummer Neal Smith – first began making albums, it was a different story. After being discovered by Frank Zappa, the band issued a pair of albums that were in a much more psychedelic/acid rock vein – 1969's *Pretties for You* and 1970's *Easy Action* – both of which went nowhere.

But once the quintet crossed paths with producer Bob Ezrin, the "Alice Cooper sound" we all know and love was born, resulting in a pair of hit albums in 1971 – *Love It to Death* and *Killer*. And in early '72, the band congregated at the Record Plant in New York City to work on the album that would become *School's Out*.

The only thing that the band needed to truly put them over the top was a top-10 hit single (up to this point, "I'm Eighteen" came closest – peaking at #21). And it turned out that the album-opening title track would indeed do the trick. One of the greatest rock anthems – and along with Pink Floyd's "Another Brick in the Wall (Part 2)," one off the greatest *anti-school* anthems – the song opens with a now instantly-recognizable riff courtesy of Mr. Buxton, before the band and Alice do an outstanding job of bottling (both lyrically and musically) the excitement that children feel upon hearing the final bell of the last day of school.

And while its riff and memorable chorus ("School's out for summer, School's out forever, School's been blown to pieces") are what sticks out the most for many, Smith's drumming also adds an interesting dynamic to the tune – which he discussed in the book *Bonzo: 30 Rock Drummers Remember the Legendary John Bonham.* "I liked pockets as well, but with the music that we had, even 'School's Out' went in and out of different beats – the chorus is like a bolero, and then the rest of the song lays in pockets and goes through changes. I'm a rudiment drummer – I took two years learning snare drum before I ever had a set of drums. I started when I was twelve years old, and then I got my first set of drums when I was fourteen. I studied those very hard."

"I was very influenced by marching bands – they're field snares and it's what I learned on and played on for two years. I had lessons in grade school and junior high and I was in marching band and orchestra, and in rock combos. Then, when I finally had a set of drums, I employed that, and that's why I always wanted to be in a band that wrote. And that's the evolution from the Nazz to Alice Cooper – when I was fortunate to join my best friends and be part of that band. It gave me the creativity to use a lot of rudiments and rhythms."

And while admittedly there were no other tunes on the album that were as concise and fiercely rocking as the title track (although "Luney Tune" and "Public Animal #9" come closest), the album can be pinpointed to as the one in which the group entered a true "cinematic" realm (obviously thanks in large part to Ezrin) – and is best experienced listened to from start to finish. Case in point, such tunes as "Gutter Cat vs. the Jets"/"Street Fight," "Alma Mater," and "Grand Finale." Other standouts include the surprisingly old time rock n' roll sounds of "Blue Turk" and the piano-led epic "My Stars."

Released on June 30, 1972, the album's cover image featured a badly abused wooden school desk (with the initials of all five Cooper members carved into it), and the early vinyl pressing of the album featured the LP wrapped in a pair of panties (made out of a paper-ish material)! Due to the success of the title track being issued as a single (which peaked at #7), the album rocketed up the charts – peaking at #2 on the *Billboard 200*, and earning platinum certification.

"Out of all the Top 40 songs that we had, the only one I was sure of was 'School's Out,' Alice told me for *Heavy Consequence* in 2021. "I said, 'If this isn't a hit, I should be selling shoes somewhere – because then I don't know anything about this business. This song has got everything. It's got every piece of what should be a hit.' And it was. 'Eighteen' was a hit...but 'School's Out' was *an anthem*. And those are the things that last for 50/60 years. It's impossible to close the show with anything except 'School's Out'."

Post-*School's Out*, the Cooper group would go on to issue arguably their best-ever album, 1973's *Billion Dollar Babies*, plus the oft-overlooked *Muscle of Love* the same year. With the band seemingly on the cusp of even larger/sustained success...the singer shockingly opted to go at it alone, while the Cooper band went their own way (with most of its members eventually uniting as the short-lived band, Billion Dollar Babies). Ezrin would continue working with Alice (including his best solo album, 1975's *Welcome to my Nightmare*), as well as leaving his stamp on additional classics by Kiss (1976's *Destroyer*) and Pink Floyd (1979's *The Wall*).

When I interviewed Ezrin for the book *The Eric Carr Story*, he saw quite a lot of similarities between early Kiss and Cooper. "Actually [Kiss and Alice Cooper] shared a lot of the same attributes. They had a great work ethic, great sense of humor. They were not 'precious' about what they were doing, but they were very serious about it. And all they wanted was to do the best they possibly could, so they could make the best stuff for their fans. That's what motivated both of them, that they were there for their fans. I think the Kiss guys are still doing that, and so is Alice. They're all great entertainers. They're all 'show people,' in the classic sense of it. They give the fans a great show."

And while Alice Cooper has been putting on a great show for decades by this point, it should not overshadow the quality of his early '70s recordings. Especially, *School's Out*.

Raw Power
(Iggy & the Stooges, 1973)

There are several albums that can be pinpointed to as contributing to the birth of punk rock. And most certainly, *Raw Power* by Iggy & the Stooges, is one of them. While it has gone on to be widely considered a classic rock recording, interestingly, the album was largely ignored upon its original release. The band (which had gone simply by "The Stooges" on their previous two LP's, 1969's self-titled debut and 1970's *Funhouse*) had experienced line-up upheaval at the time. Original bassist Dave Alexander was gone, a second guitarist, James Williamson, had joined and formed a two-guitar tandem with Ron Asheton, while singer Iggy Pop and drummer Scott Asheton remained in place. But the Stooges were dropped by their label, Elektra, after the first two albums failed to leave an impression on the charts, while several of the band members spiraled deep into drug addiction.

With the Stooges in limbo, Iggy made his way to New York City (by way of his hometown, Ypsilanti, Michigan), and received a fateful phone call – that soon-to-be-superstar/Stooges fan, David Bowie, would like to meet him. Shortly after an introduction at the hip hotspot, Max's Kansas City, Iggy signed on with Bowie's management, MainMan, and inked a recording contract with Columbia Records. And instead of inviting all of the Stooges to join him in England for this new venture, he initially only invited Williamson. But after it was determined that no British musicians that they had auditioned were up to snuff, the Asheton brothers were invited across the sea – with Ron switching over to bass.

When I spoke to James on two different occasions for *Songfacts* (in 2013 and 2018), he recalled the writing and recording of *Raw Power*. "I wrote most of that album in my room in London, on Seymour Walk. So, it was mostly written on acoustic guitar. I had a little Gibson B-25 natural, and we lived in a mews house – townhouse style – with lots of neighbors on both walls. So, I couldn't really play through an amp in there. I had to play everything acoustic. That turned out to be something I ended up doing for my entire career, because I found that the acoustic had a very clear tone. You could really hear what the music was. And then when it translated into electric, it was for all the better. That's how I wrote them…not all of them."

While the majority of *Raw Power* was rowdy hard rock with power chords/piercing solos galore (namely "Search and Destroy," "Your Pretty Face Is Going to Hell," the title track, "Shake Appeal," and "Death Trip"), there were a few numbers that dialed the intensity down (including "Penetration," "I Need Somebody" and especially, the closest thing to a ballad on the album, "Gimme Danger"). "I also liked the tonal qualities of the acoustic – you can really hear the notes quite well. I was fooling around and just came up with those chord patterns [for 'Gimme Danger'] – the beginning patterns of that song – and fleshed it out from there. It was a very convoluted process of actually stringing all that stuff together, but once it did come together, immediately it was like, a song. It was very quick from there on out."

But it turns out that one of the album's best known tracks, the ferocious album-opener, "Search and Destroy," was not written at the aforementioned location, but rather, at a rehearsal studio (R&G Jones) near Wimbledon. "Well, I had come up with kind of that 'bum bum bum bum bum bum bum' a little bit, but it was more in regard to imitating a machine gun, if you will. Because this is the era of the Vietnam War. And so we were kind of screwing around with that, and that's where that figure comes from. Then the rest of the song was around that. But I think the beginning, the 'bum bum bum bum bum bum bum, bum bum bum bum bum bum bum,' that part was the thing that really kicked off that song."

Recorded at CBS Studios in London from September 10-October 6, 1972, Williamson recounted to *Vintage Guitar* in 2018 which equipment he used for the sessions. "I was pretty sparse back in those days. What I ended up using on the tracks was my 1969 cherry burst Les Paul Custom [aka "The Leopard Lady"]. That's been the guitar I've pretty much used on every record I've ever made – up until the single with Maia last year [2016's 'Sickkk' and 'I Made a Mistake']. And then I donated that guitar – along with the acoustic guitar that I wrote all of *Raw Power* on, which was a Gibson B-25 natural – to the Rock and Roll Hall of Fame. So, I no longer

have those guitars. But I used that cherry burst and an English Vox AC30 – because we recorded in London [at CBS Studios]. That was pretty much it. I did use an occasional Marshall for solos, but I didn't use any pedals or any effects back then. So occasionally I had to bring in something that would really sustain well in the studio. But mostly, it was the AC30."

Although *Raw Power* lists Iggy Pop and David Bowie as co-producers, it was initially the band producing, as Williamson told *Songfacts*. "What happened on that album was that the management team that we had over in England was distracted by Bowie breaking in the US, and they kind of left us alone. So we went into the studio to make the record that we owed CBS and we basically had no adult supervision – we just essentially went in there and did whatever we wanted to. Consequently, there are some technical problems with that album." Eventually, these "technical problems" were sorted out when Bowie was enlisted to remix the album in one day at Western Sound Recorders, in Los Angeles, during October – leading to his production credit (despite not being present for the actual recording sessions).

Although the album failed to sell (and led to the Stooges' split a year later), by the mid-to-late '70s, it was already pointed to as a landmark proto-punk release, and an obvious influence on the classic debuts by the Ramones [1976's self-titled] and the Sex Pistols [1977's *Never Mind the Bollocks*], among others. Over the years, such artists as the Red Hot Chili Peppers, Guns N' Roses, Soundgarden, Def Leppard, Monster Magnet, and John Mellencamp have all covered tunes off *Raw Power,* while Kurt Cobain listed it as his #1 favorite recording (in the book *Journals*).

Bassist Mike Watt – who played with the reunited Stooges from 2003-2016 – offers his thoughts on *Raw Power*. "I heard it third – like in the order. It actually came out when I was in high school, and the bass was kind of small. Because the first two albums – especially *Funhouse* – Dave Alexander was the bassist. And Ronnie plays bass on *Raw Power,* and the drums are also kind of small. But in a way, as a piece, it's freaky. It's trippy. I'm talking about the David Bowie mix – the original mix. I remember Scotty telling me when he heard the test pressing, *'Frisbee time!'* They were pissed, and I understand in a way."

"But as a piece, as a whole thing, it's just so bizarre – the way the lead guitars come out of nowhere. I think it's a good thing. And Ronnie always said he liked the songs. But that's a bad record – bad meaning good. Really influential. But me playing with both guys [Ronnie and James], they're very unique people – they're not guys who learned off records, they're guys who developed their own sound."

Spectrum
(Billy Cobham, 1973)

Where was the missing link between the psychedelic stylings of Jimi Hendrix and the shredder pyrotechnics of Eddie Van Halen? You may very well be able to pinpoint it to guitarist Tommy Bolin, and specifically, the opening track, "Quadrant 4," from Billy Cobham's jazz-fusion tour de force from 1973, *Spectrum.*

As the drummer of Mahavishnu Orchestra, Cobham was quickly making a name for himself on the strength of such trailblazing jazz-fusion albums as 1971's *The Inner Mounting Flame* and 1973's *Birds of Fire.* But there wasn't a whole heck of a lot of room for collaboration within Mahavishnu, as guitarist John McLaughlin was the undisputed main songwriter. Looking to establish himself as his own band leader, Cobham set out to work on his debut solo recording.

Instead of connecting with an established guitarist for the sessions, Cobham instead enlisted the then-unknown Bolin, who was based at the time in Boulder, Colorado, freshly out of blues rockers Zephyr (and playing in a local band, Energy), but had impressed the drummer when he had heard what Bolin had contributed to demo recordings by flautist Jeremy Steig. And when Mahavishnu was passing through Colorado on tour, Cobham supposedly made a personal visit to Bolin's apartment, to invite him to New York, to provide guitar on the sessions that would result in *Spectrum.*

Despite Bolin presumably being the only musician on the sessions that did not read music, the main band – which was comprised of Cobham, Bolin, bassist Lee Sklar, and keyboardist Jan Hammer – worked at a breakneck pace, recording the entire album in a mere *three days* (May 14-16, 1973) at Electric Lady Studios. And the electrifying results speak for themselves.

The aforementioned "missing link" between JH and EVH can be heard in the raging "Quadrant 4," which begins with some rapid-fire keyboard play from Hammer (who played so fluidly that many have mistakenly assumed it was a guitar solo), before Bolin makes his grand entrance just before the 2:00 mark. For the next two minutes, Bolin simply shreds on his Strat, while also testing the limits of his tremolo bar and creating laser gun sounds with his trusty old Echoplex – resulting in one of the greatest rock guitar solos ever committed to tape.

And while there aren't any other tracks as intense as "Quadrant 4," *Spectrum* is an extremely consistent album (although admittedly, several brief "interludes" tend to interrupt the flow). Case in point, "Taurian Matador" (which sees Hammer and Bolin exchange solos back and forth), the killer groove of "Stratus" (which contains another near two-minute long wailing guitar solo), and the more laid-back yet funky album closer, "Red Baron." The only two full-length tunes on the entire album that do not utilize the six-string wizardry of Bolin are the horn-heavy title track and "Le Lis" (the latter featuring John Tropea on guitar).

When I spoke to Hammer for *Touched by Magic: The Tommy Bolin Story,* he recalled what made the recording sessions so special. "With *Spectrum*, it was a real breakthrough, and everybody was sharp and on top of things. Everybody was focused. A lot of it was not ever written. So it wasn't any handicap for [Bolin] – you hum whatever you have in mind, and it comes together in rehearsal. Even though Billy had written some things down, they were more for the other type of sessions, which Tommy wasn't on – the more jazzy things with the larger group. But as far as the things with Tommy and the four-piece band, there was a one-off riff, and just *go.*"

Seemingly upon the album's release on October 1, 1973 via Atlantic Records, *Spectrum* became an incredibly influential jazz-fusion classic – inspiring some of rock's top musicians, including Jeff Beck, as drummer Carmine Appice also remembered in *Touched by Magic.* "That Cobham album is the thing that got Jeff Beck to move on to the *Blow by Blow* [released in 1975] stuff. I was with Jeff with Beck Bogert & Appice, I had Billy's album and the Mahavishnu album, and we used to drive in the cars together. Pretty much, we would listen to Mahavishnu Orchestra and the Billy Cobham album with Tommy on it. The whole vibe of that jazz-rock mixture, Jeff really liked it."

Bolin's friend/eventual Peter Frampton bassist, Stanley

Sheldon, also explained the album's enduring influence in the book. "As far as the world of fusion goes, you can't talk about fusion music without…that's in the canon. That's one of the major influences for all – you look at Marcus Miller today, the great fusion bassist, he produced Miles' last records. But on his most recent solo outing, he covered "Red Baron" from *Spectrum*, that won a Grammy – it's called *M Squared* [released in 2002]. That record is great, and they do a version of "Red Baron" that's just awesome. I guess what I'm speaking of is the influence it had on all musicians – that one record. It really did. When I tell a musician that Tommy was my friend, they'll quote the *Spectrum* album. That touched everybody – every thinking musician, anyway."

Due in large part to his playing on *Spectrum,* Bolin became a highly sought-after guitarist, resulting in additional exceptional recordings with the likes of the James Gang (1973's *Bang!* and 1974's *Miami*), Alphonse Mouzon (1975's *Mind Transplant*), and Deep Purple (1975's *Come Taste the Band*), as well as issuing a pair of solo albums (1975's *Teaser* and 1976's *Private Eyes*). Sadly, Bolin had developed a drug addiction, and on December 4, 1976 (while on tour with Jeff Beck), died from an overdose of heroin and other substances.

But all these years later, Bolin's playing on *Spectrum* continues to endure, as explained by Greg Hampton (the producer of the 2006 Bolin compilation, *Whips and Roses I & II,* 2011's *The Definitive Teaser Collector's Edition,* and the 2012 Bolin tribute album, *Great Gypsy Soul*). "The guitar playing on *Spectrum* by Tommy Bolin truly was the beginning of the instrumental jazz/rock-fusion movement – an astounding barrage of guitar riffs and melodies, that are as memorable as any vocal melodies. It was so edgy and had such authority, and the use of the Echoplex with it…he opened my eyes to actually playing effects pedals, and to playing with natural dynamics, and in the same breath, a mad machine gun burst of unconventional notes and rock and jazz licks – that would always land just right. Right on the edge – brilliant genius."

Rock n' Roll Animal
(Lou Reed, 1974)

More so than any other decade, the 1970s were abundant with classic live albums by rockers. Case in point, the Allman Brothers' *At Fillmore East*, Deep Purple's *Made in Japan*, Kiss' *Alive!*, Peter Frampton's *Frampton Comes Alive*, and Cheap Trick's *At Budokan*. But one release that seems to get lost in the shuffle is Lou Reed's *Rock n' Roll Animal*. Before his 1972 breakthrough glam rock hit, *Transformer*, Reed was best-known for his work with proto-punks the Velvet Underground. But by the time of *Rock n' Roll Animal*, Reed had embraced classic rock sounds, thanks to the awesome guitar duo of Steve Hunter and Dick Wagner.

Reed's previous work did not rely on guitar harmonies or busy backing music (as the focus was primarily on his "street poet lyrics"). But when he enlisted Bob Ezrin to produce his lush 1973 solo effort, *Berlin*, the producer invited Hunter and Wagner to supply guitar for the album…which led to the guitar duo also backing the singer on the album's supporting tour. "With the combination of me and Steve Hunter on guitars, it was like that from the very first day," Wagner told me about how effortless it was working with Hunter during a *Songfacts* interview in 2014. "It was amazing, putting together two guitar players, and we made a conscious decision right from the beginning that we would divide up the leads and the rhythms so that neither one of us would be the dominate guitar player. It would be a pair, a duo, and it really worked great. We sounded great together. We have a similar touch of a guitar and our styles are similar, but yet different enough so you can tell."

With bassist Prakash John, keyboardist Ray Colcord, and drummer Pentti "Whitey" Glan rounding out the backing group (and for the first time in his career, Reed solely singing and not playing guitar), it was decided that the group's performance on December 21, 1973 at Howard Stein's Academy of Music in New York would be recorded and later issued as a live album. "I knew he had gone off to Europe and was kind of out of sight," rocker/poet Jim Carroll recalled in the 1998 Reed documentary, *Rock & Roll Heart*. "But then he comes back to New York and he's doing these shows at the old Academy of Music. I went to two of the shows and they were recording them for a live album, which turned out to be the *Rock n' Roll Animal* album. At the right moment, they start going into the power chords of what you couldn't mistake was 'Sweet Jane,' and Lou just kind of struts very easily out for the first time on stage. He doesn't have a guitar and he's got this spiked dog collar on, his hair is all short, and he's in these leathers, and somebody yelled out 'Heroin!' from the audience, and the first thing he said was, '*Shut the fuck up!*', picked up the mic, and started to go into the first verse of 'Sweet Jane'."

Due to most of the songs being much longer than the original versions (and almost completely re-worked musically/sometimes not even resembling the original song structure) only five songs were included on the original LP. Case in point, the aforementioned album-opener, "Sweet Jane," which begins with an instrumental interlude (featuring harmonies and carefully interwoven lines between the two guitarists) that lasts for over three minutes, before the song's familiar chords ring out. And on a rendition of the VU classic, "Heroin," the tune now stretched to over thirteen minutes in length due to a smorgasbord of soloing from about halfway through to the song's conclusion.

But one of the better examples of a complete overhaul of an earlier classic was "White Light/White Heat," which musically, had absolutely nothing to do with the noisy original, and had morphed into an uptempo funky rocker. One of the album's pleasant surprises was the *Berlin* obscurity "Lady Day" (with its slashing guitar lines), before concluding with the album's second-longest tune, the ten minute-plus "Rock n' Roll" (again, due to the addition of many a solo) – which includes an awesome phased-out funk guitar break at the 4:18 mark.

"To me, it was a blessing," Wagner reminisced about his time in Reed's band. "Because Lou Reed offered the opportunity to put this band together and for Steve and I to play together, and it really helped make our reputation. He's a great writer, Lou Reed. He's not a great singer, but what is great singing? I mean, Bob Dylan wasn't a great singer, either. But certain people do their own songs really well in a style. So I loved Lou's songs and I loved Lou, but he's not an easy character to understand. Lou was different than most people. But he's a true artist and I loved working with him." And just to clear up a possible misconception from my earlier observations and descriptions – all of the songs' lengthy durations were not due to indulgent-meandering-jam-type-soloing. No siree. From the sound of it, Hunter and Wagner seemed to have many of their guitar lines and harmonies worked out beforehand, and their solos sound inspired and focused throughout.

Released in February 1974 (exact date unknown), the album peaked at #46 on the *Billboard 200* and fared better in the UK, where it reached #26. The album would become a cult classic due to quite a few tracks being spun by FM radio – and resulted in it becoming one of Reed's best-selling albums, eventually earning gold certification. Also of note, the other tunes recorded that night that did not appear on *Animal* would later comprise 1975's *Lou Reed Live* (with two extra previously unreleased tunes, "How Do You Think It Feels" and "Caroline Says I," added to a remastered CD version of *Animal* in 2000).

Despite his backing band showing great promise, Reed instead opted to distance himself from the album and dismiss the band – as his immediate musical path took him away from guitar solos. After Hunter and Wagner's exit, they joined Alice Cooper's band, and in 1975, Reed unleashed perhaps the biggest "middle finger" release that an established rocker ever issued, *Metal Machine Music*. "He fired me at the end of the tour because he wanted to go in another direction," remembers Wagner about his exit. "He claims that he didn't like the *Rock n' Roll Animal* album, but at the time he sure loved it. I was sort of the bandleader and arranger for the band. Did most of the arrangements for the live show."

"A lot of the songs were from the Velvet Underground days, and I wanted to take them out of that placid performance of the songs and make it more for the concert stage and the stadiums, so I did some majestic arranging with some of the songs – that's what I do. Within the context of the band and how to deliver the songs, it really worked. I guess Lou doesn't really like it that much, but that's kind of a lie. You would think he would, but whatever. I don't really care. It's part of history now, it's on record. And *Rock n' Roll Animal* stands very tall, it's a big record."

And in my *Songfacts* interview with Wagner (which sadly took place a short while before his passing on July 30, 2014 at the age of 71), he could also detect the album's importance and influence on rock music. "I think that, yeah, we were very influential on a lot of bands. We still are – people still talk about *Rock n' Roll Animal*. I'm very proud of that record, without a doubt."

Kiss
(Kiss, 1974)

When conversations arise about the greatest hard rock debut albums, the usual selections immediately come to mind for many – offerings by Led Zeppelin, Van Halen, and Guns N' Roses, to name a few. But one debut that seems to get overlooked quite often is the 1974 self-titled album from Kiss.

At the time, glam rock was beginning to be phased out – David Bowie would soon stop shaving his eyebrows and drop the makeup for his streamlined "Thin White Duke" persona, Alice Cooper was about to go solo and embrace ballads, and the New York Dolls were on the cusp of imploding. Hence, '74 would not have been the most ideal time to release a debut disc from a makeup-wearing band.

Although singer/guitarist Paul Stanley and singer/bassist Gene Simmons had been playing music together for a spell in the New York City area, it was not until 1973 that they finally crossed paths with two other like-minded musicians – first drummer Peter Criss, and then lead guitarist Ace Frehley – comprising the classic Kiss line-up.

After building a local following, attracting manager Bill Aucoin, and signing with the fledgling Casablanca Records, the group – which performed with their faces disguised by makeup and dressed in costumes/platform boots – was not as "femme" as the other aforementioned glam acts, and also, rocked a heck of a lot harder (ok, ok…besides Alice Cooper from 1970-1973).

So, when the quartet arrived at Bell Sound Studios in New York City during October-November 1973 to lay down what would become their debut album, they interestingly chose not to enlist the famous producer who oversaw an early demo (Eddie Kramer), but rather, hooked up with the less-renowned production duo of Kenny Kerner and Richie Wise.

Speaking to *Songfacts* in 2013, Wise looked back on the sessions. "I remember being out in the studio with them trying to work out some better arrangements for the songs, making them more available to the listener, put in the verses, choruses, bridges, repeats, whatever, in the right places."

"I worked very closely with Ace playing guitar," he continued, "because as a guitar player I was able to piece together some nice guitar solos for him and work with him on some of that stuff. The vocals went really smooth. I don't have any negative feelings at all. The first album was a breeze to do. I think we recorded it in six days and mixed it in six or seven days. It took about 13 days from start to finish to do it. It was done quickly and I'm very happy about that one."

Instead of kicking things off with a tune that served as their live-opener for the next two years ("Deuce"), another rockin' tune, "Strutter," got the nod. Also included was Kiss' first-ever single, "Nothin' to Lose" (which sees Simmons sing the verses with Stanley joining in at parts, before Criss handles lead scat vocals on the chorus).

"Firehouse" would soon become a concert highlight (due to Simmons breathing fire at the song's conclusion), while the Frehley-penned "Cold Gin" quickly became another Kiss classic (although it would take Frehley a few more albums before he would gather enough courage to begin singing songs he wrote – Simmons handles vocals here). And closing side one was the song that Stanley played for Simmons the first time they ever met, "Let Me Know" (then known as "Sunday Driver").

Side two kicks off with the throwaway cover of "Kissin' Time" (made famous by teen idol Bobby Rydell in 1959), which was included at the behest of Casablanca Records head, Neil Bogart. But up next, we get one of the album's best tunes, "Deuce." While the song's lyrics don't necessarily make a whole hell of a lot of sense, the track has certainly whipped countless concert goers into a frenzy over the years.

"Love Theme from Kiss" is one of the few times Kiss ever went instrumental (and is the sole tune on the album credited to all four members concerning authorship), while "100,000 Years" would soon become a concert highlight (onstage, it would include a drum solo by Criss and a stage rap by Stanley, enthusing the merits of rock n' roll). Wrapping things up would be an epic, "Black Diamond," which would also become a crucial component to Kiss concerts – serving as the last song performed each night (during which Criss' drum riser would…rise).

In addition to the quality of the material, what has made Kiss' debut age so well throughout the years is the way it was recorded and produced – keeping things close to how the quartet sounded live. "Without the volume," was what Wise recalled being the LP's sonic key to *Songfacts*. "The album was done very organically, which I liked. We didn't go for a bombastingly crazy, overly distorted sound. Things were kept real. There was a minimum of effects used, so therefore the instruments stayed pretty close by, in your face. That album has a nice big sound to it without being loud, and without being super distorted."

Released on February 18th, 1974 (some sources cite February 8th), the album did not exactly set the charts alight – peaking at a meagre #87 on the *Billboard* chart. But it did spend an impressive 22 weeks on the tally, and eventually, obtained gold certification. However, it is impossible to calculate just how many subsequent renowned rock musicians were inspired and influenced by this particular recording. And a year-and-a-half later, most of these ditties were included as even higher-energy renditions on their commercial breakthrough, *Alive!*

So, the next time you find yourself involved in a "greatest hard rock debut album debate," consider that song-for-song, Kiss' debut is right up there among the Rock & Roll Hall of Fame group's top albums, with the band still performing four tracks off the disc 45 years later on their "End of the Road" farewell tour.

If nothing else, the debut disc tops Gene Simmons' list of Kiss albums. "The first record is my favorite because it has so many memories," he stated on *Good Morning America* in late 2018 while promoting the band's farewell tour. "You know when a dream starts to come true? You dream big and you have that first record, and you hold it in your hands. I bought our first record, and I went, 'Wow, I'm in Kiss.'"

Queen II
(Queen, 1974)

Out of all the albums from Queen's glory period (1973-1980, i.e., pre-*Hot Space*), the one I find myself listening to the most is probably the most obscure – and lowest-selling – of the bunch...*Queen II*. Part of the reason is if you think back to what rock music resembled at the time, *no one* sounded like this – Brian May's multi-tracked guitars, the group's trademark vocal harmonies, the ability to somehow blur the lines between heavy metal, prog rock, and glam rock (sometimes all within the same song), etc.

"I liked Queen because they were *a metal band*," Twisted Sister's Dee Snider once told me, in the book *Long Live Queen: Rock Royalty Discuss Freddie, Brian, John & Roger.* "And when Freddie came out – and there's nothing wrong with that – and started taking control more and more, and the band became more and more flamboyant, and less metal, when 'Bicycle Race' and 'Fat Bottomed Girls' came out, it was like, they jumped the shark for me. *Queen II* is my favorite Queen album, and that is their least popular record. They play nothing off that record. It was one of their biggest disappointments – they put so much into that album, and the public didn't receive it well. *I* received it well. Axl Rose, it is one of his favorite Queen albums. But they started to realize that they had to commercialize a little with the third album, *Sheer Heart Attack.* But *Queen II* is my favorite."

Although Queen – justifiably – would eventually become one of the world's most popular rock bands, it's hard to believe that their first few releases did not exactly set the world on fire sales-wise. The group – singer Freddie Mercury, guitarist Brian May, bassist John Deacon, and drummer Roger Taylor – released their self-titled debut in 1973, and while it was indeed an outstanding album (why it is never mentioned in the "greatest rock debuts of all-time" debates is befuddling), it was a bomb commercially. So, it would make sense for the band to offer an easier-to-digest sophomore album, right? *Wrong.*

Recorded between August 1973 and February 1974 at Trident Studios in London, the group was co-producing once again with Roy Thomas Baker – along with a rather obscure name, Robin Geoffrey Cable. *Queen II* begins "the white side" (rather than "side one") with a somber-sounding instrumental, "Procession" – which is comprised solely of what sounds like a heartbeat and a string orchestra comprised solely of May's Red Special guitar.

"Brian May opened our ears to the guitar orchestra," violinist/luthier Mark Wood raved in the same *Long Live Queen* book. "It was never done before in rock to this extent. He is a brilliant musician and composer. The guitar orchestra in 'Procession' on *Queen II* is astounding. He was a total influence on me, but remember, Brian was highly influenced by classical violin music, too. You can hear it in his vibrato and slurring of his note choices." The guitarist of the *We Will Rock You* musical and Meat Loaf's band, Paul Crook, also points to "Procession" as his gateway into the world of Queen. "When I first heard Queen, I believe the first song I heard was 'Procession' off of *Queen II*. I think that's what did it for me. Hearing the harmony guitar, and going, 'What the fuck is that sound'?"

And then, the first tune to feature the exceptional vocals of Freddie was a rocker, "Father to Son," which lyrically seems to focus on things being passed down from generation to generation (on the male side of things). But instead of following in a hard rockin' path, "White Queen" was a gorgeous ballad, which begins with acoustic guitar, before slowly building into a grand composition. The underrated melodic rocker, "Some Day One Day," was the first Queen tune to ever feature May on lead vocals, before Taylor gets his allotted "one tune to sing per album" with another rocker, "Loser in the End."

"The black side" (side two) begins with one of the heaviest tunes Queen ever recorded, "Ogre Battle," which was surprisingly penned entirely by Mercury ("surprisingly" because the singer/pianist has become best known for penning Queen's more pop-sounding tunes – "Killer Queen," "We Are the Champions," "Bicycle Race," etc.) and features some of their most fairy tale-y lyrics ever. Case in point, "He gives a great big cry and he can swallow up the ocean, With a mighty tongue he catches flies and the palm of his hand incredible size."

The tune has gone on to receive great praise by several renowned rockers over the years, such as the singer on the first two Iron Maiden albums, Paul Di'Anno: "To me, the first thrash metal song I ever heard was by Queen, 'Ogre Battle'." And also, King's X singer/bassist, Doug Pinnick: "The other thing that really impressed me about Queen was 'Ogre Battle.' It was *so* fast for the time. Now, it's not fast at all, but when it came on with the high harmonies, I lost my mind when I heard 'Ogre Battle,' because it was so heavy and so melodic, and so beautiful at the same time."

One of the artsier tunes on *II* follows with "The Fairy Feller's Master-Stroke" (a tune whose title was borrowed by the name of a famous painting by artist Richard Dadd), and as Joe Russo – who assumes the role of Mercury in the tribute band, Almost Queen – explains, is an absolute vocal tour de force. "In the beginning, the richness of *Queen I* and *Queen II* is I think a tribute to him – the vocal overlays. You can't believe how many vocal parts are on some of those songs. Y'know, 'The Fairy Feller's Master-Stroke' – you're talking like, *40 vocal parts* on it." A tune comprised solely of voices and piano, "Nevermore," is next, before another one of my favorite tunes on the album arrives, the 6 minute and 32 second opus, "The March of the Black Queen."

"By *A Night at the Opera,* Roy Thomas Baker's production was certainly perfected by then," adds Joe Russo once more. "But *Queen II* has some *really* great parts to it. And there are a lot of parallels with stuff like 'March of the Black Queen' and 'Bohemian Rhapsody' – with the drama of the song and different parts and different movements. There are ballads on *Queen II,* but I think the sound – and of course, the studio quality – made it a little better. But it was really perfected by the time they got to *A Night at the Opera.* I would absolutely say that's the masterpiece."

"Black Queen" also features some great May guitar work throughout, which was appreciated by latter-day Judas Priest guitarist Richie Faulkner. "The solos in 'March of the Black Queen,' 'The Fairy Feller's Master-Stroke,' right up until 'These Are the

Days of Our Lives' – he was a very 'musical' guitar player. He said so much. He wasn't a flash guitar player all the time. He could play fast stuff, but it was what he was emoting with the notes that he was using was what connected with me most. So like I said, 'March of the Black Queen.' All of it man, is pretty inspiring stuff for me as a guitar player."

"Black Queen" leads directly into "Funny How Love Is" (which leads to some – well, at least *me* – considering "Black Queen" and "FHLI" as one single, long composition), before the album wraps up with what would become Queen's first-ever hit single in their homeland of the United Kingdom, the piano-led rocker, "Seven Seas of Rhye." The tune was "previewed" at the very end of their debut (as a brief instrumental), before transforming into a more fully realized tune with vocals on *II*, and serving as an introduction to the band for many of their subsequently longest-tenured British fans – thanks to it being issued as the album's lone single, and peaking at #10 on the UK chart.

"I believe the first time I heard Queen would have been 'Seven Seas of Rhye' – on the radio," recalls Diamond Head guitarist Brian Tatler. "The first thing that impressed me was the guitars all over it." And even original Sex Pistols bassist, Glen Matlock, admitted to being a "Rhye guy." "I did like the track 'Seven Seas of Rhye.' It had a good groove, and it was exciting."

And finally, the iconic cover image of *Queen II* – photographed by one of the greatest rock lensmen of all-time, Mick Rock, who was kind enough to discuss his memories of the photo session with me for *Songfacts* in 2020 (just a year before his passing). "I had been in France at the Château d'Hérouville with David [Bowie] for *Pin-Ups*. That was an album where I didn't shoot the front cover but I did shoot the photos on the back of the cover and the inner sleeve. And after that, I did Mott the Hoople's *All the Young Dudes*, so I was all over that scene at that moment in time and became 'the glam photographer,' as I also shot Roxy Music. And Queen."

"There was a guy [Ken Scott] who was David's engineer and had co-produced *Ziggy Stardust* and *Hunky Dory*, and he worked for a company called Trident Audio Productions. They had a studio in the middle of London, in Soho. I had built a little notoriety because of my work with David, Lou [Reed], and Iggy [Pop]. And Queen – and very much Freddie – wanted to get a slice of that glam stuff. I remember going and they played me *Queen II*, and I said, 'Wow...that's kind of like *Ziggy Stardust* meets Led Zeppelin.' They loved that, and that probably clinched the deal."

"I remember coming across a photo of Marlene Dietrich on the set of *Shanghai Express*. I showed it to Freddie and said, 'Freddie, you could be Marlene Dietrich! How do you fancy that?' And he loved it. They hadn't had any success particularly – this was only their second album – but they were very confident that they were going to do well – certainly Freddie was. Anyway, I sold him on the idea. The theme was black and white, so I shot two set-ups: There was the black set-up and the white set-up, and they weren't sure what the front cover should be. In the end, the white photo ended up on the inside of the gatefold spread. But that shot, the rest of the band was a little bit timid about it because they thought it looked very pretentious. Freddie said, 'Pretentious? Yes, of course we're pretentious...because we are that good'!"

"Freddie was kind of the 'visual guru' of the band because he'd been to art college, whereas Roger was a dentist, Brian was some kind of astrophysicist, and John was very quiet. Anyway, that became the cover, and of course they copied it for the 'Bohemian Rhapsody' video. Like the *Transformer* shot for Lou and the *Raw Power* shot for Iggy, it stayed around and became their definitive image. There was a ladder involved to get the right angle. When I shot it, I shot it in black and white, I shot it in color, I shot it with their hands in different positions. Mostly I shot them with the hands as you see them, but there were little variations, and Brian and Roger changed sides. Some images just stay around, and that one definitely stayed around."

Original Judas Priest guitarist KK Downing recalls being one of the lucky few to first hear the album *prior* to its release. "We actually were in Trident Studios, and Queen had just wrapped up – they were working down there with Roy Thomas Baker – and we went into that studio to do a few overdubs. I think Queen had just finished mixing *Queen II* there. We actually listened to the album on a great big pair of Cadac speakers – which were about six-foot tall, maybe more – in this room. I was absolutely blown away with how fantastic it sounded."

Released on March 8, 1974, *Queen II* would climb all the way to #5 on the UK album chart (thanks to the success of the aforementioned "Seven Seas of Rhye" single and a memorable performance on *Top of the Pops*), but only manage #49 in the US. However, it *did* help set the stage for the next two albums that served as Queen's global breakthrough, *Sheer Heart Attack* and *A Night at the Opera* – the latter of which spawned "Bohemian Rhapsody."

"The thing that was so important about Queen to me was how every album takes you on a journey," adds radio personality Matt Pinfield. "From *Queen II* on, I felt like they approached every record in the way that *Sgt. Pepper* was – in the sense that, 'Here we are, we're going on a trip right now. We're taking you on a journey – *a musical journey.*' The way the songs would weave together so brilliantly, and you'd turn the record over – back then, it was vinyl, of course – and you start the next part of the journey. That's why they're one of my favorite bands of all-time. They were so ambitious, but delivered. It was one thing to be ambitious, but it's another to be able to deliver incredible songs like that. And back in those days, they weren't waiting three years to make each record – they had an album coming out just about every year from '73 on."

And while Queen would soon conquer the charts with such hit singles as "Killer Queen," "Bohemian Rhapsody" and "Somebody to Love," there are still quite a few renowned rockers who prefer the group's earlier, not as easily digestible recordings. Rick Springfield: "Actually, my favorite albums of theirs are from before they became huge – *Queen II* and *Sheer Heart Attack*." Ronni Le Tekrø: "*Queen II*, because of its musically diverse color." Mark Wood: "I loved *Queen II*, and that album sealed my ears forever with their greatness." And lastly, one more quote from Matt Pinfield, which neatly sums up *Queen II*: "The first album, I loved.

By the time of *Queen II,* they were making their albums very conceptual. The albums took you on this incredible journey."

Red
(King Crimson, 1974)

By 1974, there had been moments where prog bands rocked hard (Yes' "Heart of the Sunrise" immediately comes to mind). However, no band had yet truly merged the complexity of prog rock with the mighty riffs of heavy metal. That all changed with the arrival of King Crimson's seventh studio album overall, *Red.*

Formed during 1968 in London as a multi-membered band, Crimson issued one of prog's all-time classic recordings right off the bat, with 1969's *In the Court of the Crimson King* (which spawned the classic tunes "21st Century Schizoid Man" and the title track) – and featured a pre-ELP Greg Lake on vocals and bass. The album also proved to be a hit on both sides of the Atlantic – peaking at #5 in the UK and #28 in the US, and earning gold certification in both countries. But the longer the band went on throughout the early '70s, the height of the band's chart-placements dwindled, and its members exited one by one (all except for guitarist Robert Fripp). By 1973's *Larks' Tongues in Aspic*, singer/bassist John Wetton and former Yes drummer Bill Bruford were now part of the line-up (among others), and by *Red*, the group's line-up had whittled down to a trio of Wetton-Fripp-Bruford.

"As the band progressed, we sort of developed unbelievably," Wetton told *Songfacts* in 2014. "We were starting to be a really good live band during *Starless and Bible Black*. You can tell that when we started interspersing bits of improvisation with real studio tracks. And then by *Red*, we're actually a fully-fledged, in-your-face, shit-kicking unit, because we'd been on the road for three years. And that does things to you. So when we recorded *Red*, all we needed was a set-up where we could play it live, basically. We used our live engineer, George Chkiantz, at the Olympic Studios and we set the band up in a live room so that all we had to do was play it, because we'd played it a thousand times before on the road, and it worked."

And as Wetton already stated, most of *Red* would be recorded at Olympic Studios in London (from July-August, 1974) with the band also handling production duties. And it didn't take long to realize that this was an entirely different-sounding Crimson when compared to their earlier efforts – especially with the album-opening, Sabbath-y, all-instrumental title track. And in the same *Songfacts* chat, Wetton explained the song's heaviness was no accident. "We'd learned how to be in-your-face on the road. There are some gigs that you play where you can't be a namby pamby. You can't be pussy-footing around. You've got to hit people really hard, and we'd learned how to do that."

"It's just purely from road experience: You go on stage opening up for ZZ Top in Texas, you can't go on the English flowers of the poet's society. It ain't going to work. You've got to come on like a ton of bricks. And by the time Crimson finished, that's exactly what we were. And, yeah, a lot of it was killer metal from the guitar department, and for the bass, sure. We'd virtually learned to do it as a three-piece by the end. David [Cross, the band's violinist], I like David a lot, but he was becoming more and more ineffectual as the tour went on. At that point you either grasp it or you run away screaming."

Later in the album, a similar-sounding, heavy tune rears its head, "One More Red Nightmare." But this time, contains singing/lyrics. And Wetton explained the tune's lyrical inspiration – "At that time we were taking about three flights a day. If we had air miles in those days, I'd *still* be flying on them! This went on for months and months and months on end. It goes without saying that we knew airline crews personally. We'd walk on the plane, 'Oh, hi Joe. Hi Cindy, how you doing? How are the kids?' It's just incredible the amount of flying that that band did. And we had some pretty hairy experiences. 'One More Red Nightmare' is just that. It's one of my pre-Joni Mitchell lyrics. It's kind of arty."

But not all of *Red* was heavy. Case in point, a pair of tunes that touched upon many moods – "Fallen Angel" and "Starless," which saw a chap by the name of Richard Palmer-James earn a songwriting credit on both. "I learned a lot from Richard Palmer-James," admitted Wetton. "He's a superb lyricist. I went to school with him. Where he crafts the lyric, I just chuck it out. I just throw the stuff out, and if there's anything clever in my lyrics, it's completely by coincidence or accident. Richard is a wonderful poet."

"At that time, I was collaborating with Richard on a lot of the lyrics. For instance, we wrote 'Starless' in rehearsal, and we went on the road with it. The lyric that I started singing on the road, by the time we got to record it, it was almost finished. It just kind of evolved on the road. I gave it to Richard and I said, 'Can you just put that into some kind of order, because it's just a lot of jumbled unconnected ideas,' and he crafted it into the lyric that we now know as 'Starless.' It was just beautiful. But when I gave it to him it was just a load of unconnected phrases that sounded good when you sang them. So we kind of wrote that one together."

"We did the same thing with 'Fallen Angel.' We never played that on the road, but I had ideas for that and Richard just finished them off and we collaborated on some stuff." Also included on *Red* would be an entirely improvised tune, "Providence," which was recorded live at a gig at the Palace Theater in Providence (hence its name!), Rhode Island, on June 30, 1974.

Released on October 6, 1974, *Red* would feature a black and white shot of the three Crimsons on the cover (although it should be noted that while several other musicians lent a hand in the recording – particularly horn-blowers – they were not considered full-fledged members by this stage). And despite the LP being a strong and rocking one, it failed to storm the charts – peaking at just #45 in the UK and #66 in the US. The reason? Although King Crimson seemed to be entering a very interesting musical phase, it all came to an abrupt halt on September 25, 1974, when the band split (less than two weeks before *Red* was to be issued). Crimson would issue a posthumous live album in 1975 (*USA*), while Wetton and Bruford would unite as UK, issuing their self-titled debut in 1978. And as you'll read in a bit, Fripp would unite once again with Bruford for a "new look/sounding Crimson" shortly after the dawn of the '80s.

However, over the years *Red* has received its rightly-deserved praise – resulting in an expanded *40th Anniversary Edition* in 2009. "I think *Red* is a great-sounding album, and it's basically only three people," explained Wetton. "Sure, we do little overdubs and there are guests, but essentially, it's three people. The noise that you hear is three people. And when Steven [Wilson, of Porcupine Tree] did the remix and the remaster, the 5.2 of *Red* [as part of the *40th Anniversary Edition*], they had the playback in this big sort of church hall in North London. And Steve Wilson came up to me and he said, 'Sounds great, doesn't it?' I said, 'Yeah, Steve. It does sound great. But it sounded great in 1974, actually'."

"And I'm not demeaning anything that he's done, but it sounded fucking great in '74. It's bound to sound good. I think there were other albums of King Crimson that would benefit a lot more from Steven Wilson's touch, like *Lark's Tongues in Aspic*, which is actually very badly recorded. And I think that would benefit an awful lot more from Steven's touch than, say, *Red*, which was actually recorded pretty much as we played it. By the time we did *Red* we were fairly confident, and you can hear that just listening to the record. The confidence just kind of spews out from the record. Just such a pity the band had to end there for me – I thought we could have done a lot more with that line-up."

Sadly, any chance of the *Red*-era Crimson line-up reuniting for one last go-round was extinguished in 2017, when Wetton passed away from cancer (at the age of 67).

Blow by Blow
(Jeff Beck, 1975)

Although there had already been quite a few all-instrumental/guitar-heavy albums by the mid-70's (the Ventures, the Shadows, Mahavishnu Orchestra, etc.), there is no denying that Jeff Beck's first all-instrumental offering, *Blow by Blow*, was the one that introduced jazz-fusion – with an added healthy helping of funk – to rock guitarists on a mass-scale.

By the time of the album's arrival, Beck had been considered one of rock's top guitar talents for years. Born on June 24, 1944 in Wallington, Surrey, England, Beck first rose to prominence as Eric Clapton's replacement in the influential psych-pop-rock band the Yardbirds, before helping trailblaze hard rock/heavy metal with the Jeff Beck Group (whose original line-up featured such then-unknowns as Rod Stewart on vocals and Ron Wood on bass) and Beck Bogert & Appice.

And as the drummer in BBA, Carmine Appice, recounted in the earlier entry for Billy Cobham's *Spectrum*, Beck had become inspired by that particular album – and especially, the guitar work of Tommy Bolin. Even Beck's future keyboardist, Jan Hammer, recalled Bolin's influence on Beck in the book *Touched by Magic: The Tommy Bolin Story*. "We always talk about influences – how Jeff [Beck] influenced me, and how I influenced him. But definitely, you can hear after he saw and heard Tommy that there was something that also added another ingredient to what Jeff was about. A definite influence happened."

So for the second album ever credited solely to Beck (although many consider 1968's *Truth* to be a Jeff Beck Group release, only the guitarist was credited on its cover), the guitarist decided to shake things up – the most obvious move being the hiring of Beatles producer George Martin to oversee the sessions, which took place during October 1974 at AIR in London. And the second change was to close the chapter on his association with the short-lived BBA project – by enlisting keyboardist Max Middleton (who had previously played on Beck's *Rough and Ready* and *The Orange Album*), bassist Phil Chen, and drummer Richard Bailey to back him on the sessions.

And the results were marvelous – proving that you did not always need a singer to hold the listener's attention if the guitar provided memorable melodies (in place of where vocals would usually go) and the music was performed at a high level, but didn't get weighed down with show off-y chops (but rather, playing what fit the songs best). Case in point, such funky workouts as "You Know What I Mean," "Constipated Duck," and "Air Blower" (the latter of which dare I say…approaches disco territory!). But Beck mixes it up throughout – especially on a relaxed, slightly reggae-ish cover of the Beatles' "She's a Woman" (which sees Beck utilize a talk box a year before Peter Frampton would popularize it on *Frampton Comes Alive*) and on the eight minute-plus album closer ballad, "Diamond Dust," which includes a symphony backing Beck.

And while those tunes were certainly fine and dandy, I saved the album's true standouts for this part. Firstly, the uptempo "Scatterbrain" – which features a repetitive line which creates instrumental tension to great effect (but if I may offer a suggestion, be sure to check out a killer rendition of this tune on the 1977 release, *Jeff Beck with the Jan Hammer Group Live*, which outdoes the studio version). And then a pair of tunes penned by Stevie Wonder – which opened side two back in the days of vinyl/cassettes – "'Cause We've Ended as Lovers" and "Thelonius."

The former tune is a ballad (which was originally recorded by Wonder's former wife, Syreeta Wright, on 1974's *Stevie Wonder Presents: Syreeta*), and may very well be Beck's all-time best track – as his guitar simply sings for nearly six minutes. And the latter composition is a fierce funk jam, which supposedly features Wonder himself (uncredited) on clavinet. And then another gem – "Freeway Jam." Penned entirely by Middleton, its funk groove slowly builds until Beck finally introduces the song's main melody just before the 1:35 mark, and later, offers a simply scintillating solo.

Released on March 29, 1975 via Epic, the album's cover featured a painting of Beck playing a Gibson Les Paul by John

Collier. And Beck expert Wolf Marshall discussed that particular instrument in the book, *Iconic Guitar Gear*. "He had a certain Les Paul that was put together by Seymour Duncan – which looked black, but it was actually a dark brown oxblood colored Les Paul. It's a conversion from an early '50s model – it's not a Standard – but it has humbucker pickups I believe, and Seymour Duncan did those." Chart-wise, *Blow by Blow* blew up – peaking at #4 on the *Billboard 200*, and earning platinum certification. Rightfully, the album has gone on to be widely considered a landmark album.

"There are not too many guys who have the technical facility to play like Beck," former *Guitar Player* editor Jas Obrecht explained in the book *Shredders! The Oral History of Speed Guitar (and More)*. "The closest one I heard back then was Eric Johnson, on that *Seven Worlds* tape that he did in the mid 1970s. There's some beautifully played Beck-ian stuff on there. But Beck, especially during the jazz-rock fusion period that gave us *Blow by Blow* and *Wired*, was really a breed apart from everyone else. He was using Sir George Martin as his producer, and he was exploring jazz veins. And Beck often played without a pick, which was rare during that time. Everybody idolized Beck for his articulate approach to playing notes, his fire, his passion, and the sheer force of his personality. Jeff Beck is a class by himself, and I personally think of him as the best electric guitarist to come out of Great Britain."

Former Michael Jackson guitarist (and even an eventual member of Beck's band), Jennifer Batten, also holds the album in high regard. "It was the *Blow by Blow* record on the radio that opened up my mind to just so many possibilities and genres. He hit everything from jazz to funk rock. I mean, he got in *DownBeat* magazine with that. It was basically a rock record, but it did touch into jazz and funk, and even reggae. So that just blew my mind. At first, I'd listen to it a lot, and then I started to carve into it and learn some of the stuff. I remember during GIT that year, Steve Lynch was also influenced by Beck. Our assignment was to transcribe a song, and play it live. And his choice was ''Cause We've Ended as Lovers' from *Blow by Blow*. Just to have that in my face and hear it live sent me into another level of getting into Jeff. One of the things I did after school was over was to carve into *Blow by Blow* and *Wired*, and learn all of the solos on both of those records. So all those years later, to get a chance to play with him was completely unexpected, and completely joyful."

Lastly, you can certainly make the claim that it was Joe Satriani who carried the torch of Beck's all-instrumental recordings a decade after *Blow by Blow* – particularly on such releases as *Surfing with the Alien*. And Satch is also quick to list Beck as an inspiration. "I grew up learning how to play with Jeff Beck records. We weren't doing anything new – there had been tons of classical and jazz instrumental guitar records. I grew up listening to Wes Montgomery jazz records. There were the Ventures and the Shadows. We weren't doing anything new conceptually – at all, as a matter of fact."

"And we grew up listening to those Jeff Beck instrumental records and every time we listened to a record – whether it was instrumental guitar from the 50s, like George Van Eps, or from the 60s, like Wes Montgomery and the Ventures and Shadows, and then Jeff Beck and John McLaughlin and Al Di Meola – those were the things that I think gave us confidence to try our fingers at it, you know what I mean?"

Ritchie Blackmore's Rainbow
(Rainbow, 1975)

By the dawn of 1975, there were few hard rock/heavy metal bands as immensely popular as Deep Purple. Case in point – their albums were instant hits, they headlined arenas and stadiums throughout the world, and also, had recently unleashed one of rock's all-time great tunes, "Smoke on the Water." And they also pulled off the rare feat of remaining popular after switching key members (in 1973, singer Ian Gillan and bassist Roger Glover were replaced by David Coverdale and Glenn Hughes, respectively).

Still, Purple guitarist Ritchie Blackmore was not content. Supposedly not happy that more R&B and funk elements were working their way into the band's high-decibel sound (give a listen to such tunes as "Hold On" and "You Can't Do It Right" off *Stormbringer* for the proof), he surprisingly exited Purple and sought to form a band that would be more rockin'. And this led to the formation of Rainbow – and their classic debut album, *Ritchie Blackmore's Rainbow*.

And it turns out that Blackmore did not have to search far for new bandmates. Impressed with a band that had previously opened for Purple on tour, Elf, he inquired if all of the group would like to join him in his new project – keyboardist Micky Lee Soule, bassist Craig Gruber, and drummer Gary Driscoll…and a then largely-unknown singer by the name of Ronnie James Dio (Elf's guitarist at the time, Steve Edwards, was not invited to remain on onboard for the new band, however).

The newly-formed band opted to retain the engineer-turned-producer of Purple's last few albums, Martin Birch (who would be listed on the subsequent debut as a co-producer – along with Blackmore and Dio), and laid down their repertoire at Musicland Studios, in Munich, West Germany, from February 20 through March 14, 1975.

Kicking things off is one of Rainbow's best-known tunes, "Man on the Silver Mountain" – which contains an outstanding/swirling Blackmore riff (the amount of classic guitar bits he constructed throughout the '70s remains staggering) and an awesome guitar solo, and also does a dandy of a job introducing

Dio as the group's vocalist and lyricist. "Self Portrait" kicks off with apparently the most popular piece of percussion for '70s rock drummers – the tapping of a cowbell – and while not as stellar as the album's opener, succeeds in keeping things rocking along.

A cover of an obscure tune by British prog-rockers Quartermass, entitled "Black Sheep of the Family" is next – a tune that supposedly Blackmore unsuccessfully tried to get his former band to take on. But to be totally honest...the tune was a throwaway – it's hard to hear some of the tune's silly lyrics ("I've got half a pound of rice, a beard full of lice") and not think that they would have been much better off composing another original tune – especially since they had a very strong songwriter/lyricist in the ranks, in the form of Dio.

And then next is another all-time Rainbow classic – the gorgeous ballad, "Catch the Rainbow." And speaking of lyrics...it contains some of Dio's best, while musically, it bares somewhat of a resemblance at points (particularly in Blackmore's guitar work) to Jimi Hendrix's "Little Wing."

Back in the vinyl daze, side two kicked off with one of the album's hardest rocking tunes, "Snake Charmer" – which also showed that Dio was quite talented at creating memorable vocal melodies throughout. Up next, "The Temple of the King" is a bit reminiscent of the style that Blackmore would eventually pursue further with his Renaissance-folk outfit, Blackmore's Night (although admittedly, is a touch too "electric" for the mostly acoustic-based Blackmore's Night).

"If You Don't Like Rock n' Roll" features a topic that seemed to be quite important to the lads in Rainbow, as another tune issued just three years later, "Long Live Rock n' Roll," featured a similar lyrical sentiment. That said, like "Black Sheep," the tune comes off as a throwaway. But things get back on track for the album's final two tunes.

"Sixteenth Century Greensleeves" certainly has a strong strut to it, and also features one of the boldest opening lyrics of any song on the album – "It's only been an hour since he locked her in the tower" (which also signaled the "gothic/castle/damsel in distress" brand of lyric writing that Dio would favor throughout his career). And closing things is a surprise all-instrumental reworking of the Yardbirds' "Still I'm Sad" – which shows that the band had already gelled into a tight n' rocking machine (and once again, features Driscoll riding the cowbell).

Ritchie Blackmore's Rainbow was issued on August 4, 1975 (to put it all in perspective, Blackmore's last performance with Purple occurred on April 7...so that makes it less than four months that Rainbow was formed, the material recorded, and released), and was a near top-10 hit in the UK by peaking at #11, while reaching a respectable – but certainly not on par with Purple – #30 in the US. However, those who figured that this would be the line-up that Blackmore would stick with would be sadly mistaken. He would quickly dismiss almost all of the members – only Dio would be left in attendance by the time a sophomore effort, *Rising*, would appear a year later.

While Rainbow would go in an increasingly more commercial direction after Dio exited in 1979 (he would join Black Sabbath shortly thereafter, before embarking on a successful solo career) and enjoy near-top-of-the-chart success in England, *Ritchie Blackmore's Rainbow* remains one of the band's finest offerings.

Ramones
(Ramones, 1976)

Sure, there had been several albums issued prior to 1976 that certainly resembled what we now all know as "punk rock" (Iggy & the Stooges' *Raw Power*, the New York Dolls' self-titled debut, the Dictators' *Go Girl Crazy!*, etc.). But it seems to be widely agreed that it was not until the Ramones' self-titled debut that punk rock truly became, well...*punk rock*. And there are several reasons for this – first off, it includes quite possibly the greatest punk rock anthem of all-time, nearly every song is played fast/kept short and sweet (the longest tune clocked in at 2 minutes and 35 seconds), while the group sported what would soon come to be known as the universal "punk rock uniform" on the album cover.

Formed in 1974 in Forest Hills, Queens, New York, the group was comprised of neighborhood chums Joey Ramone (real name: Jeffrey Hyman) on vocals, Johnny Ramone (John Cummings) on guitar, Dee Dee Ramone (Douglas Colvin) on bass, and Tommy Ramone (Thomas Erdelyi) on drums. When I spoke to the man who would eventually replace Tommy on drums, Marky Ramone (real name: Marc Bell), for *Long Island Pulse* in 2015, he explained how they all eventually shared the last name. "We were *not* brothers! The name 'Ramone' came from Paul McCartney. When he used to check into hotel rooms when he was in the Silver Beatles, before the Beatles, he thought it was an exotic name, so he used Paul Ramon."

And in the same interview, Marky was also kind enough to describe the personalities of the Ramones (all except for the chap he replaced). "Joey was very quiet, but when he went on stage, he transformed into a great, histrionic singer. Johnny was very business-like, very astute at knowing the business, which was important. And Dee Dee was the main songwriter and a wild, crazy guy – that's why we were very friendly. We were the closest in the band, me and Dee Dee. Every one of us was different."

Building a following and eventually a buzz by regularly playing CBGB's in the Bowery of New York City (along with Television, Talking Heads, Blondie, Patti Smith Group, Richard

Hell & the Voidoids, etc.), the Ramones eventually caught the attention of Seymour Stein, who signed them to Sire, and the group entered Plaza Sound in Manhattan to record what would be their classic debut. The sessions would last from February 2 though 19, 1976, with Craig Leon being listed as producer (and Tommy Ramone serving as associate producer).

"It was kind of strange," Tommy recalled to me back in 2007 for *Classic Rock,* about the studio that the album was recorded in. "We were put into this really interesting studio, that was a beautiful art deco radio station, that was converted into a recording studio in the Radio City Music Hall building. It was a beautiful studio, but we were separated – we were each put in different rooms. It was a strange experience making that record. We did that record really fast – that whole record cost $6,000. We did it very quickly and without too much fanfare."

And the album (originally comprised of 21 songs that blew by at a brisk 29 minutes and 4 seconds) starts off with the tune that I declared earlier as "quite possibly the greatest punk rock anthem of all-time" – "Blitzkrieg Bop." While the main songwriters of the original Ramones were thought to be Joey, Johnny, and Dee Dee, it was in fact Tommy that penned the majority of the tune by himself. "It's my song," Tommy explained. "Dee Dee came up with the title, and changed a line from 'They're shouting in the back now' to 'Shoot 'em in the back now.' The rest of the song is mine."

With most mid-70's punkers drawing inspiration from the Stooges and the Dolls, Erdelyi explained that the Ramones were busy studying an unlikely source. "We were looking for a chant-type song, because the Bay City Rollers had a huge hit at the time with 'Saturday Night.' I was trying to think of ideas for something like that. Coming home from the grocery store one day, I just thought of a chant – 'Hey! Ho! Let's go!' – which basically comes from a song called 'Walkin' the Dog' by Rufus Thomas, where he goes, 'Hi ho's nipped her toes.' When we were kids we used to goof around – when Mick Jagger sang the song for the Rolling Stones, it sounded like he was saying *'Hey ho.'* It was a silly thing, but I remembered that from the past."

Erdelyi figures that the song was written sometime in 1974 – shortly after the Ramones formed – and recalls where the germ of the musical idea for the song came to him. "The actual music and melody, I was fooling around with a guitar at Arturo's loft – Arturo Vega was our lighting guy – and I just started playing the riff. That song slowly came together. I went home, I liked that riff, and just wrote the lyrics." Which leads to the subject of the song's lyrics. Many have tried to decipher the song's true meaning unsuccessfully over the years, but Erdelyi sets the record straight once and for all. "The lyrics are basically about people going to a concert and having a great time." 'Nuff said.

And while "Blitzkrieg" remains the album's best-known composition, from start to finish, the debut is quite possibly the Ramones' most consistent studio album. Truly, you can randomly select any tune here and it's a winner, but if I was pressed to select the crème de la crème, you can't do wrong with such punk thrashers as "Judy Is a Punk," "Chain Saw" (which begins with the soothing sounds of…a chainsaw!), and "Now I Wanna Sniff Some Glue," as well as more melodic tunes such as "I Wanna Be Your Boyfriend," "Havana Affair," and "Listen to My Heart." But certainly one of my all-time favorite Ramones tracks would be "53rd and 3rd." Although the Ramones usually focused on lighthearted topics lyrically, this tune was an obvious exception – which details a male prostitute murdering one of his clients, to prove he's no "sissy."

Released on April 23, 1976, the album featured a black and white photo of the band shot by Roberta Bayley, standing in front of a brick wall, and as I mentioned earlier, sporting what would soon become "the punk rock uniform" – denim jeans (usually torn at the knees), sneakers, t-shirts, and black leather jackets. Upon its initial release, the album failed to leave much of an impression on the charts (peaking at only #111 on the *Billboard 200*), but sold steadily over the years – eventually earning gold certification in the US and silver certification in the UK, and has since been widely recognized as a classic and highly influential rock album.

And although punk rock was accepted by the mainstream seemingly upon arrival in the UK (thanks to the Sex Pistols and the Clash), it took far longer for this back-to-basics sound/approach to be embraced in the US (not until the '90s, thanks to Nirvana and Green Day). Which is surprising, because if you take an early Ramones song and slow it down, it could potentially sound like a Black Sabbath song, and if you took a Black Sabbath song and sped it up, it could sound like the Ramones. And I even had the opportunity to run this theory by Marky in the aforementioned *Songfacts* chat, to which he replied, "Yeah, but I don't think they could play as fast as us, but we could play as slow as them!"

Also, while we are on the topic of "early Ramones," in addition to their instantly recognizable fashion choices, another object that became closely associated with the band visually was a specific uncommon guitar that Johnny would perform his all-downstroked, speedy rhythm guitar work on. "The original punk rock guitar architect played the California-made Mosrite Ventures II guitar," radio personality Matt Pinfield explained in the book *Iconic Guitar Gear.*

"Named for the guitar series specifically made for the legendary 1960's king of the American instrumental groups, the Ventures, who scored huge hits with 'Walk Don't Run,' and the original theme song for the TV show, *Hawaii Five-O.* Especially designed for their member, Nokie Edwards, a man in Japan who was called 'The King of Guitars' (and later did some acting in the show *Deadwood*). It's easy-to-navigate neck was perfect for playing fast at breakneck speeds and made it the perfect guitar for Johnny Ramone – who inspired an endless number of young punks to pick up and play the guitar emulating his 'couldn't give a fuck' guitar as a weapon buzzsaw style. *Fast and loud.*"

Lastly, did Tommy (who was the last living original Ramones member, until his passing on July 11, 2014 at the age of 65) agree that "Blitzkrieg Bop" is the greatest Ramones song? "No, I don't. There's so many great Ramones songs – 'Rockaway Beach,' 'Cretin Hop.' I think 'Blitzkrieg Bop'...it's hard to say, since I wrote the song. I'm very self-conscious about it. But people seem to like it." Quite the understatement.

Rising
(Rainbow, 1976)

Throughout the course of Rainbow's history, one thing always seemed inevitable – except for Ritchie Blackmore, band members would come and go like the wind. And one of the quickest/most extensive overhauls took place after the band's first album, 1975's *Ritchie Blackmore's Rainbow,* when the former Deep Purple guitarist promptly sacked the album's bassist, keyboardist, and drummer – only retaining the singer (a then-largely unknown Ronnie James Dio). And while their debut was not as hard rocking as his previous band's output from 1970-1974 was, the line-up that he assembled for Rainbow's sophomore effort, *Rising,* changed all of that in a jiffy.

Despite being a largely newly-assembled band (bassist Jimmy Bain, keyboardist Tony Carey, and drummer Cozy Powell were the recent arrivals), musically and stylistically, it sounded as if they gelled automatically. The resulting *Rising* is largely considered to feature Rainbow's best line-up (which, as expected, was in place for just this one album), and also, widely praised as one of heavy metal's all-time great recordings. Recorded at Musicland Studios, in Munich, Germany, and produced by Martin Birch, the band laid down the tracks at a rapid pace – completing recording during a single month (February 1976).

When I interviewed Carey for the book, *The Other Side of Rainbow,* he offered a glimpse into the album's recording sessions. "It was quick. We knew most of the material, because we had played it live or played it in rehearsals. We were at one of the little villages around Munich, and we rented out a pub – a country bar – to rehearse, and we rehearsed for a couple of days. And then we arrived in the studio, and a lot of the stuff was one or two takes for the band. I didn't play live with the band – I overdubbed everything I played. They played just as a trio – with Ritchie, Jimmy, and Cozy, and of course, Ronnie overdubbed, and I overdubbed. Really quick. In and out."

And it certainly didn't hurt that the quality of the compositions were amongst the best of Rainbow's entire career. By and large, the first side of the vinyl version collected the more succinct songs – "Tarot Woman," "Run with the Wolf," "Starstruck," and "Do You Close Your Eyes." And while the "side one" songs did indeed feature some splendid six-string work from Blackmore (namely two tunes that saw him break out the old slide – "Wolf" and "Starstruck"), he was saving the best for last, upon inspection of the flipside. Comprised of only two tracks, "Stargazer" and "A Light in the Black" (with each stretching past the eight-minute mark), it's difficult to pick which song contained Blackmore's most sterling solos…perhaps it's best to merely call it a draw.

During the same interview, Carey discussed his favorites. "I like the two that we never played live the best – 'Tarot Woman' and 'Run with the Wolf,' because they have a really bluesy groove. 'Starstruck' I like, too – it's not the best lyric. 'Do You Close Your Eyes' is better than throwaway lyrics. The throwaway lyrics happened later – when I heard 'All Night Long,' I thought it was the silliest song I'd ever heard. But for just music, 'Tarot Woman' and 'Run with the Wolf' were my two favorites, probably. 'Stargazer' is an epic song, but as a keyboard player, there's not much to do in 'Stargazer' – it's all parts. There is no room for improvising. And I like the stuff I can improvise on. 'A Light in the Black' was really fun to play – it was the first thing I ever even heard at that tempo. It was like bebop or jazz – that was an enormous tempo. Really, really fast."

40 years after the album's release, Carey still had recollections of which songs worked live, and which did not. "The reason that 'Tarot Woman' and 'Run with the Wolf' didn't work live is because a lot of these old live recordings were really rough, and one of the roughest things about them is the tempos were always terrible. They were really too fast. I've heard recordings of 'Man on the Silver Mountain' that are twice the speed of the record. And the record's got this big, fat rock n' roll pocket, and it's fabulous. And then live, it sounded like two rabbits fucking. It was too fast. But if you're actually in the audience and watching it, then that's exciting. It makes it exciting – you don't care. But in an analytical sense, is this groovy? No, it's not groovy. *It's too fast.* And every time we

tried to play 'Tarot Woman' – which wasn't very often, we gave that up right away – it was always too fast. It didn't have that pocket. And the same with 'Run with the Wolf.' And 'A Light in the Black' we played a few times, but then we had to drop it, because it was too demanding – even for Cozy Powell, who was like *The Six Million Dollar Man.* He was a bionic drummer, and even *he* couldn't do that – with that double-bass drum thing for twelve minutes."

While *Rising* did not exactly storm the charts Stateside upon its release (peaking at only #48), it was a far bigger hit in the UK (where it reached #11), and shortly thereafter/ever since, has been heralded as a definitive heavy metal recording (coming in at #1 on *Kerrang! Magazine's* "All-Time Top 100 HM Albums" list in October 1981 – above the likes of *Back in Black, Led Zeppelin IV,* and *Paranoid*). And to this day, it is deemed an all-time classic, as confirmed by metal expert Eddie Trunk. "*Rising* definitely. It's a tough question, but *Rising* I think stands as the definitive Rainbow record, and a lot of that has to do with the fact that 'Stargazer' is on it."

Hotel California
(Eagles, 1976)

1976 was quite a year for the Eagles. In that year alone, they issued two albums that at the time of this book's release are the #2 and #3 best-selling US rock albums of *all-time* – *Their Greatest Hits (1971-1975)* at 41.2 million and *Hotel California* at 21.8 million (and in case you were wondering, *Thriller* is numero uno, at a cool 50.2 million).

Originally formed in 1971 in Los Angeles, band members would come and go, with singer/guitarist Glenn Frey and singer/drummer Don Henley being the chief songwriters/mainstays – before the "*Hotel California* line-up" was solidified in 1975 with guitarists Don Felder and Joe Walsh, plus bassist Randy Meisner. But from their formation to the point of writing the material for what would become *Hotel California*, a slight stylistic shift had occurred, as Felder explained in *The Yacht Rock Book*.

"When I first heard the Eagles, it was definitely 'country rock.' And it was more focused on country than on rock. When I joined the band, it was my objective – at the behest of both Glenn and Don – to shift from a country feel into more of a rock/R&B feel. That was sort of why I was brought into the band in the first place. And then I do know quite a few people that have their large yachts, and I don't know if it was because I was in attendance or aboard their vessel or the fact that they just liked that music, but I have heard the Eagles' music on *a lot* of yachts! Not only on the ones I was on, but echoing through the harbors from somebody having a party. I would say the Eagles' music was all three – country rock, soft rock, *and* yacht rock."

Working once again with producer Bill Szymczyk, the sessions for their fifth studio album overall lasted from March through October 1976, at two studios – Criteria (in Miami) and Record Plant (in Los Angeles). And prior to entering the studio, Felder had demoed several tunes for consideration – with one just happening to be one of the most celebrated and instantly recognizable rock tunes of all-time, which would serve as the album's opener. "I had rented a house on the beach in Malibu," Felder also recalled in *The Yacht Rock Book*. "I think it was '74,

'75 – and was just sitting on a couch on a beautiful July or August day, with my young kids playing in the sand on a little swing set, out front on the beach. The beautiful Southern Pacific was sparkling with Southern California sunlight. I was sitting on the couch, playing guitar, and out rolled that original progression. So I played it four/five/six times so I would remember it, and in my back bedroom of this rented house, I set up this little four-track reel-to-reel tape recorder in my daughter's bedroom – she was one year old at the time. When she was awake, I could go back and make these music tracks. I went back and recorded some of that progression, then just turned it off."

"Later, when we started writing songs for what was going to become the *Hotel California* record, I went back and started listening to a bunch of these ideas. I think I had six, eight, ten, fifteen different song ideas. I sat down and started finishing these ideas, by starting with a drum machine, playing a rhythm guitar, playing a bass on it. Pretty much building the track – almost exactly what you hear on the Eagles' version now of 'Hotel California,' without a few 'Walsh-isms.' I was trying to write something that Joe and I could play together on the end of that song. It was like what we had been doing in Joe Walsh & Friends, before Joe joined the band. I wanted to play against him on something, so I thought that track would be a good way to give us that foundation to play on."

"So I made up this demo that had me playing kind of both parts – me and Joe – some of which Joe ended up playing in his solos and I had written on the demo. And I had to play my part exactly like I played it on the demo, because Henley wouldn't let me play anything but what he had been listening to on the cassette. So I submitted several songs, gave it to Randy, Joe, Glenn, and Don, and said, 'If there's anything on these cassettes you want to finish writing, let me know, and we'll get together and start writing.' So, Henley called me up and said, 'I really like that song that sounds like a Mexican reggae.' It was the only song idea on that cassette that sounded like that as he described. I said, 'Oh, that's great. Let's get together.' He, Glenn, and I sat down and started talking about what it should be about."

"I don't remember if it was Glenn or Don that came up with 'Hotel California,' but we were having this discussion about none of us being from California. We had all driven in on Route 66 at night, and you can see the lights of Los Angeles hovering on the horizon for about seventy miles away at night – if it's a clear night coming through the desert. And when we got here, everybody was in search of that *dream*. And we were somehow, like a genie, rewarded with this dream, that so many of thousands – if not millions – of people have pursued here. *And here we were.* So we wanted to write a song about that."

"Henley, being the brilliant lyricist that he was, took that idea and wrote just stellar, picture postcard lyrics of the storyline that runs through that song. And obviously saying it like everything else he does – impeccably and superbly in tune. As soon as you hear his voice, you know exactly who it is. The whole combination of writing, lyrics, guitar playing, the production that Bill Szymczyk helped put together on the project. It was just a magical combination for that particular album. To me, it seemed like that record was sort of the crescendo – or climax – of the Eagles' writing and production." As a result, the tune would be credited to Felder, Henley, and Frey.

But the group's country leanings were still on display on specific tunes – most notably on one of the album's other best-known tunes, "New Kid in Town," as well as "Wasted Time," "Try and Love Again," and "The Last Resort." Also included were a few tunes that were symphonic and a bit shmaltzy (a reprise of "Wasted Time" and "Pretty Maids All in a Row") – but were balanced out by two more rockers, which happened to also be amongst the LP's strongest selections.

First of which was the riff rocker "Life in the Fast Lane" – a tune credited to Henley, Frey, and Walsh, which as its title alludes to, is about a couple who lead a wild and reckless lifestyle. And according to Felder, so was the band at the time. "I think it's being quite polite to say 'a lot of partying.' I think there was *massive* amounts of partying, all types of levels of it. Abusing ourselves with drugs and alcohol, abusing ourselves with the level at which we were working. We had very little time off – we were always on the road or in the studio. There was a lot of women involved in the whole thing that was going on. There was *a lot* of partying."

"We used to have a phrase that if somebody had just gone to the bathroom and done some cocaine and had come out and you could still see white powder around their nose, it was called, 'You're showing.' During the filming of that 'Hotel California' video, while Joe and I are playing the end of the solo, I lean over to him – jokingly – and say, 'You're showing.' [Laughs] It was just a way to play with him, like, 'Oh my God...we're being filmed and I've got blow on my nose'!"

And then the *other* rocker being "Victim of Love." "It was on that same reel as 'Hotel California' – it was another one of the demos that was on that reel," recalls Felder. "It was probably one of the hardest rock tracks at the time that the Eagles had attempted to record. And I had played drums on a lot of the demos that I made, although I'm not a great drummer, but I had to play simple enough parts that Don could sing and play drums at the same time. If it was a complicated drumbeat, it makes it too complex to be able to sing and play drums at the same time. So, I tried to make it pretty simple drum-wise. But hard-hitting. It was one of the tracks that was on that cassette that I gave to Don, and me and Glenn and JD Souther really liked that song."

"I had written the melody pretty much for the verses – you can hear the opening guitar part is the melody for the verses. And I had a different melody for the chorus. When we got together, we sat down with Don, Glenn, and JD Souther, to re-write the lyrics for that song. And sitting around – I think it was at Glenn's house – we were trying to think of a hook or a word or a catch or something. So JD said, 'What about the word 'victim'?' And I said, 'Ooo, I like that. That's great. That's a really strong word to base a song on.' And JD said, 'Well yeah, but...victim of what?' And Henley said, '*Victim of love.*' That stuck, and we were off to the races – writing lyrics that would lead you into that chorus, which was 'Victim of Love.' It turned out that JD, Don, and Glenn wound up writing most of the lyrics to that song – not all of the lyrics – and I wrote the music and the melody."

Released on December 8, 1976, both the *Hotel California* album and its title track single would reach the top of the *Billboard 200* and *Hot 100*, respectively – with two more singles hitting the charts, as well ("New Kid in Town" peaking at #1 and "Life in the Fast Lane" reaching #11). And as you could probably figure out with the earlier mention of it being one of the greatest selling albums ever, *Hotel California* came in as the #4 top-selling album of 1977, and has continued to reappear on the charts ever since.

And there is also one more item forever associated with the album – its iconic cover image of the Beverly Hills Hotel at sunset, taken by photographer David Alexander. Felder: "When they first showed me that picture of it, I went, 'What hotel is that?' They said, 'The Beverly Hills Hotel on Sunset.' I went, *'No it's not.'* Because from the street, it looks like about a fifteen-foot hedge – like a privacy screen. So unless you drive onto the property, you don't even see the hotel. The only way you would get that – as it was explained to me, later – that they had rented a cherry picker and parked it across the street, and unbeknownst to the Beverly Hills Hotel, they erected this cherry picker and the photographer took a bunch of pictures right at sunset as the lights were coming on at the hotel. I think it was Kosh [aka John Kosh] that was the director of that artwork. It turned out to be – in a nutshell – the perfect image to capture the concept of *Hotel California*."

"The inside cover [of the gatefold], we wanted it to be much more sleazy looking than the Beverly Hills Hotel – which is really more typical of old Spanish architecture. And yet, we wanted to staff the lobby – in this old, kind of seedy hotel, I think it was the Lido Hotel, in a pretty shady area – with people that were either guests coming in or at a party or bellmen, and make it look like a live staff shot in the middle of this hotel, that we were standing there, checking in to. Or checking out – however you wanted to read it."

"I remember doing that photo session. We took a lot of different shots and angles on that, but that one somehow wound up with what people seem to claim is some lady in one of the windows above us all – on the second story, in like an alcove or something. I don't remember anything about the woman being up there. But if you look carefully, you can see some female figure up there – *supposedly*. But they were all people that we knew – it was business managers, lawyers, our makeup people, and our PR people. All the people that were part of the Eagles company and business we invited to be a part of that shoot. Now that I look back, I still recognize all the people that were involved in that shoot."

And while the Eagles would continue to soar and score another #1 album (1979's *The Long Run*), before splitting up and reuniting in 1994, Felder – and probably most Eagles fans – feels that *Hotel California* was the band's peak. "The Eagles had an immense catalogue of great songs. And on every record, we tried to raise the bar to a higher level of songwriting, a higher level of recording and production, and a higher level of performance. So, every new Eagles record that came out was better than the last one. Until we finished *Hotel California*, and had to top that, I thought that was kind of the crescendo or the climax of the creative part of that band. It was almost like a level so high that we couldn't get over it. As Glenn liked to say, 'We created a monster, and it ate us.' He had a great way of saying a very humorous catchphrase that was right on the money and very truthful."

Never Mind the Bollocks...Here's the Sex Pistols (Sex Pistols, 1977)

Grown men wearing capes. Stadium-sized concerts that seemed to be an excuse for over-indulgent, never-ending soloing. Lyrics that had nothing to do with reality. Rock stars being chauffeured around in limos and living in castles. Any (or all) of the above could be selected as an accurate description of the state of rock music by the mid 1970's. Thankfully, the punk rock movement offered a much-needed alternative. And while several bands had already issued recordings that could be classified as "punk rock" (especially the Ramones' self-titled debut), the first one that left a real impression on the charts – and whose creators received the most amount of press coverage – was *Never Mind the Bollocks...Here's the Sex Pistols,* by the Sex Pistols.

Formed in 1975 in London, England, the original Pistols line-up was comprised of singer John "Johnny Rotten" Lydon, guitarist Steve Jones, bassist Glen Matlock, and drummer Paul Cook, and seemed to immediately attract a following with other disenfranchised youth. With a fashion sense that was the opposite of your Yeses and Zeppelins (short/spiky hair, torn clothing, etc.), the band certainly stuck out from the rest. But while their shenanigans resulted in publicity galore (including an appearance on live British TV in December 1976, during which two members swore – prompting nationwide outrage), the Pistols found it hard to build a lasting relationship with a record label, EMI and A&M both had brief affiliations with the band (resulting in two classic singles, "Anarchy in the UK" and "God Save the Queen," respectively), before each grew cowardly and dropped them quickly in succession.

Finally, Warner Bros. proved to be a label courageous enough to take the band on for their full-length debut. One teeny problem – one of the band's main songwriters, Matlock, had exited the band, and was replaced by a chap who appeared to possess very little bass talent...Sid Vicious. As a result, Jones pulled double-duty on the debut's recording sessions, playing guitar *and* bass (although Matlock did appear on one track, when the single version of "Anarchy" was recycled for *Bollocks*). Working with producers

Chris Thomas and Bill Price, the main sessions for the album took place from March-August 1977, at Wessex Sound Studio in London.

Speaking to the Ultimate Guitar site in 2010, Jones recalled the equipment he utilized on the album – "I used a '74 Gibson Les Paul, a white Custom and I also had a black one while we were doing *Never Mind The Bollocks*, it was a Les Paul Black Beauty but I'm not sure what year that guitar was. I only had one amp and it was a Fender Twin and that was used on everything. I only used one effect pedal and it was on 'Anarchy in the UK,' it was a MXR Phase 45. That was the only thing I added on my end. Bass-wise I used a Fender Precision through an Ampeg amp."

And in these very pages [of *Vintage Guitar*], Jones recalled how he obtained the white Custom Les Paul – "It used to belong to Sylvain Sylvain from the New York Dolls. I think he got it at Manny's, I believe – a guitar shop in New York. Then [Pistols manager] Malcolm McLaren started managing the Dolls for like ten minutes, and I don't know how Malcolm acquired it, but he brought it back from New York and he gave it to me." Unfortunately, the whereabouts of this now-iconic instrument (which sported two decals of what appeared to be '50s era pin-up models) are unknown. "It just went to the wayside like everything else – in a drug haze. There was a guy managing the Professionals [Jones' post-Pistols group, in the early '80s], it ended up with him, and my amp. He claimed it was money that was owed to him – which is suspect, I don't believe that. I just believe he decided to take it. When all the rest of the band went to go back to England, I decided to stay in New York, and all the equipment went back there. And I didn't go back for like, twelve years. So, I guess the manager guy sold it to somebody."

Front to back, there is not a single weak track on *Bollocks*, which showcases Jones' knack for coming up with power chord progressions that instantly stick in your noggin (namely the aforementioned "Anarchy" and "Queen," as well as "Holidays in the Sun," "Pretty Vacant," "Liar," and "Problems"). And as a reaction to all the indulgent rock guitar soloing at the time, Jones kept his leads to a minimum (and very basic) – "'Problems' has a good, long guitar solo. There are a few. It's got two little sections in 'Anarchy,' where there's two little moments. I would barely say they were guitar solos – they're just like parts, more than anything else. But 'Anarchy' was the only track that actually had a foot pedal on it – it has a Phase 90 on it. [Note: Jones earlier said it was a Phase 45, and it has also been noted that it could have possibly been a Phase 100] I had it worked out before we recorded it, because we used to play it live."

Released on October 28, 1977, the album rocketed to the top of the UK album charts, while peaking at a meagre #106 in the States. But only a few months after the album's release, the band was kaput – resulting in *Bollocks* being their sole full-length studio recording. The album proved to be a steady seller, however (eventually earning platinum certification in both the UK and US) while both Megadeth and Mötley Crüe would take turns covering "Anarchy," plus Kurt Cobain once listing it as one of his all-time favorite albums, and being included as part of *Rolling Stone's* 500 Greatest Albums of All Time in 2012 (coming in at #41).

Discussing the material that comprised the album in 2018, Matlock is still pleased. "I think it stands up as well as anything by Gene Vincent, Little Richard, or Elvis' *Sun Sessions*. I think anything that was done well at the time should sound as fresh and vital as the day it was made – regardless of the current musical climate. And I think it does."

News of the World
(Queen, 1977)

Seemingly overnight, rock music had changed come 1977. Just two years ago, it was seemingly the norm to be a rock band that indulged in never-ending solos, extended song suites that took up entire sides of LP's, and offered bombastic concerts in arenas or stadiums. The emergence of punk rock altered all that – bringing it back to a much more real, raw, and focused approach. And some of rock's "old guard" took note, and used punk's emergence as an inspiration to get back to basics – and there is probably not a better example than Queen's sixth studio effort, *News of the World.*

From the time of *Queen II* (which we discussed a ways back in this little old book) up to this point in the band's career, the British band had fast become one of the world's top rock acts – on the strength of such now-classic albums as *Sheer Heart Attack*, *A Night at the Opera*, and *A Day at the Races*, plus the hit singles "Killer Queen," "Bohemian Rhapsody," and "Somebody to Love." And while there were unmistakable prog-y moments on their earlier albums (especially "The Prophets Song" and "Bohemian Rhapsody," both off *Opera*), by *Races*, it was clear that the band – singer/pianist Freddie Mercury, guitarist Brian May, bassist John Deacon, and drummer Roger Taylor – were taking steps toward a shorter and more focused approach with their songwriting. And as with all Queen albums, all four members contributed in the songwriting department.

Recorded from July 6 through September 16, 1977 at a pair of London studios – Sarm and Wessex – the production team of *Races* was united once more (the band and Mike Stone). And as original Sex Pistols bassist Glen Matlock told me in the book *Long Live Queen: Rock Royalty Discuss Freddie, Brian, John & Roger*, he had an unexpected encounter with a certain Queen member at Wessex. "Actually the funny thing is we had been in a studio called Lansdowne, which is a very stottie, BBC-ish kind of place in London, in Holland Park, and then moved to a studio called Wessex [to record 'Anarchy in the UK'], where a lot of things were done – the Clash did their stuff there. When we went to check it out, there were two rooms there – a big room and a little room. And we went into the big room, opened the door – because the red "DO NOT ENTER" sign wasn't on – and it was Queen's room! And Freddie Mercury was in full-flight, and they got annoyed with us. We said, 'Well, don't blame us...*you* didn't have the red light on!' So, we got around that, and we went into the smaller room, out the back, a few days later."

"I remember going out to get a beer out of the fridge, and as I opened the door, there is somebody bent over, listening through the keyhole...and it was Freddie Mercury! I said, 'Oh, Freddie!' And he goes, 'Oh, oh...dear, where's the bathroom?' And I said, 'It's just behind you. You've been in here two months!' Really, he could have asked nice and possibly come in. He wanted to find out what it was all about. So, that was quite funny."

Kicking things off is quite possibly the greatest-ever one-two punch album opener – "We Will Rock You" and "We Are the Champions." Concerning the inspiration behind "We Will Rock You," as actor Gwilym Lee (playing the role of Brian May, who penned the tune) explained in the 2018 film, *Bohemian Rhapsody*, "I want to give the audience a song that they can perform. What can I do?" *STOMP STOMP, CLAP! STOMP STOMP, CLAP!* As a result, there is no percussion nor bass in the tune, just the sound of many a customer stomping and clapping in unison, vocals, and at the very end, a guitar solo (one of May's very best).

The Mercury-penned "We Are the Champions" is a rather self-explanatory number from its title alone, and would soon serve as the permanent set closer of Queen concerts (not counting a pre-recorded rendition of "God Save the Queen" which would play over the PA as the band thanked the audience/took a bow). And it turns out the tune was a particular favorite of Cinderella's Tom Keifer – "There was something about *News of the World* with 'We Will Rock You,' and I loved 'We Are the Champions' – I'm a sucker for ballads, and I just loved the positive attitude of that. I always thought that song had a great attitude to it. That's probably one of my favorites of theirs."

And then, one of the most intensely rocking tunes Queen ever created – "Sheer Heart Attack" (imagine how many geezers over the years have purchased the 1974 album of the same name in hopes of locating this tune...and were left empty-handed!). Penned entirely by Taylor – who also played rhythm guitar and bass, and even shared the vocals with Mercury – the tune was obviously Queen's "answer" to punk rock. And by golly, it worked! *"News of the World* was the only Queen album I ever owned," admits Primus' Les Claypool. "But it was a *spectacular* Queen album. I always liked 'Sheer Heart Attack.' When I was a kid, I was like, 'Oh my God! *This song is amazing!'* Before we heard any punk or anything, we were like, 'How the hell do they play so fast'?" And according to Anthrax's Charlie Benante, the tune pushed the boundaries *so* far, that it just may have birthed another rock subgenre. "'Sheer Heart Attack' predates thrash metal, and I always said Queen had these riffs that were very 'thrash metal'."

Since there was no possible way to top the previous number, the next tune, "All Dead, All Dead," is compositionally and sonically on the complete opposite end of the spectrum from "Sheer Heart Attack" – an admittedly rather depressing piano-led ballad sung by May (which lyrically is supposedly about the death of May's pet cat) – followed by one of Queen's most underrated tracks, the Deacon-penned "Spread Your Wings." Lyrically the tune tells the story of a down-on-his-luck fellow named Sammy, and sonically, narrowly misses being filed under the "power ballad" category. And while the tune certainly hits the mark – and coulda/shoulda been a hit – the on-stage rendition of the tune included on *Live Killers* two years later is probably even better than the studio version. Go ahead, compare the two if you don't believe me!

While "Another One Bites the Dust" is often credited as Queen's first foray into dance sounds, there were a few instances in the '70s when they got surprisingly funky, and the Taylor-penned (and side one closer) "Fight from the Inside" does contain an unmistakable dance-vibe – but May's guitar work balances the funk with the rock. Opening the second side is certainly one of Queen's most overtly sexual songs (perhaps only outdone a few years later by "Body Language"), "Get Down, Make Love." Just how steamy does this Freddie tune get? Sample lyric: "You take my body, I give you heat, You say you're hungry, I give you meat, I suck your mind, You blow my head, Make love, Inside your bed." *Yowza!*

And quite a few rockers fancy this tune, including Anthrax's Charlie Benante: "One word comes to mind about 'Get Down, Make Love' – SEX! This wasn't an ordinary song. The verses were spastic and the chorus was big and catchy – and then there is the middle section that sounds like a noise orgasm. I love the way Queen sound, they always had 'their sound.' I don't know what it was that set them apart from the rest – when you heard Queen, you knew who it was. Freddie was such an amazing singer, he could incorporate anything and make it sound like Queen. I have many more Queen favorites – this one is in my top-5. Nine Inch Nails did a killer cover of this." Also, Ty Tabor of King's X – "'Get Down, Make Love' had so much freaky guitar stuff. It was one of the most heavy things I'd ever heard in my life. Just genius heavy stuff – subtle things on guitar I'd never heard anybody do before. And then, it would kick in, and Freddie's voice."

Another underrated number, the surprisingly bluesy rocker "Sleeping on the Sidewalk," follows. Sung and penned by May, the tune features great guitar work throughout (especially the solo), and tells the tale of an unnamed trumpeter – all we know is he was "a city boy" who makes it big…and ultimately rejects fame. And yet another tune that seems to always get lost in the shuffle but is one that I have found myself appreciating more and more over the years – the Deacon-penned "Who Needs You." If I may make a point – the thing about Queen that set them apart from the pack was the wide range of styles they could not only take on, but completely make their own. And here, it's Calypso – complete with outstanding flamenco guitar work by May.

The argument could be made that *News of the World* is amongst Queen's hardest rocking albums, and the May-authored "It's Late" most certainly rocks. *Hard.* Clocking in at 6:26, the tune is the longest on the album, and musically, contains a riff towards the beginning which sounds like a not-so-distant relative of Led

Zeppelin's "Ten Years Gone." Also, the tune is notable for the fact that May is heard "tapping" the solo on his guitar's fretboard (a year before a certain Dutch-Eurasian guitarist perfected the technique and revolutionized rock guitar). Closing the album would be another glum-sounding number, Mercury's "My Melancholy Blues." Not containing one iota of May's Red Special at all, it's a bare-bones composition (featuring just voice, piano, what sounds like either a fretless or upright bass, and drums played with brushes), that wouldn't have sounded out of place performed late night by a jazz band at a smoky lounge.

News of the World (whose title probably came from a now-defunct British tabloid of the same name) would also feature one of the more unforgettable cover images – a painting of a robot holding or dropping the dead/bloodied members of Queen! As it turns out, the painting was done by sci-fi artist Frank Kelly Freas. Originally appearing on the cover of the October 1953 issue of *Astounding Science Fiction* (but obviously without the Queen members in the android's hand – originally holding just a single unlucky bloke), Freas agreed to re-do part of the painting to now include the deceased Queen members.

And since he is such a mega-Queen fan, why not let Charlie Benante share his thoughts once again, but this time concerning the *NotW* cover? "This is probably one of my favorite album covers. Growing up and coming from an artist background, this cover would always speak to me. I always wanted to know why this robot has killed Queen. [Laughs] And is he sorry for doing it? Because the look on his face is somewhat of, 'Oh no. What did I do?' But then you turn it over [Note: actually, it's when you look inside the gatefold of the LP], and you see him cracking a hole in an arena, and you see the people running, and you say, 'Was he just misunderstood...or was he on a mission to wipe out civilization?' But the shit that was on that record was some of the greatest music that they ever made."

Released on October 28, 1977, *News of the World* would become a worldwide hit (peaking at #3 in the US and #4 in the UK), while "We Are the Champions" would be issued as a single with "We Will Rock You" as the b-side – with many radio stations playing both tunes together as one – and peaked at #4 in the US and #2 in the UK. Other singles included "Spread Your Wings" (which would reach #34 in the UK) and "It's Late" (reaching a disappointing #74 in the US). Additionally, the album would solidify Queen as a worldwide arena (and soon, *stadium*) headliner.

And the album certainly left its mark on fellow musicians. "They've got classic songs that just have some killer riffs," explains Dimebag Darrell's partner, Rita Haney. "*News of the World* was one of our favorite records – it's on our jukebox." And Joseph Russo (the man who assumes the role of Freddie in the tribute band, Almost Queen) remains in awe. "They picked up with *News of the World,* and their intention with that was to get back to their original rock roots, and play a four-piece album. If you listen to that album, it's all straight rockers – bass, guitar, drums, and piano. It was such a big departure from *A Night at the Opera/A Day at the Races* – where everything was so flamboyant and big, and operatic. And believe me, I love *News of the World* – I just got the new 40th anniversary box set, and it's fantastic. There are a lot of studio cuts and working cuts. It's really wonderful."

Lastly, let's let Enuff Z'Nuff's Chip Z'Nuff provide the final *News of the World*, shall we? "One of their most underrated releases, *News of the World,* which came out in 1977, had the two big smash hits 'We Will Rock You' and 'We Are the Champions,' but the rest of that record is an absolute masterpiece. 'Spread Your Wings,' 'Get Down, Make Love,' 'Fight from the Inside,' and 'Sleeping on the Sidewalk'...all the band members contributed to the writing on the record, that featured a bridge truck full of hooks and mind-boggling songcraft. Nobody was doing what these cats were doing. Whatever they were drinking, please give me a sip!"

Van Halen
(Van Halen, 1978)

There are only a few select albums that pinpoint where a major shift in rock music occurred. Van Halen's classic self-titled debut is certainly one such release. Admittedly, it did not have the "beyond music implications" as say, *Meet the Beatles!* or *Nevermind* (meaning an album that affects fashion, advertising, politics, etc.). But from a musical and a guitar standpoint? *No question.* And as with many trailblazers, the band (and their guitarist) spawned an infinite amount of copycats who lacked the originality and pizazz of the originator – which of course, was not VH's fault.

The Pasadena, California group had been comprised of singer David Lee Roth, guitarist Eddie Van Halen, bassist Michael Anthony (real name: Michael Anthony Sobolewski), and drummer Alex Van Halen since 1974. And after toiling away playing backyard parties, high schools, and clubs on the Sunset Strip (and at least one close-call with stardom – Gene Simmons unsuccessfully trying to get them a record deal), Van Halen finally signed on the dotted line with Warner Bros. in 1977, and from August-September 1977, recorded what would be their debut LP at Sunset Sound Recorders in Hollywood, with Ted Templeman producing (a chap best known for his work with the Doobie Brothers and Montrose).

Now, before we dive deep into the album track-by-track, we should address the earlier claim concerning how the album would change the direction of rock from a guitar standpoint. And this was due to not one but *two* groundbreaking innovations courtesy of Eddie. First off, his two-handed tapping technique – which soon, seemingly every bloody rock guitarist would adapt into their own playing style.

"Most people think that the tapping and all that stuff had been in Ed's hands at least a year or maybe a couple of years before he even went in the studio to record the first record," explained former *Guitar World* editor Brad Tolinski in the book *Iconic Guitar Gear*. "And that would be wrong. When you listen to those early bootlegs of Van Halen, you really don't hear Ed tapping. You don't even hear him tapping on the demos for Warner Bros. And you don't hear him tapping on the Gene Simmons demos. You don't really hear him doing it until around the time of the first record."

"So, what's really fascinating to me is there was this moment in time where the band gets signed – Ted Templeman signs Van Halen. And they have like, two or three months before they go in the studio – because Templeman is finishing up a Doobie Brothers record. And the record label is basically saying, 'Look guys, we don't want you to play clubs. We don't want you to be out there until the record is done.' So, there's this couple month period where the band was essentially hiding. And I think that that's where Ed starts thinking very deeply about, 'OK. This is going to be my big shot. My big statement. I've been working on all these ideas. I've got a couple of months on my hands…let me see what I can do with all this crap.' That's when he gets serious. That's when the tapping really starts coming into focus."

Secondly, the creation of Ed's iconic homemade instrument, which again, would soon lead to other guitarists copying its look, gadgetry, and creative approach. "He goes and builds his first Frankenstein," adds Tolinski. "He messes around with it – he's got some guitars that were bits and pieces leading up to the Frankenstein. But he doesn't really create the Frankenstein until this period before they start recording the record. So, he's putting together all the bits and pieces of knowledge and all the things he's been thinking about for the last five, six, seven years – whatever it was – since he started playing guitar. They all start coming together in this one incredible, explosive, fertile moment in time – where Ed's really going to make *his statement*. None of the guitars that he had at that point were doing quite what he wanted them to do. And he's like, 'I've got to figure that out, because I'm going to be recording an album and that's going to be *for real'*."

"So, he sort of starts from scratch. He has a Strat – he doesn't really like the way it sounds. He's like, 'I'm done grabbing from guitars that I have. I want to just start fresh and find a neck and find a body that I really like – and put it together that way.' So he goes to Charvel and he finds a body that looks good to him. I think it's an ash body. He takes that and it's cheap, and the other thing about that was he didn't have a lot of money – his family had the smallest house on the block, sort of had to make do. So, he found a body that he could afford, found a neck that he liked, and put them together. It's as simple as that. The fact that they were cheap was neither here nor there – I mean, that was a plus, right? He just wanted what he wanted – he was going to paint it anyway. And he knew he was going to chisel the fuck out of it – because he was going to put in his pickups. So…why would he want a super-fancy body or neck? Some of this stuff is not such a mystery – it's just economics. It's just where he was at the time and how he was going to get this sound."

However, after all that detailed info, it turned out that EVH used two guitars to record the debut – Frankenstein, as well as an Ibanez Destroyer (the latter of which did not have a tremolo bar – unlike the other aforementioned instrument) whose original shape had been altered, and is often referred to as "the Shark." And both would be decorated with randomly-placed lines of electrical tape. And while we've spent the past few pages discussing the greatness of Eddie, now would the right time to discuss the greatness of the other VH members. I've often felt that if his brother was not in the band, Alex Van Halen would have received a heck of a lot more accolades for his outstanding drumming (listen to the beginning of "Hot for Teacher" off *1984* for the proof). Similarly, Michael Anthony is quite possibly the best back-up singer of any rock band ever, and bass-wise, was wise to keep things simple, to allow EVH to dazzle over top of everything else.

And while Roth himself would probably even admit he is not in the same Mercury/Dio/Halford category of extraordinarily talented rock vocalists, he certainly fits in the Jagger/Cooper/Stanley category. Meaning, that while they are not exceptionally technically-gifted vocally, their personality comes through in their singing style, which sets them apart from the rest of the pack – resulting in them having their own instantly recognizable style, as well. And to catch my drift regarding how Diamond Dave is one of a kind vocally, I wholeheartedly suggest you locate on YouTube the "vocals only" version of "Runnin' with the Devil." Trust me, you'll thank me later.

OK, so now that we have that out of the way, let's get down to the real nitty gritty – *the debut's tunes.* Except for two selections, all were credited as being penned by the entire band. Starting things off is the sound of a blaring car horn, before we're greeted by the aforementioned mid-paced rocker, "Runnin' with the Devil," which is one of the few times on the album where it is a showcase for DLR rather than EVH (along with a tune we will get to in a few, "Devil" features one of the guitarist's more simpler solos). "Dave is Dave," said Blue Öyster Cult singer/guitarist Eric Bloom, in the book *MTV Ruled the World.* "He's very flamboyant, and 'I want to hump your leg.' [Laughs] Especially as a young man back then. It's just great, and he got away with that stuff, whereas many other acts couldn't, because he wore his sexuality on his sleeve. Plus, on top of that, he's one fantastic frontman." And in the same book, Loverboy singer Mike Reno had nothing but high praise for his fellow vocalist – "I think at that time, if I were to think of California, I would think of David Lee Roth and Van Halen. They were the bad boys. They were the hardest rockin' guys out there."

And wouldn't ya know it, right after I'm done with my spiel about the vocals...it's right back to guitar! Of course, I'm talking about probably the greatest rock guitar solo ever captured on record, "Eruption" – which except for some brief appearances by drums and bass at the beginning, is almost entirely an unaccompanied Eddie solo. This was the tune that really showed the world that rock guitar had *not* been taken to the max, and that there was most definitely more ground to be broken – particularly the precise speed of soloing, tapping, and the introduction of "the whammy bar dive bomb."

"I was at a raging party the first time someone put on the first Van Halen record," recalls Billy Idol guitarist Steve Stevens, in the book *Shredders.* "And it got to 'Eruption,' and I literally ran across the room – this is the days of turntables – lifted up the needle and put it back on, and asked the person whose party it was, 'Who the fuck is this?!' Eddie was a total, complete assault. Not only technically, but the sound of his guitar was astounding at that point."

"His playing, especially on the instrumental, 'Eruption,' upped the game for everyone," added former *Guitar Player* editor Jas Obrecht in the same book. "The technique of tapping the fingerboard had been around for decades, but it was sparsely practiced, and almost always as a novelty. Eddie brought finger tapping into mainstream rock'n'roll. Within six months of the release of the first Van Halen album, young guitarists all across the country and in Europe – and especially Japan – were sporting copycat guitars and playing pale versions of 'Eruption.' But no one surpassed the original, because the real genius of Eddie Van Halen has always been in his hands and his imagination. I saw this myself one day in 1980, when Eddie showed me how he plays 'Eruption.' He did this with an unplugged Strat, and you know what? *The whole song was there.*"

Up next was the rare instance of a cover song *possibly* topping the original (and the original was bloody outstanding to begin with) – the Kinks' "You Really Got Me." If I were to pick the other standout guitar solo on the album besides "Eruption," it would probably be the one included here – as Eddie also inserts turbo-charged guitar licks between most of Roth's vocal lines. Up next was another tune that has gone on to be a VH classic, "Ain't Talkin' 'Bout Love," which according to Tolinski, was the group's tribute to a then-still emerging rock sub-genre. "Right around the time Ed was creating his guitar, he, Al, and Dave would go to the clubs in LA. And they sort of dug punk rock. They were curious at least. You always hear that Ed said, 'Well, 'Ain't Talkin' 'Bout Love' was a tribute to our version of a punk rock song."

As a result, the tune contains one of the simpler guitar solos on the album (which was supposedly overdubbed with an electric sitar). Which brings up a point concerning what separated EVH from the majority of the shredders that came in his wake – he always played what was best for the song, and kept things tasteful and memorable. In fact, I defy you to locate a solo on any Van Halen album that you cannot sing along to, whereas his copycats seemed to be just focusing exclusively on the speed and tapping aspects – with little expression on the instrument. I interviewed Eddie's son, Wolfgang, in 2021 for *Songfacts,* and asked, "While it seems like the primary focus of what made your father such an iconic guitar player was his soloing, he was such a phenomenal rhythm player." He agreed. "Everybody focuses on the tapping and the fast stuff, but his real strength was in his rhythm playing and his songwriting."

Y&T singer/guitarist Dave Meniketti praised the song's guitar work in *Shredders*, as did Diamond Head's Brian Tatler. Meniketti: "With his tone, he was doing a lot of semi-muting picking stuff, that was really distinctive for the style of songs that they were doing – such as 'Ain't Takin' 'Bout Love,' where it's obvious he's not just picking the strings in a standard way. He is, but he's using his palm to 'mute pick' a lot, as well. That's part of what he was doing, as well. Again, not unusual, but given with that and all the other things he was doing, it made for a distinctive sound for him."

Tatler: "There is very little or no double tracking on the first six Van Halen albums – he could perform in the studio, which I found really difficult to do. He would throw little licks in as he went through the track. I could not do that – I would have to concentrate on getting a rhythm track down, then add a solo. But Eddie seemed to be able to do it all in one, giving it a very loose feel. Incredible stuff. How did he manage to get such a brilliant riff out of just an A-minor chord in 'Ain't Talkin' 'Bout Love'?"

The remainder of the album seemed to be split 50/50 between heavy metal headbangers ("I'm the One," "Atomic Punk," "On Fire") and more melodic offerings ("Jamie's Cryin'," "Feel Your Love Tonight," "Little Dreamer"), as well as a tune that merged both approaches together, and would serve as an in-concert vehicle for DLR to strap on an acoustic guitar and chat with the audience at the beginning, "Ice Cream Man" (originally penned by blues singer/guitarist John Brim). But don't be misled – the tune also contains another standout solo, which in 2020, Steel Panther guitarist Satchel picked as his #5 "favorite Eddie Van Halen solo" for *Guitar World.* "OK…the first lick in the solo is iconic. And not easy to play, either. But again, the whole solo just grooves and fits so perfectly. And Eddie somehow made a simple 12-bar blues progression sound so heavy metal and exciting."

Released on February 10, 1978 (and featuring a cover of all four members posing/occupying a quarter space, with the soon-to-be iconic VH logo in the middle), the album was an immediate hit (reaching #19 on the *Billboard 200*) – thanks largely to the success of the lead-off single, "You Really Got Me" (#36 on the *Billboard Hot 100*). But over the years, the album kept selling…and selling…and selling. At last count, it was awarded the prestigious Diamond Award by the RIAA (meaning 10 million copies sold in the US alone).

Perhaps rockabilly guitarist Reverend Horton Heat summed up Van Halen's debut best, when he once told me, "I remember when that record came out, it was like a bomb going off. I mean, *everybody* got that record. They were like, almost instantly one of the biggest bands in the world."

Live and Dangerous
(Thin Lizzy, 1978)

Like Kiss, Peter Frampton, and Cheap Trick, Thin Lizzy issued an exceptional live album during the '70s. But *unlike* Kiss, Peter Frampton, and Cheap Trick, the recording in question – *Live and Dangerous* – did not conquer the charts. That is...*at least not Stateside*. But this was certainly not because of the quality of the material nor the performances, as nearly every expected Lizzy classic gets an airing here, and just about every single rendition outdoes the original studio version.

Originally formed in Dublin, Ireland in 1969, it was not until 1974 that the line-up that would be featured on *Live and Dangerous* (and which many consider to be the definitive Lizzy line-up) was put in place – singer/bassist Phil Lynott, guitarists Scott Gorham and Brian Robertson, and drummer Brian Downey. And soon after, the quartet scored their breakthrough with 1976's *Jailbreak*, and the anthemic worldwide hit, "The Boys Are Back in Town." While *Jailbreak* would be their highpoint chart-wise Stateside (the album peaked at #18 and the single at #12), they continued to crank out the hits throughout other parts of the world. And with the Lynott-Gorham-Robertson-Downey line-up having issued five albums by 1978, the time sure felt right to issue Lizzy's first live LP.

Tony Visconti – the co-producer of the group's last studio effort, *Bad Reputation* – was back on board again to oversee the recordings (with Lizzy also earning a production credit). And selections from a total of three shows would ultimately comprise the tracklist – Hammersmith Odeon in London, England (November 14, 1976), Tower Theatre in Philadelphia, Pennsylvania (October 20 and 21, 1977), and Seneca College Fieldhouse in Toronto, Canada (October 28, 1977). And as with seemingly the majority of live albums released in the '70s, there was allegedly quite a lot of overdubbing and fixer-upping in the studio afterwards.

Kicking things off is the tune custom-made for serving as a Lizzy concert opener, "Jailbreak." And while the studio version is one of the few Lizzy ditties to not include a guitar solo, this live version corrects that problem once and for all – with a wah-drenched Robertson solo. Up next, one of the album's standouts – particularly from a guitar standpoint – "Emerald." "That was a riff that Phil had," Gorham recalled in a *Songfacts* interview from 2013. "It's got the real sort of Irish-y feel in it. Brian Robertson and I, we came up with the harmony guitars in there. But the main riff came straight out of Phil. It's a song about ancient times in ancient Ireland, talking about the warring clans and all that."

And in the same interview, Gorham explained the awesome "guitar duel" between he and Robertson at the end, which was taken to new heights on this live rendition. "It was the first time that Brian Robertson and I did the bounce off lead guitar thing where he starts, I start, he starts, I start...the back and forth. That's the first time we actually got that one together. It felt so good and it felt so right, so we then started to try that out on a couple of other songs. That was kind of a launching pad for that style of writing between the two guitarists."

Up next is the underrated melodic tune, "Southbound," which contains some gorgeous guitar harmony work between the two guitarists – a style that was not all that common at the time within hard rock/heavy metal, but certainly bands like Iron Maiden and Metallica would study this Lizzy trademark and make it their own in the '80s. "The inspiration comes from the left, it comes from the right, it comes right down the middle," Gorham told *Vintage Guitar* in 2019, about how Lizzy guitarists create their harmonies.

"Sometimes you have a harmony line before the song has even been written, and you're looking for a place to put this into. Other times, the harmony line almost writes itself – just because of the chord pattern, the sequence that you're in. Sometimes, I'll start a line off, and Christian, Damon, or whoever will say, 'That needs a harmony part there,' or I'll say the same thing to their line. There's no real one certain way of doing it. And you don't just put it in for the sake of you've got two guitars. It definitely melodically has to fit, or it just sounds forced and there's no point in it."

Side one of the vinyl version ends with a bang – a turbo-charged rendition of the Bob Seger obscurity, "Rosalie" (with a bit of Lizzy's "Cowboy Song" added in, resulting in the tune being listed as "Rosalie/Cowgirl's Song"). The quartet cools things down a bit with the laidback funk groove of "Dancing in the Moonlight (It's Caught Me in Its Spotlight)," before the uptempo "Massacre" (which the aforementioned Maiden would later cover in 1988, as the b-side for their "Can I Play with Madness?" single – and as a sidenote, kickstarted yours truly's interest in the Lizzies) reintroduces the rock.

And then…another one of the set's standouts, the ballad "Still in Love with You," which features soulful vocals from Lynott, and a simply outstanding solo once more from Robertson. Gorham: "Brian Robertson, it was he and I that started this whole Thin Lizzy guitar style of playing. And I had a great time with Brian – I thought he was just a magnificent player. He was a really young guy, but was really fiery and a lot of energy."

Closing out side two would be another funky number, the amusingly-titled "Johnny the Fox Meets Jimmy the Weed" – which leads to the question, who came up with the titles and lyrics in Lizzy? "That was 100% Phil," Gorham admitted. "If he was struggling, like, say for a word to rhyme somewhere, you'd throw a word out and he might use that, but it's like in Black Star Riders, Ricky's such a great lyricist that none of us want to go into that area at all. It was the same with Phil, he was such a master at that side of it, there wasn't any real point of the rest of us trying to hone in on it."

Perhaps the greatest example of a *Live and Dangerous* rendition outdoing its sleepy studio version is "Cowboy Song" which simply explodes after its relaxed intro, and leads directly into Lizzy's best-known tune, the anthemic "The Boys Are Back in Town," and the rocking "Don't Believe a Word." One of Lizzy's more underrated/oft-overlooked tunes is next, "Warrior," which once more, features outstanding guitar work from start to finish from Gorham and Robertson. "That's just a lick and a chord pattern that I had," recalls Gorham. "We were at a rehearsal and I just started playing it. Phil looked up and said, 'What's that?' And I said, 'Well, it's a riff and a groove I have.' He goes, 'OK, man. Let's try to develop that.' And he and I, we just sat down and started developing it, put the different licks in there. We'd developed a solo spot and I said, 'I think Brian Robertson will be perfect for this, rather than my guitar.' That's how that song came about, with Phil perking up his ears when I started to play the opening line for that particular song, 'Warrior'." And then wrapping up side three would be the previously unrecorded "Are You Ready" – a straight-ahead, seemingly made-for-the-stage rocker (and soon after, would be utilized as a set-opener).

Side four would focus mostly on tackling pre-*Jailbreak* material, such as the guitar-heavy n' bluesy "Suicide," "Sha La La" (which includes an unaccompanied drum solo by Downey smack dab in the middle of it), a previously unrecorded tune penned by the *Live and Dangerous*-era Lizzy line-up, the almost Blues Brothers-esque "Baby Drives Me Crazy" (which features a then-unknown Huey Lewis on harmonica), before the album concludes with a rendition of the early Lizzy classic, "The Rocker."

While *Live and Dangerous* gets my vote – and I'm sure most other Lizzy fanatics – as the band's definitive live concert recording, in 2009, another vintage Lizzy live set was issued, *Still Dangerous*, which documented a single show (Philadelphia's Tower Theatre on October 20, 1977) that was originally broadcast on the radio via the *King Biscuit Flower Hour*. And unlike *Live and Dangerous*, this one did *not* receive an excessive amount of overdubs.

When I asked Gorham if he preferred *Live and Dangerous* or *Still Dangerous* during an interview for *Goldmine* the same year as the latter album's release, he responded, "Sometimes I have to watch myself [with this question], because I know how near and dear the *Live And Dangerous* album is to a lot of people. But I think that the *Still Dangerous* album is a better album. The playing is probably a little better, and the production is definitely better, with Glyn Johns. If it's not better than *Live And Dangerous*, then it certainly stands up shoulder-to-shoulder next to it."

Released on June 2, 1978, *Live and Dangerous* was a huge hit in the UK (peaking at #2 on the charts), while frustratingly performing far below expectations Stateside (#84). Lizzy would continue on until 1983, before Lynott (who was addicted to hard drugs for the last few years of his life) sadly died on January 4, 1986, at the age of 36 – extinguishing any hope of a reunion of Lizzy's *Live and Dangerous* line-up. But since Lynott's passing, appreciation for the band and the talents of the singer/bassist/poet has only increased. And when I spoke with Lynott's mother, Philomena, for *Rolling Stone* in 2005 about the unveiling of a statue of her son on Harry Street in Dublin, Ireland, she also recognized his one-of-a-kind talents. "I'm tired of picking up magazines and reading, 'Phil Lynott: rock star who died of the drugs.' I'd like him to be remembered as a wonderful son, a kind and gentle soul, a great musician, poet, songwriter, lyricist. That's 'mother' talking, but I *know* he was great."

The Cars
(The Cars, 1978)

There are only a few albums in rock history that you can say are perfect – or at the very least, *near* perfect – in so much that you can listen to them from beginning to end, without feeling the urge to utilize the fast forward button at some point. In my humble opinion, the Cars' self-titled debut is most certainly one of them – as it automatically placed the band as one of the leaders of the "new wave movement," and contains countless tracks that are still spun on classic rock radio to this day.

Hailing from Boston, the Cars' roots stretch back to a folky band by the name of Milkwood, which contained two members that would eventually prove essential to the Cars' story – Ric Ocasek (real name: Richard Otcasek) and Ben Orr (real name: Benjamin Orzechowski). By the mid '70s, Milkwood was no more, and the duo continued on as the more rockin' Cap'n Swing – with Ocasek on vocals/rhythm guitar and Orr on vocals/bass, plus additional members Elliot Easton on guitar, Greg Hawkes on keyboards, and David Robinson on drums. And when it came to deciding who sang what, Ocasek and Orr split the vocal duties 50/50 (with the former singing on the quirkier tunes, and the latter on the more easily-digestible compositions).

However, the band was not collaborative. "Our band never jammed – I wrote all the songs," Ocasek told me back in 1997, for the now-defunct publication, *The Island Ear*. "I put them down on tape, with the parts on, and people learned the songs. I've never done a song by jamming with somebody else; I don't like the idea of it. I don't like to write with others, it's probably my least favorite thing to do. I started the Cars to play music that I wrote, just like I've started any band that I've ever had in my life – to do music I wrote. I form bands to play my songs."

And when you heard the quality of the material that Ocasek was penning at this stage, it's understandable why he had assumed full control – especially with such tunes as "Just What I Needed." Ocasek: "Our demo tape got played on the radio – 'Just What I Needed' became a hit before it was even on a record. WBCN in Boston was playing it, and it became the most requested song.

Record companies started coming around asking, 'What label are they on?' So then we had 20 labels chasing us around Boston."

With the songs and sound already in place – a merger of new wave (Hawkes' synths, Ocasek's muted/down-picked power chords) and arena rock (stadium-ready choruses, Easton's guitar heroics), a record deal with Queen's then-US label, Elektra, was soon secured, with the group flying to England to work with another Queen-connection, producer Roy Thomas Baker. As Hawkes recounted to *Classic Rock* in 2006, "That was way exciting – we got to go to London, recording at AIR Studios, George Martin's studio. Which was a thrill – got to meet him there. The studio was great, getting to work with Roy Baker was great. We did it in like twelve or fourteen recording days, and then mixing was approximately a day per song. We had the whole thing recorded and mixed during February 1978."

Released on June 6, 1978, The Cars' self-titled debut contained such new wave anthems as "Good Times Roll," "My Best Friend's Girl," "You're All I've Got Tonight," and the aforementioned "Just What I Needed" (the latter of which contained a now-classic synth break from Hawkes). Also rounding out the nine-track LP were such quirky numbers as "I'm in Touch with Your World," "Don't Cha Stop," and "Moving in Stereo" (the latter of which was later utilized as an instrumental in an unforgettable scene in the 1982 film, *Fast Times at Ridgemont High*), as well as the melodic album closer, "All Mixed Up," plus the album's most underrated tune, "Bye Bye Love."

"We opened for about anybody in the beginning," Ocasek once told me about the tour in support of *The Cars*. "We opened for bands that we really hated, like Styx. I remember opening for Styx for about a week, and we kept winning over the show, and they got mad. And that would keep happening for bands that we'd open for. And then halfway through the tour we started headlining. But in the beginning we took whatever we could get. Most of those bands would go watch us on the side of the stage to see what the fuck was going on. And it seemed that the people were relating to us and not relating to them. So they all got a little pissed."

As a result of a heavy touring schedule and radio embracing the band, the Cars' debut was an immediate hit – peaking at #18 Stateside, and enjoying immense staying power (coming in at #4 and #48 on the 1979 and 1980 "year-end charts" for *Billboard*, and at last count in 1995, certified 6x platinum). The Cars would go on to carve out a successful career (particularly the 1984 Mutt Lange-produced mega-hit, *Heartbeat City*), before splitting in 1988 and eventually being inducted into the Rock and Roll Hall of Fame in 2018. Sadly, with both Orr and Ocasek having passed away (in 2000 and 2019, respectively), the possibility of a reunion of the original Cars line-up has been extinguished. But listening back to *The Cars* today, it's plainly evident that it remains one of the greatest rock n' roll debuts. *Ever.*

Some Girls
(Rolling Stones, 1978)

To repeat a similar point I made in the entry for Queen's *News of the World*, by the late '70s – whether you liked it or not – punk rock had affected just about all forms of rock music. And funny enough, many of the same veteran acts that the young punks criticized for becoming too bloated, grandiose, and out of touch suddenly became more focused and concise in their songwriting and approach. The biggest rock band on the planet that was still a working/functioning act at the time would have been the Rolling Stones – who instead of turning a blind eye to the message and vibe of this young/upstart style, used it as an inspiration on *Some Girls* (their most inspired and simply *best* album since 1972's *Exile on Main St.*).

Furthermore, additional pats on the back are in order for the Stones being able to issue a new album *at all*. Case in point, the threat of one of their co-founding members, Keith Richards, receiving a lengthy jail term in the near future hung overhead (after being busted in Toronto during February of 1977 for "possession of heroin for the purpose of trafficking," upon being caught with 22 grams of heroin and 5 grams of cocaine). Nevertheless, by October 10, 1977, the Stones – singer Mick Jagger, guitarists Richards and Ronnie Wood, bassist Bill Wyman, and drummer Charlie Watts – began work on a follow-up to 1976's somewhat lackluster *Black and Blue* at Pathé Marconi in Paris (with the sessions running until March 2, 1978). And once again, the Glimmer Twins (aka Jagger and Richards) would be producing – and aside from a single track, would co-pen every single song.

With disco sweeping the world by this time – thanks to the immense popularity of the *Saturday Night Fever* film and its Bee Gees-heavy soundtrack – quite a few rockers took a "dance detour" around this time. In case you forgot, I'm talking about Blondie with "Heart of Glass," Rod Stewart with "Da Ya Think I'm Sexy?", Kiss with "I Was Made for Lovin' You," Queen with "Another One Bites the Dust," and…the Stones with "Miss You." But unlike the majority of the other tunes mentioned, "Miss You" (most memorable for Jagger's perfectly-placed multitude of "Ooo's" throughout) was much more laidback – so perhaps "funk" rather than "disco" is a more fitting description.

For the remainder of the album, most of the tunes can be neatly categorized into two categories – rockers that sound like what you'd expect from the Stones ("When the Whip Comes Down," the title track) and tunes that contain an unmistakable punk edge ("Lies," "Respectable"). Also included are a few surprises, such as the country-ish "Far Away Eyes" and a cover of a tune that the Temptations scored a #1 hit with back in 1971, "Just My Imagination (Running Away with Me)." Plus, the seemingly obligatory one tune per Stones album in which Richards was permitted to sing lead on, "Before They Make Me Run" – which lyrically seems to be his reply to the sticky legal situation he found himself in at the time.

And while the album was a pretty darn consistent listen from beginning to end, the argument could be made that the Stones "back loaded" *Some Girls* a bit, as the two best tunes reside at the rear – "Beast of Burden" and "Shattered." The former being another laidback funk workout, and the latter managing to be both funky *and* punky. In fact, some punk purists may argue with the following observation/claim, but here it goes anyway – a tune such as "Shattered" sounds an awful lot like the punk-meets-funk style that the Clash would soon start adopting themselves from *London Calling* and onward. Mere coincidence or genuine influence?

Released on June 9, 1978, the album was a worldwide smash – hitting #1 in the US and #2 in the UK, and going on to sell a whopping 6 million copies in the US. But the LP came with a bit more controversy than your average Stones release. Firstly, its cover design – which resembled what looked like either a hairstyle or wig ad for women. Several faces were featured on the cover modeling different hairstyles – including such female celebs as Lucille Ball, Farrah Fawcett, Judy Garland, Raquel Welch, and Marilyn Monroe, as well as the Stones members. Since the photos of the celebs were used without permission, lawyers soon came a-callin', and the cover was quickly recalled and altered.

Secondly, when Reverend Jesse Jackson publicly took offense to the lyric "Black girls just want to get fucked all night/I just don't have that much jam" in the title track. But all seemed to be forgiven after a public apology was issued by the president of Rolling Stones Records, Earl McGrath. And in case you were wondering about Richards and his aforementioned legal troubles – they *didn't* make him run. In October '78, he pleaded guilty to possession of heroin and was given a suspended sentence and placed on probation for a year (in addition to continuing a drug rehabilitation program and performing a benefit concert for the Canadian National Institute for the Blind).

Looking back at their long n' lengthy discography, I'd be bold enough to declare that *Some Girls* was the last Stones album that I'd feel comfortable/confident putting in the same category as *Sticky Fingers* and *Exile on Main St.* – as an offering that captured the band both inspired *and* focused, from both a songwriting and performance perspective (although admittedly, 1981's *Tattoo You* comes mighty close, as well). And in 2011, *Some Girls* deservedly received the "deluxe edition" treatment, which featured a bonus disc of twelve previously unreleased tunes from the album's sessions, while a great concert performance filmed from this era was issued the same year on DVD – *Some Girls: Live in Texas '78.*

Jethro Tull's Ian Anderson   Billy Cobham

Jeff Beck   Deep Purple/Rainbow's Ritchie Blackmore

(Photos by Bill O'Leary)

Blue Öyster Cult

The Scorpions

(Photos by Bill O'Leary)

Queen's Freddie Mercury

(Photo by Bill O'Leary)

Queen's Brian May

(Photo by Bill O'Leary)

Freddie

(Photos by Bill O'Leary)

Queen's Brian May, John Deacon, Roger Taylor

(Photos by Bill O'Leary)

Van Halen's David Lee Roth

Van Halen's Eddie Van Halen

(Photos by Bill O'Leary)

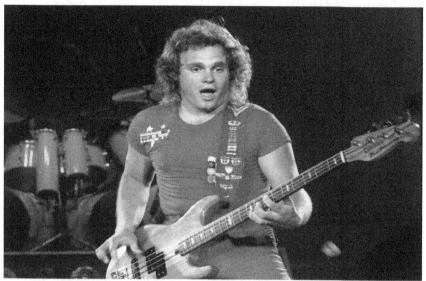

Van Halen's Michael Anthony

Van Halen's Alex Van Halen

(Photos by Bill O'Leary)

Cheap Trick

(Photos by Bill O'Leary)

Cheap Trick's Rick Nielsen

(Photo by Bill O'Leary)

UFO's Michael Schenker

(Photo by Bill O'Leary)

Pink Floyd

(Photos by Bill O'Leary)

Rush's Alex Lifeson

Rush's Geddy Lee

(Photos by Bill O'Leary)

Rush's Neil Peart

(Photo by Bill O'Leary)

Judas Priest's Rob Halford and Glenn Tipton

(Photo by Bill O'Leary)

Judas Priest's KK Downing

(Photo by Bill O'Leary)

AC/DC

(Photos by Bill O'Leary)

AC/DC's Malcolm Young

(Photo by Bill O'Leary)

Randy Rhoads

Ozzy Osbourne

(Photos by Bill O'Leary)

King Crimson's Adrian Belew

The Police

(Photos by Bill O'Leary)

At Budokan
(Cheap Trick, 1978)

It seemed like just before the '70s drew to a close, any rock artists that had not yet got around to issuing a live album rushed to squeeze one in before the dawn of the '80s. But it turned out that one of the greatest rock concert recordings of all-time, Cheap Trick's *At Budokan*, was a happy accident. Initially released solely for the Japanese market (where Cheap Trick was exceedingly more popular than in any other area on the planet), it was selling so extraordinarily well as an import Stateside, that a wiseman (or wisewoman) at Columbia Records decided it deserved a proper worldwide release. And the rest, as they say…is history.

Hailing from Rockford, Illinois, the definitive Cheap Trick line-up was in place by 1974 – singer/guitarist Robin Zander, guitarist Rick Nielsen, bassist Tom Petersson, and drummer Bun E. Carlos (real name: Brad M. Carlson). After toiling away for a few years playing locally, the quartet signed with Columbia Records – issuing their self-titled debut in 1977. And the group would soon become best known for two traits – penning incredibly hook-y power pop (that could lean toward the punkier side of things at times) and possessing an interesting look (where Zander and Petersson represented the good-looking "rock stars," while Nielsen and Carlos represented the uncool "oddballs").

And while they did issue three studio LP's that were indeed jolly good – the aforementioned self-titled debut (my personal fave CT studio effort), plus 1977's *In Color* and 1978's *Heaven Tonight* – something was amiss. Namely, fans who were lucky to catch the band live during this era soon discovered that there was simply no comparison between how Cheap Trick's tunes sounded live as opposed to in the cold confines of a recording studio. So, a decision was made to record two nights when they headlined the Nippon Budokan in Tokyo (a hallowed hall when it came to rock n' roll, as the biggest of the big had played there previously – the Beatles, Led Zeppelin, Deep Purple, Queen, Kiss, etc.), on April 28 and 30, 1978.

Listing "Cheap Trick" as the sole producer, you can certainly say that similarly to my previous entry for Thin Lizzy's

Live and Dangerous, the live renditions of all the tunes on *At Budokan* prove to be superior to the much more reserved studio versions. And this is evident right from the get-go with the seemingly custom-made show opener, "Hello There" (particularly with its straight-to-the-point-lyrics, "Hello there ladies and gentlemen, Hello there ladies and gents, Are you ready to rock? Are you ready or not?"), followed by another tune that shines in a live setting, "Come On, Come On." "Lookout" fulfilled the purpose of "incentive" for fans who already owned all their studio albums (as Nielsen says on record, "This is a brand new one"), as did the surprisingly over nine-minute jamfest, "Need Your Love" (which would eventually appear as a not nearly as good studio version on their next album, *Dream Police*) – with the *In Color* tune, "Big Eyes," sandwiched in between.

Opening side two was a surprise (and again, previously unrecorded) cover of Fats Domino's "Ain't That a Shame" – which begins with an extended/anticipation-building intro. When interviewing Carlos for the book *John Winston Ono Lennon*, he recounted how the band came to cover the tune. "In '75, I remember Tom got in the car one night – we were going to a gig, and he goes, 'I saw this thing on TV last night – *Roots: John Lennon Sings the Great Rock & Roll Hits*!' We thought he was just pulling our leg – because Tom used to make up the wildest shit and tell you with a straight face. Then about a week later, I see this ad on TV for the album. I immediately picked up the phone and ordered two copies. Lo and behold, then the thing got injuncted! About a week after it got injuncted, my two copies showed up in the mail. That's where we got 'Ain't That a Shame' and stuff like that. We'd sit around after gigs at our buddy's house at 1:00 or 2:00 in the morning and put that record on, and just be in ecstasy. That was like *the coolest* record ever."

Up next was the tune that would finally introduce Cheap Trick to the masses (and one of Mike Damone's favorites), "I Want You to Want Me." If you were to compare this superior/amped-up live rendition to the lackluster studio version on *In Color*, you'll be absolutely flabbergasted. "It turned out that the studio version was produced not the way we would have done it," Petersson told *Classic Rock* in 2006. "And we've never done it since like that anyway – with a little 'Shakey's Pizza Parlor piano' and twinky little sounds. It was like, 'Ugh'."

Concerning the song's original creation, Petersson recalled in the same *Classic Rock* piece, "My recollection is that he [Nielsen] just did that song as a bit of a joke, because at the time when we had done that song, there was a lot of pop music on the radio. ABBA, and all sorts of things – disco. He thought, 'I'm just going to do an over-the-top pop song, I just want to do one that's so silly – total pop – and then we'll do a heavy version of it.' He didn't know what was going to happen with it. The idea was to have it like a heavy metal pop song. Cheap Trick doing ABBA – except a very heavy version."

Nielsen explained his unique perspective of penning the song as, "I just pictured myself in a big, overstuffed chair, and my dad turned on the TV, there were like three stations. I wanted to watch Gabby Hayes – he was a cowboy – I always wanted what wasn't there, so I think that's what's got me inquisitive throughout my whole life. When you wanted Gabby, Gabby's not there, when you want your dad, your dad is not there. It was the easiest lyric I could think of, and I wish I were that stupid more often. It's like Van Morrison – some of this old songs, it didn't matter what the lyrics meant. It's how they sounded."

Up next was another one of the album's undisputed standouts – one of the all-time great teen anthems, "Surrender." Best known for its killer chorus ("Mommy's alright, Daddy's alright; They just seem a little weird; Surrender, surrender; But don't give yourself away") and also mentioning a certain other famous rock band ("Got my Kiss records out!"), the tune also turned up around the same time in a key scene in the cult classic film, *Over the Edge* (as did "Hello There"). And I'll give ya an interesting bit to keep an ear out for the next time the *At Budokan* version comes on – Carlos drops a beat during a crucial drum fill, around the 2:22 mark. For all intents and purposes, a reprise of "Hello There" appears under the title of "Goodbye" (with its lyrics altered to reflect the conclusion of a concert…rather than its birth), before "Clock Strikes Ten" wraps things up. A largely forgettable tune when originally included on *In Color* (largely due to its subpar lyrics), "CST" improves exponentially here.

As previously stated, *At Budokan* was originally issued in Japan (in October '78) before finally enjoying a Stateside release a few months later (February '79). And as with their previous two albums, the front cover of *At Budokan* only featured the two "handsome" members, while the other "nerdy" members were allotted to the back cover. "We did that for Japan only, and that was the understanding through the whole project," Carlos remembered in an interview with *Long Island Pulse* in 2016. "After it came out in Japan it was still the understanding for about the next six months. And then its fame kind of overtook us, so we put it out in the US thinking it was going to sell a few hundred thousand copies while we were in Europe and Asia touring. And then when we got back the label said, 'This thing is taking off'!"

And take off it did. Once the stellar live rendition of "I Want You to Want Me" was issued as a single in April '79, Cheap Trick finally had a hit on their hands – peaking at #7 on the *Billboard Hot 100*. And as a result, *At Budokan* scaled the *Billboard 200* all the way to #4 (and came in at an impressive #13 on *Billboard's* year-end charts), and at last count, was certified 3x platinum. "That was surprising – we didn't have any idea," admits Petersson. "What we think are going to be hits, we kind of go both ways – we think everything should be a hit, or we don't really expect it. So, it's always something [that] is a surprise I've found – like that live record. And it shouldn't be a surprise, because that's how we were signed to a record label – people saw us live, and that was a strong suit of ours. When we did 'I Want You To Want Me' on the second album, it sounded nothing like us, and it wasn't successful. So it turned out that the live thing worked."

And if you're wondering what happened to the rest of the material that did not make the cut on the single disc *At Budokan*, it has surfaced several times over the years in different configurations. First in 1994 on another single disc, *Budokan II,* then in 1998 as *At Budokan: The Complete Concert*, and then as a mammoth 4-disc set in 2008 to mark its 30th anniversary, simply titled *Budokan!* And time and time again, Cheap Trick has proven to be oh so much better on stage than in the studio, as such other stellar concert recordings as 1999's *Music for Hangovers*, 2001's *Silver*, 2019's *Are You Ready? Live 12/31/1979*, and 2021's *Out To Get You!: Live 1977* have demonstrated.

Looking back on Cheap Trick's career today, it's understandable to state that it was a double-edged sword to have such an exceptional, high-energy live album as your commercial breakthrough – for the simple reason that it would be near-impossible to top. But Carlos disagrees. "The live album wasn't the problem. The problem was we already had the next record ready to go, *Dream Police*. And we were looking forward to playing the new songs because we'd been doing the other stuff for a while. Suddenly, everything got delayed and postponed for six months or a year. And then the workload tripled. It was like, 'Pack your bag. You're not going to see home for a couple of years.' And at that point we hadn't been home for a couple of years – maybe a week a year. Things got more hectic and the days got twice as long."

Strangers in the Night
(UFO, 1979)

Whad'ya know...*another* classic live album appeared just before the '70s drew to a close! This time, it was UFO's turn with the double LP, *Strangers in the Night*, compiled from performances recorded on October 13 and 18, 1978 from a pair of venues (International Amphitheatre, Chicago and Louisville Gardens, Louisville). And like most of the previous concert albums included in this book, the more energetic renditions here certainly outdo the more staid original studio versions.

To put it all in perspective, UFO began issuing albums in the early '70s as a "space rock" band (hence...their name), and endured several members coming and going, before their best-known line-up took shape and shifted towards an arena rock sound – singer Phil Mogg, guitarist Michael Schenker, keyboardist/guitarist Paul Raymond, bassist Pete Way, and drummer Andy Parker. And it was this era of the group that issued their best, most-focused, and hardest-rocking albums yet, 1977's *Lights Out* and 1978's *Obsession*. With the band touring hard alongside some of the era's best bands (Rush, Thin Lizzy, AC/DC, etc.), UFO had built themselves a sizeable following – particularly in Chicago – and appeared poised to become a leading hard rock force.

As with all live albums of the '70s, it's hard to tell how much "studio doctoring" was done on *Strangers in the Night* post-recording (producers of this era should be ashamed with the annoying trend of inserting additional loud crowd noise throughout some of these recordings). The proof that there was some post-recording fixer uppers was when in 2020 a deluxe edition of the album was issued, which added several other shows from the tour, and if you are to compare the show from Youngstown, Ohio from October 15, 1978 to *Strangers*, there is indeed a noticeable difference. But regardless, producer Ron Nevison did a good job of not going overboard post-production (and here's an interesting factoid: a then-unknown Mike Clink served as assistant engineer...who would go on to produce *Appetite for Destruction* eight years later).

The album's original tracklisting (as a 1999 reissue shuffled it around considerably) began with the rocking "Natural Thing," brought the tempo down a bit with "Out in the Street," before offering up the anthemic "Only You Can Rock Me," and closing side one with the fan favorite, "Doctor Doctor" (a tune in which Iron Maiden would eventually adopt as the selection played over the PA before hitting the stage).

The second side doesn't disappoint with such further rockers as "Mother Mary," "This Kid's," and "Love to Love" – the last tune serving as a near eight-minute epic, which starts with great mood-setting keyboards courtesy of Raymond (it should be noted that UFO were one of the few hard rock bands of the era that was able to truly enhance their sound with keyboards...perhaps the Cars being the only other). But it is side three which is the best of all four – although only comprised of two tunes, "Lights Out" and "Rock Bottom."

Both tracks are a showcase for the outstanding guitar talents of Schenker, who makes his Flying V sing n' scream in his allotted solo spots. "On songs like 'Only You Can Rock Me' or 'Lights Out,' Pete Way would come up with [sings melody], and that was it," Schenker once explained to me in a *Songfacts* interview, about the UFO songwriting process. "Then I get inspired by that and find the additional parts. Or in the other song, that kind of happened quite a few times, too, that Pete came up with, like, 'Only You Can Rock Me,' for instance. But that was it. And then I added all the other pieces to it."

In the same interview, I mentioned to Schenker how the studio and live versions of "Rock Bottom" are so different, as the latter includes a long guitar solo section which also includes some nifty interplay between guitar and keyboard. His reply? "Well, 'Rock Bottom' has that piece in the middle of free expression, and it's perfect for me because I love pure self-expression. It's a really, really good part to play over that particular chord there, and it leaves a lot of space to come up with a whole bunch of creative ideas. Over the years, the solos have changed. I keep the basic structure of it, but there is a lot of space to put new 'sparks' on here and there and keep it fresh. It's always enjoyable to play over and over and over, because I can be very creative with it on the spot. That's a very fascinating, enjoyable part of music for me."

The tunes "Too Hot to Handle," "I'm a Loser," "Let It Roll," and "Shoot Shoot" fill out side four, and while "Handle" and "Roll" are certainly winners, one can't help but wonder why stronger selections that have appeared on other live releases (from this tour) did not make the cut, especially "Cherry" and "Pack It Up (And Go)." But regardless, when the album was released on January 2, 1979, it cracked the UK top-10 (#7), while just missing the top-40 Stateside (#42). However...by the time *Strangers* hit the shelves, Schenker had exited the band for good. "All of a sudden, I was a major influence," Schenker also told me for *Vintage Rock*. "People were saying 'Schenker is God,' and I thought, 'What is this? This is rubbish.' After *Strangers in the Night* and *Lovedrive* [the latter a Scorpions studio album that Schenker played on around this time], I had enough of that, and I wanted to continue focusing on music."

Afterwards, Schenker would carry on as the leader of the Michael Schenker Group (aka "MSG"), while UFO enlisted Paul Chapman as Schenker's replacement, and issued several underrated studio offerings (particularly *No Place to Run* and *The Wild, the Willing and the Innocent*). But neither Schenker nor UFO were able to truly break through worldwide post-*Strangers* – which leads one to wonder what could have been if the Schenker line-up remained together just a bit longer.

Regardless, at least two UFO members still hold the album in high regard. When I asked Way what his favorite UFO album was for *BraveWords* in 2014, he replied, "Probably *Strangers in the Night*, because the fact that it's a double album, it does span quite a lot of what we were trying to achieve. And also, the fact that we're playing in a great big auditorium. It was the end result of an awful lot of work, and an awful lot of enjoyment doing that." And Schenker once shared a similar sentiment – "One of the best live rock albums of all time!"

And perhaps the gent who has single-handedly kept the cult surrounding *Strangers in the Night* alive has been radio personality Eddie Trunk. Never bashful about listing it as one of his favorite albums of all-time, which he did for *Classic Rock* in 2016 (as part of a list entitled "The 11 Records That Changed My Life"), and said, "*Strangers in the Night* definitely has to be in there, as well. I got into UFO because of *The Wild, the Willing and the Innocent*, but *Strangers*, to this day, to me, is the greatest live album of all time. And also, probably my favorite album of all time. *Strangers* to me is just as good as it gets in terms of performance, songs, energy – it's the ultimate melodic hard rock. I have introduced so many people to that record in the last 15-20 years."

Highway to Hell
(AC/DC, 1979)

Were they metal? Boogie? Punk? Rock 'n' roll? It was hard to put your finger on just which style of rock AC/DC specialized in throughout their first few studio offerings with singer Bon Scott. But one thing was for certain – they were rapidly building a large and loyal fanbase throughout the world, and it seemed to all coalesce in what would turn out to be the band's last album with Scott, 1979's *Highway to Hell*.

Already stars back home in their native Australia, AC/DC – who were comprised of Scott, the brother/guitar duo of Angus and Malcolm Young, bassist Cliff Williams (who replaced Mark Evans in '77), and drummer Phil Rudd – were several albums into their recording career. While their early albums would be issued under different titles and varied track listings, AC/DC's Stateside discography included 1976's *High Voltage*, 1977's *Let There Be Rock*, plus 1978's *Powerage* and *If You Want Blood You've Got It* (another album from '76, *Dirty Deeds Done Dirt Cheap*, would not see the light of day in the United States until '81).

The quintet certainly had the tunes (heck, they'd already unleashed the likes of "TNT," "Whole Lotta Rosie," and "Sin City," for crying out loud!), but production-wise, it was still a bit rough around the edges (as the band had worked exclusively with the production duo of Harry Vanda and George Young – yep, another Young brother – up to this point). And all you had to do was give a listen to FM radio at the time, to discover that you needed a major league-sounding production to gain entry onto the airwaves (Boston, Queen, The Cars, Styx, Pink Floyd, etc.). And it just so happened that AC/DC had found their man – Robert John "Mutt" Lange.

Now considered one of rock's all-time great producers due to his impeccable track record of churning out mega-sellers with the biggest names of rock and pop (Def Leppard, Bryan Adams, Shania Twain, Muse, etc.), at the time, Mutt had yet to make the jump to the big time – having worked with the likes of Graham Parker, the Outlaws, and the Boomtown Rats. But from the first notes of the album-opening title track of *Highway to Hell*, it was undeniable that this was the best-sounding AC/DC album yet – powerful and clear, without forfeiting any of the raunch of the group's earlier work (Bon's vocal delivery and lyrics made sure of the latter). Also, unlike many other rock acts at the time that were opting to reach the mainstream via either a ballad or a disco tune, AC/DC was one of the few – perhaps other than only the Ramones – that offered 100% rawk.

In the book *AC/DC: Album by Album* by Martin Popoff, former *Guitar World* Editor-in-Chief Brad Tolinski explained, "That higher level of discipline on *Highway to Hell*, that sort of lifts them from being this great little high-energy pub rock band into something worthier of the arenas. And that little bit of spit and polish on the choruses, like you hear on [the song] 'Highway to Hell,' makes it just a little bit better for radio, too."

And while the anthemic title track and its instantly recognizable guitar chord progression remains the album's best-known tune – with its lyrics recounting what it was like being in a touring rock band – the album is chock full of other prime cuts. Case in point, a song that would gain repeated performances onstage ("Shot Down in Flames"), as well as tunes that dip deep into Bon's trademark lyrical sleaze ("Girls Got Rhythm," "Walk All Over You," "Touch Too Much," "Beating Around the Bush," "Love Hungry Man"). Admittedly, the second side of the album is padded with filler (namely "Get It Hot" and "If You Want Blood"), and also contains one of AC/DC's most notorious tunes of all-time.

The lyrics of the album-closing tune, "Night Prowler," detail the thoughts of a deranged stalker/murderer, and upon the album's release and for a few years afterwards, didn't receive much attention (because, quite frankly, it was not one of the band's better nor more memorable tunes). But all that changed in 1985, when serial killer Richard Ramirez was nicknamed the "Night Stalker" (turns out he was a big-time AC/DC fan) – after carrying out multiple grisly murders, before being apprehended and eventually, incarcerated. Interestingly, the last words Scott ever spoke on an AC/DC album were in tribute to Mork from Ork (a character portrayed by Robin Williams, from the TV comedy *Mork and Mindy*) – "Shazbot" and "Nanu Nanu."

Released on July 27, 1979, and sporting an album cover that featured a painting of the band staring and sneering (with Angus transformed into a devil), *Highway to Hell* became AC/DC's first top-20 album in the US, peaking at #17 (chart-wise, it was a quantum leap for the group, as their previous two albums, *Powerage* and *Blood*, topped out at #133 and #113, respectively), and at last count, was certified 7x platinum. As a result of the album's success, AC/DC became one of the most sought-after opening acts by rock's biggest names at the time – including sharing stages with Ted Nugent on an arena tour (including the group's first-ever appearance at Madison Square Garden), the Who (stadiums in Europe), and as part of the Bill Graham's Day on the Green Festival in Oakland.

But as stated earlier, *Highway to Hell* would sadly prove to be Bon's last album with AC/DC, as he would die on February 19, 1980, at the age of 33, from alcohol poisoning (as is officially reported) – although author Jesse Fink claims in the book *Bon: The Last Highway: The Untold Story of Bon Scott and AC/DC's Back in Black* that it was a heroin overdose. The surviving members of AC/DC would opt to carry on – enlisting singer Brian Johnson, uniting once more with Mutt behind the board, and issuing the blockbuster *Back in Black* just five months after Bon's passing. That album has been certified 22x platinum in the US alone.

Highway to Hell certainly left its mark on subsequent rockers – including former Iron Maiden singer Paul Di'Anno, who recounted in the book *Iron Maiden '80 '81*, that Bon Scott was an influence on him vocally. "I went to Bon's grave about five years ago in Perth, and I cried like a baby," Di'Anno recounted. "I just couldn't deal with it. And I was even more upset when I got to Fremantle, and there's a statue of him. You can't say nothing bad about Bon Scott in front of me – I'll punch ya!"

Although it is four decades old, *Highway to Hell* still rocks, ferociously – as Keith Roth, host of the Sirius XM channel *Ozzy's Boneyard* stated, "Hard to believe it's been 40 years since the release of *Highway to Hell*. AC/DC started building a lot of traction amongst my keg party comrades. We were licking our lips after *Powerage*, and what they delivered was from another planet. Sounds as fresh and exciting today as the first time you heard it. Bon Scott left us with the ultimate parting gift!"

The Wall
(Pink Floyd, 1979)

Sure, there had been albums issued prior to 1979 that were meant to be listened to as an entire "piece," and took you on a true musical journey (the Who's *Tommy* immediately comes to mind). But one of the very best – especially when listened to on headphones – was Pink Floyd's 2-LP masterpiece, *The Wall.* A concept album or "rock opera" (in other words, it tells a story throughout all of the tracks), *The Wall* is widely considered not only one of the very best of this story-telling album genre, but also, is one of the greatest plain old *rock albums* ever.

Originally formed in London circa 1965, Pink Floyd was first and foremost a psychedelic band early on (especially when singer/guitarist/songwriter Syd Barrett was in charge). But by '68, Barrett went bye-bye, and Floyd's best-known line-up was in place – singer/bassist Roger Waters, singer/guitarist David Gilmour, keyboardist Richard Wright, and drummer Nick Mason. The band slowly morphed into one of the top prog rock and arena rock bands by the late '70s, due to the enormous success of such classic LP's as 1973's *The Dark Side of the Moon*, 1975's *Wish You Were Here*, and 1977's *Animals.*

As mentioned in previous entries, the arrival of the punk movement seemingly inspired many veteran rock bands to suddenly tighten up their song arrangements and dramatically dial down the bombast. Hence, Floyd would shun the looong compositions that comprised *Animals,* and shall we say…"trimmed the fat" for its follow-up. And instead of producing themselves on their eleventh studio album (as they had done on *Animals*), Alice Cooper/Lou Reed/Kiss producer Bob Ezrin would oversee the sessions – along with Waters, Gilmour, and a bloke by the name of James Guthrie.

And as also previously mentioned, the resulting album *The Wall* had a story running through it – supposedly inspired by Waters' unhappiness with how popular and out of touch Floyd had become when the group had toured strictly enormodomes in support of *Animals* (and in particular, an incident that occurred on the tour's last date on July 6, 1977 at Olympic Stadium in Montreal, when Waters supposedly spat on overexuberant fans in the front row). But also, it was clear that former member Barrett had an influence on bits of the storyline, to boot – particularly that by this point, he had become a "rock n' roll casualty" due to either mental illness or overdoing it with drugs (or perhaps a mixture of both).

The sessions would run for nearly a year (from December 1978 through November 1979), while five different recording studios would be utilized – Britannia Row (London), Super Bear (Nice, France), Miraval (Correns, France), 30th Street (New York), and Producers Workshop (Los Angeles). And while sessions were taking place at Producers Workshop, Toni Tennille (of Captain and Tennille fame) dropped by to provide backing vocals on several tracks – along with Beach Boy Bruce Johnston. She recounted what she saw that day in *The Yacht Rock Book,* which completely caught her off guard (and not in the way you'd assume a recording session with one of the world's top rock bands during the decadent '70s to be like).

"The session was set for a Sunday morning – which I thought was kind of odd, for a rock group. Not for me, because I have always been a day person. I think we met there around 11:00 in the morning, at a prominent but not huge studio in LA, Producers Workshop. I walk in with Daryl [Dragon, aka 'The Captain'] – Daryl came along because he just wanted to watch. And David Gilmour met us at the door when we came into the studio. He introduced himself with a big smile and said, 'I am so excited that you're here! I just saw you on television this morning.' And I thought, 'What in the world could he have been watching on television on Sunday morning that we were on?' He said, 'I was watching *Kids Are People Too* with my kids.' And that was a kids show that we had guested on. And I thought, *'Well, there goes your rock image right out the window'.*"

"I have to say, there wasn't a groupie in sight, and it was one of the most professional sessions I've ever been in. It was beautifully handled. People always ask, 'Which songs did you sing on?' Well, I don't know, because they didn't have names then – they would just say, 'Here is the track, and this is what we want you to sing on this track,' and we did it. It was fun and it was just lovely the way they appreciated what we did and respected what we did."

Now, if I were to dissect/analyze each of the album's 26 tracks in detail – which by the way, *Waters wrote 23 of* – it would take all bloody day. *But...*an overview is certainly doable (especially in the space allotted for this entry). Kicking things off with a surprising bang (literally, 16 seconds in) is "In the Flesh?" – which shows that while bass is the instrument Waters is most associated with, he was also an underrated riff-writer. Immediately afterward, several tracks are used primarily to tell the story of the early years of the main protagonist (who simply goes by the name "Pink") – "The Thin Ice," "Another Brick in the Wall, Part 1," and "The Happiest Days of Our Lives" – before the album's best-known tune appears.

Of course, that would be "Another Brick in the Wall, Part 2" – which contains surprisingly funky music, and it's anti-mean teacher message sung by a kids chorus in heavy British accents ("We don't need no education, We don't need no thought control, No dark sarcasm in the classroom, Teacher leave them kids alone"). Also included is one of Gilmour's best solos (who as with many all-time great rock guitarists, you can seemingly sing along to all of Gilmour's solos).

Further "table setter tunes" occur ("Mother," "Goodbye Blue Sky," "Empty Spaces"), before another standout track is delivered, the rocking "Young Lust" – the first tune credited to someone *other* than just Waters, as Gilmour gets a co-credit – which leads into "One of My Turns" (a tune perhaps best known for having the good fortune of being the b-side of "Another Brick in the Wall, Part 2"). And before you knew it, the first record wrapped up with further "story pieces" – "Don't Leave Me Now," "Another Brick in the Wall, Part 3," and "Goodbye Cruel World."

The sublime sound of acoustic guitar and fretless bass greets us in the opening of LP #2 – with another standout, the mid-paced "Hey You" (which contains another memorable lyric: "And the worms ate into his brain"). More "table setters" continue to set the table – "Is There Anybody Out There?", "Nobody Home," "Vera," and "Bring the Boys Back Home" – before another one of the album's best tunes arrives, "Comfortably Numb." The second composition of *The Wall* to be co-credited to Waters and Gilmour, it's certainly the album's most melodic tune, and features quite possibly Gilmour's best-ever solo in the middle, as well as another wailing solo at the end.

"The Show Must Go" and a re-appearance of "In the Flesh" (although with different lyrics – some of which could be interpreted as quite racist and homophobic if one did not realize it is being sung from the perspective of a crazed character smitten with megalomania) start the final side. Then another one of the set's best tunes, "Run Like Hell" (probably yours truly's favorite of the bunch, and the third Gilmour co-songwriting credit) – which saw Gilmour utilize a delay effect to create the song's famous guitar part. But according to Guitareo.com, it was not just *one* effects pedal.

"For 'Run Like Hell,' he used two delays in tandem. The main delay was set to 380ms with 7-8 repeats and the level set to unity with the guitar. The second delay was set to 507ms and mixed to be quieter." Good luck making sense of that scientific gibberish, dear reader! The sinister "Waiting for the Worms" sees Gilmour and Waters trade off lead vocals (and once more, not exactly PC-friendly lyrics…but again, sung from the perspective of a geezer who has completely lost his marbles by this point in the storyline), before *The Wall* wraps up with three ditties, "Stop," the Waters/Ezrin collab "The Trial," and "Outside the Wall."

While chatting with the engineer of *The Dark Side of the Moon* for *Songfacts* in 2019, Alan Parsons, I asked, "How would you compare working with Pink Floyd on *The Dark Side of the Moon* to working with The Beatles?" (as that lucky bugger also worked with the Fab Four on *Abbey Road* and *Let It Be*). He replied, "Pretty different. The only similarity is that they both liked to use the studio to its fullest, and they were always looking for new effects and new sounds. But that was the beauty of working with those guys: There were always new horizons to discover in sound."

And certainly, Floyd was still looking for "new effects and new sounds" on *The Wall*, and had found a kindred spirit in Ezrin, as sounds and various bits of dialogue are used to great effect throughout the album. Case in point – a plane approaching a crash landing (the album opening "In the Flesh?"), a mad teacher shouting ("Another Brick in the Wall, Part 2"), a child admiring a plane overhead ("Goodbye Blue Sky"), a phone operator unable to connect a call ("Young Lust"), and a chatterbox groupie ("One of My Turns"), among other unexpected audio delights.

Also accompanying *The Wall* was some of the best artwork and packaging of any rock album, ever – courtesy of illustrator/cartoonist Gerald Scarfe. The original front and back cover only featured the illustration of a white brick wall, with stickers affixed to the front over the cellophane (stating the band's name and album title in messily-drawn black ink), and the tracklisting affixed as a sticker on the back cover. And when you opened it up, the gatefold featured random bricks missing, with Scarfe-drawn cartoons to represent certain characters of the storyline – Pink's mother, the nasty school teacher, worms, a jail cell, and even an enormous toches dressed up as a judge (yes, you read that right!).

Released on November 30, 1979, *The Wall* was an absolute blockbuster, and served as the first true rock mega-seller of the '80s – peaking at #1 in just about every single country in the world (surprisingly, it reached *only* #3 in one of their strongest markets…the group's homeland of the UK), while "Another Brick in the Wall, Part 2" topped both the US and UK singles charts. And *The Wall* proved to have a long shelf life – serving as the #1 selling album of the year in *Billboard*, and at last count, certified 23x platinum in the US (with worldwide sales reaching an estimated 30 million).

As a result of the album's massive success, the band would perform *The Wall* in its entirety via a highly theatrical stage show. And rather than tour the world, it would be performed for several nights in a handful of locations (Los Angeles, New York, London, and West Germany) at various points in 1980 and 1981. Additionally, *The Wall* would be made into a 1982 movie starring Bob Geldof in the role of Pink (mixed with animation).

However, the massive success of *The Wall* did not lead to peace and harmony between Waters and the other three Floyds, and by 1985, he was out of the band (with the other three carrying on). However, Waters would perform *The Wall* in its entirety at several different points in his career (playing to capacity crowds worldwide). And in 2000, a live recording comprised of selections from the group's performances at Earls Court Exhibition Centre, in London, England from August 7-9, 1980 and June 14-17, 1981 served as the basis for the *Is There Anybody Out There? The Wall Live 1980-81* double-disc release.

Pretenders
(Pretenders, 1979)

As the '70s drew dangerously close to becoming the '80s, the music biz coined a new phrase that they felt would be a bit more appealing and not as extreme as "punk rock" – *new wave*. While some chose to categorize a band such as the Pretenders as a "new wave band," make no mistake about it, certain tunes on their classic self-titled debut openly embraced good old fashioned punk rock. Heck, they even hired one of the two producers of the bloody Sex Pistols' *Never Mind the Bollocks* album as their producer!

Although thought of primarily as a British band – which they mostly were, as guitarist James Honeyman-Scott, bassist Pete Farndon, and drummer Martin Chambers all hailed from Hereford, England – their singer/guitarist, Chrissie Hynde, was born and raised in Akron, Ohio. Shortly after attending Kent State (where she was schoolmates with Devo's Gerald Casale, and witnessed first-hand the horrific Kent State shootings), Hynde moved to London, wrote for *NME*, and befriended bands who were part of the nascent British punk scene – particularly, the Pistols and the Clash.

By 1978, all the pieces of the aforementioned classic Pretenders line-up were finally in place. A deal was soon done with Real/Sire Records in 1979, and after Nick Lowe produced a cover of the Kinks obscurity "Stop Your Sobbing," the quartet got to work on their full-length – with Chris Thomas taking Lowe's place behind the mixing desk, and with two London studios utilized (Wessex and AIR).

Kicking things off would be one of the tunes alluded to in the intro that could certainly be classified as "good old fashioned punk rock" – "Precious" (due to the tune's power chord progression and Hynde's use of certain dirty words that would have resulted in a trip to the principal's office a few years earlier). The punk vibe continues on "The Phone Call," before another one of Hynde's songwriting weapons comes into use – *melodicism* – in the form of the much more laidback "Up the Neck" (its title possibly a reference to the song's ending...in which the sound of a guitar stretching to the upper reaches of its neck can be identified).

New wave bands didn't seem to have very many true guitar heroes…and then along came Honeyman-Scott. While there was never any confusion between him and your typical heavy metal shredder, his tasteful/melodic style of soloing added a crucial element to the band, on tracks such as "Kid" and "Private Life" (more on those selections in a bit). But undoubtedly, his best guitar solo can be found in the album's hardest rocker, "Tattooed Love Boys," which perfectly suits Hynde's sexually-charged lyrics.

Akin to David Gilmour's approach on Pink Floyd's "Another Brick in the Wall (Part 2)," Honeyman-Scott plays short, easily digestible phrases – ones that you'll be able to hum along to after just a few listens. But while Gilmour's "Brick" solo is about laying it way back, Honeyman-Scott sounds like he's slashing at the strings and attempting to choke the life out of his guitar. And the solo is not a traditional one – ten lead breaks are included as a sort of "call and response" between the lead and rhythm guitars. And what better way to end it all than with a bit of the ol' toggle-switch flick (something that Kiss' Ace Frehley helped popularize in the '70s on his Les Paul).

Next up is the mood-shifting instrumental, "Space Invader" (I guess the band had become smitten at the time – like seemingly the rest of the world – with the similarly-named arcade game), which turns out to be one of two instances on the entire LP that Hynde is not listed as a songwriter (Farndon and Honeyman-Scott get all the cred). A return to uptempo rock n' roll occurs with "The Wait" – a tune whose chord progression sounds similar to something that Nirvana would have concocted a decade or so later, before the aforementioned cover of the Kinks' "Stop Your Sobbing" (penned by Ray Davies, who was soon to be the father of Hynde's daughter, Natalie) closes side one.

Another of the album's highlights, "Kid," starts the second half (continuing in the tuneful direction of "Sobbing") and as previously mentioned, contains some great/tasteful guitar work throughout – particularly Honeyman-Scott's sparkling (almost country-ish) solo. Come 1979, reggae sounds had become quite popular within rock (most notably with the Police and the Clash, as well as such two-tone/ska bands as the Specials and the Selecter), and the next two tunes reflect this – "Private Life" and the album's big hit "Brass in Pocket" (the latter co-penned by Hynde and Honeyman-Scott, and containing a phrase so memorable, "I'm special!", that some were led to believe it was the title of the bleeding song). Also, the tune features a standout vocal performance by Hynde – one of rock's more underrated singers.

"Lovers of Today" is an extended ballad – featuring another standout guitar solo (although not every tune on the album featured a lead break, Honeyman-Scott consistently knocked it out of the park on the ones that did), before the album closes with "Mystery Achievement." Probably the most upbeat ditty on the entire album, the tune is one of the few to be driven by Farndon's bouncy bass, mentions the phrase "Cuban slide" (which would also be recycled as the title of a b-side). Additionally, the tune begins with a driving drum beat that Culture Club quite possibly had "studied" for their own tune a few years later, "Church of the Poison Mind."

Also, it bears mentioning that although MTV was still a few years away from changing the course of rock music, the band was wise (or lucky?) enough to film a trio of imaginative videos for tracks off the debut – "Brass in Pocket" (which shows Hynde working as a waitress in a dreary diner, with the other members playing the roles of customers), "Kid" (which takes place at a carnival), and "Tattooed Love Boys" (performance footage mixed with images of the band members' silhouettes behind a large sheet of paper). As a result, when MTV was launched and was in desperate need of videos to play, these three clips (as well as a few from their next album) were heavily rotated/helped spread the word.

Released on December 27, 1979, *The Pretenders* became a worldwide hit – topping the charts in the UK and peaking at #9 in the US, undoubtedly due to the success of the "Brass in Pocket" single (UK: #1, US: #14), and earning platinum certification in the country that Hynde originally called home. And it turned out that the band had amassed a healthy amount of non-LP b-sides, demos, and radio sessions from this golden era – as evidenced by a 2006 reissue of *The Pretenders*, which featured an entire extra disc of these long-unheard artifacts.

The Pretenders would also follow in the tradition of perfect (i.e., not a single stinker track) debut rock albums of the late '70s – *Never Mind the Bollocks, Van Halen, The Cars*, etc. However, it did not signal the beginning of a long tenure for the band's original line-up. Although a strong follow-up would be issued, 1981's *The Pretenders II*, Honeyman-Scott was found dead from a cocaine overdose (at the age of 25) on June 16, 1982, while Farndon would also be found dead – drowning in a bathtub after a heroin overdose (at the age of 30) on April 14, 1983. Hynde and Chambers would continue on however, and score another sizable hit with 1984's *Learning to Crawl*. But without question, their self-titled debut remains their tour de force.

Permanent Waves
(Rush, 1980)

By the dawn of the '80s, despite never having a studio album that cracked the top-10 in the United States (heck, also make that the top-20...and the top-30), Canadian rockers Rush were already headlining arenas throughout North America. But the first offering of the '80s from Geddy Lee (vocals/bass), Alex Lifeson (guitar), and Neil Peart (drums) would change all that – once and for all. Of course, I'm talking about their now-classic seventh studio effort overall, *Permanent Waves*.

Up to *Permanent Waves*, Rush was known mostly as a prog band which was certainly closer to the heavy metal side of things than say, Yes was. But like Yes, Rush had a soft-spot for including extended compositions on their albums – that often showcased all three members' instrumental talents. But a funny thing happened during 1979 (the first year in their recording career that no Rush album was released) – the trio discovered new wave. Especially such groundbreaking acts as the Police, Talking Heads, and Devo. And as a result, while the material on *Permanent Waves* still contained tricky bits and instrumental virtuosity, it now featured elements of this aforementioned musical sub-genre – especially the faux-reggae sounds of Sting and co.

Once again working with producer Terry Brown (who had been on board since '75), *Permanent Waves* would also be the first Rush album to be recorded at Le Studio, in Morin-Heights, Quebec, Canada (a studio that Rush would revisit for their next few albums) – with sessions taking place from September through October 1979. And the "ready for the '80s Rush" gets off to a rousing start, with one of their all-time best tracks, "The Spirit of Radio." Opening with a whirling guitar lick that was created to resemble radio waves bouncing around, the song was one of Rush's most commercial-sounding yet – which fit in perfectly with what rock radio was spinning at the time (Styx, Kansas, Journey, etc.). And Rush's discovery of reggae sounds was most clearly detected during the bit at the 3:50 mark (the "For the words of the profits were written on the studio wall" part).

As the title states, lyrically, "The Spirit of Radio" reminisces about the free-form/anything-goes format of FM radio circa the early '70s, and how it was moving more towards of a regulated format by the '80s (before long, radio playlists would become *entirely* programmed). When released as a single, "TSoR" was an undisputed success – becoming Rush's highest charting single to that point in the US (#51), Canada (#22), and the UK (#13).

How do you follow the album's best song? By offering up the album's *second* best song! Although never issued as a single, "Freewill" was certainly deserving – with a memorable chorus and lyrics focusing on freedom of choice (which interestingly, was a topic that the aforesaid Devo would also home in on that same year, with their album and song of the same name). But the album is truly a showcase for Lifeson. While not thought of first and foremost as a "shredder," Lifeson lets his fingers fly on the fretboard throughout the solo in "Freewill" – as he activates hyperspeed for much of it.

Up next, "Jacob's Ladder" remains one of the more underrated/overlooked of the extended Rush compositions. Perhaps due to the fact that unlike such previous lengthy ditties as "2112" and "Hemispheres," it doesn't wallop you over the noggin from the get-go – but rather, builds slowly. But like the others, the seven-and-a-half minute-long tune navigates through quite a few twists and turns compositionally. Another underrated tune follows, "Entre Nous" – which is French for "between us" (I guess the beginning of the chorus, "Just between us" should have been a hint, eh?). Another tune that was highly melodic and seemingly custom-made for early '80s rock radio, "Entre Nous" surprisingly did not leave any sort of impression on the singles charts worldwide, and as a result, has seemingly all but slipped through the cracks subsequently.

"Different Strings" comes off closest to a throwaway on the album, but ultimately, serves as a bit of a "pallet cleanser" for the album's grand finale, "Natural Science." The album's lengthiest tune (clocking in at a whopping nine minutes and 20 seconds), the tune is split into three parts – "I. Tide Pools," "II. Hyperspace," and "III. Permanent Waves" – similarly to how Rush's previous extended ditties were also divided into multiple-titled mini-sections.

Lyrically, "DS" is seemingly about how mankind was becoming obsessed with technology over the simpler things in life, like nature (which probably fits the modern day better than ever by how utterly mesmerized we've become with iPhones and other gadgets). And wouldn't you know it – *another* nod to reggae appears seemingly out of nowhere, at the 5:07 mark!

Released on January 14, 1980, *Permanent Waves* provided a quantum leap for Rush on the album charts Stateside, where it rocketed all the way up to #4 (compared to the mere #47 placing that their previous album, *Hemispheres*, topped off at), while pushing one digit higher in both Canada and the UK. And its cover image remains one of Rush's best – showing the hazardous effects of a hurricane, with Canadian model Paula Turnbull superimposed over it (with her skirt blowing up, to reenact the classic Marilyn Monroe pose from her 1954 film, *The Seven Year Itch*).

Listening back to the album almost exactly 40 years later at the time of this article's writing, it remains one of Rush's finest – and one of the few times that a veteran rock band managed to alter their sound/remain current without it being a blatant attempt at crass commercialization…due to a decidedly organic approach. In fact, you could make the argument that *Permanent Waves* signaled the mainstream moving to Rush – rather than Rush moving to the mainstream.

Glass Houses
(Billy Joel, 1980)

I hate to keep bringing up a point that has certainly been well-taken by this stage of this book, but it bears repeating for this entry – circa the late '70s/early '80s, it was abundantly clear how much punk rock and new wave had influenced established rock artists (Queen's *News of the World*, Rolling Stones' *Some Girls*, Rush's *Permanent Waves*, etc.). And as it turned out, it also made its presence felt on certain pop-rock artists, as well – especially Billy Joel, and his blockbuster seventh studio album, *Glass Houses*.

By the close of the '70s, the Long Island, NY native had become one of the world's top singer-songwriters, on the strength of such now-classic albums as 1977's *The Stranger* and 1978's *52nd Street*. And in the process, had also assembled a stellar backing band, which included Russell Javors (guitar), Doug Stegmeyer (bass), Richie Cannata (saxophone), and Liberty DeVitto (drums). But thus far, aside from the rockin' "Big Shot," the singer/pianist had mostly scored hits with ballads ("Just the Way You Are," "She's Always a Woman") or pop ("My Life," "Movin' Out"). However, that would all change with Joel's first offering of the '80s.

Recorded during 1979 at A&R Recording Studio in New York City, DeVitto recalled in *The Yacht Rock Book* what a typical recording session by the BJ Band around this time was like…and how nutrition played an important part. "Billy wanted a regimented time in the studio. We would start at noon, and if we didn't get anything by say, 7:00 or 8:00, we would go home. Billy would come in with an idea for a song, and we would run it through. Then, if it flew with the band, we would leave the recording studio and go in the control room, and Billy, you'd see him at the piano, starting to write down words."

"A short time later, we would come back in the studio, and there was a song. And then we would arrange our parts – put that all together. So by that time, it's like, 4:00, 5:00. Everybody's getting hungry, but we'd want to record the song. That's when the 'pre-food take' would happen. The food would come in, we'd be hungry, like 'We *really* want to get to the food,' then we'd go in and eat, and then the 'post-food take' would happen. Usually, the pre-food take won."

"There was a great Chinese restaurant across the street from the studio at the time. The studio was on Seventh Avenue and 52nd Street in Manhattan. There were always great restaurants around there. A lot of them are gone now – the Stage Deli, the Carnegie Deli, and this one particular Chinese restaurant that was there, that is now gone. Chinese food was #1, then deli food all the time. And we always had peanut butter and jelly with Wonder Bread on the table. Any time we wanted to have that, we'd have it. And a bowl full of candy! I would say something like 'You May Be Right' was a pre-food take, definitely. Most of the songs were pre-food takes, because you could tell the energy on the tracks. If it was a real high-energy tune, it was probably a pre-food take. A post-food take would have been 'Until The Night,' maybe. 'Honesty' – those kind of things."

While Joel would be credited as the sole author of all the material on *Glass Houses*, the drummer recalls all of the band members contributing their part – as well as assisting others. "He wrote the words and chords to the songs. Like, he could sit down at the piano and play the song. If there was a drum part, we created that; guitar parts; Richie created his sax parts. Actually, everybody created something for something else. Like, the song on the *Glass Houses* album called 'Through the Long Night' – I remember Russell sitting in the control room, motioning what I should play on the drums. And when I did it, it sounded great."

And as with the previous two records, *Glass Houses* would be produced by Phil Ramone. "Phil taught us how to play in the studio," DeVitto added in a chat with *Songfacts* in 2016. "I consider myself a live drummer – I put a lot of energy behind it and a lot of excitement when I'm playing live – it's what I think people pick up on. Phil taught us what counts, what doesn't count, what you can do, what you can't do in a studio. And he was so good to us, that we used to call him 'Uncle Phil.' It felt like a family when we went into the studio. There was no fear of anything. It was great."

"There were songs that Billy would come in with maybe just a verse to it, and Phil could direct him on where to go on the chorus, or flip things around. The first thing he taught us was that people want to hear just 'two and four.' That's all people like to hear – just the basic beat. They love to catch on to that. You need to have a great melody, great lyrics, and a great beat, and that's what does it. That's what Phil taught us."

Taking a gander at the tracklisting today, it's clear that "the piano man" opted to front-load *Glass Houses,* as all five tunes on side one of the LP/cassette were issued as singles. Opening with a sound effect of glass shattering, "You May Be Right" contained an unmistakable Stones-y swagger (particularly in the guitar work). "That was an interesting one, because I played the alto on that," explained Cannata about the tune, in *The Yacht Rock Book.* "And that took a minute to find...all the solos that I played for Billy were first/second take – there wasn't a lot of time spent."

"That one, we spent a little bit of time on it, because Billy thought maybe it should be a guitar solo, maybe it should be a harp solo, and we went round and round about what it was going to be – after the guitar solo. It's a split solo. And I ended up playing an alto sax on it, which I don't usually play that much. Even when I play that solo live, I play it on tenor. Again, a great song. And if you look deeply into his lyrics...y'know, Billy's brilliant. He's absolutely fantastic. It was what was happening back then in his life, and he wrote about it."

Up next was "Sometimes a Fantasy" – a tune that saw Billy and the boys distinctly hone in on new wave (and more precisely, the Cars, especially in the use of muted/staccato power chords and an unmistakable Ric Ocasek-like vocal approach), and lyrically, seems to deal with talking dirty on the phone with your significant other. The breezy acoustic guitar strum of "Don't Ask Me Why" sounds like it would have fit perfectly on the aforementioned prior few albums (and contains an instantly memorable vocal melody), before the album's best-known tune appears, "It's Still Rock and Roll to Me."

"When he wrote 'It's Still Rock And Roll To Me,' I was actually the last one to come to the studio," remembers DeVitto. "As I'm walking down the hall, Richie runs up to me and says, 'Wait until you hear this song! *You will love it!*' And it was great. And that little drum fill that is in the middle, that everybody does the air drums to when we played it live – I kind of stole that from [John Lennon's] 'Instant Karma.' Because Alan White played drums on 'Instant Karma,' and he does that straight four fill and a shuffle. And I told him once – I said, 'Alan, I stole that from you.' And he put his hands out, like he wanted money." [Laughs]

The tune also features some superb horn blowing by Cannata. "Before that solo, Billy says to me, 'Rico, play something that somebody's going to remember in twenty years.' And being in my twenties, I'm going, *'Twenty years from now?* I'll be in my forties...that's ridiculous'! What I had in my head was not what I played. I played something similar. And before that solo, Billy says, *'Alright, Rico,'* which made me even more so that person 'Rico,' and kids came to the shows with 'ALRIGHT RICO!' banners. And here it is forty years later, and we're *still* talking about it. That just happened – hardly anything was really planned."

Side one would close with "All for Leyna," which includes a tip of the cap to another then-thriving new wave band – the Police (particularly, the guitar in the verses). And while side two would not include any tunes that became hits – "I Don't Want to Be Alone," "Sleeping With the Television On," "C'était Toi (You Were the One)," "Close to the Borderline," and "Through the Long Night" – the material still fits well stylistically with the first half. And concerning the album's closing tune, DeVitto remembers it being inspired by a certain fabulous four-piece.

"Billy always loved the Beatles. The Beatles were always an influence. In fact, I think 'My Life' was kind of written like a McCartney song – lighthearted, but it's got great chords in it. As a matter of fact, on *Glass Houses*, when we do a song called 'Through the Long Night,' the guitars are on one side and the vocals are on the other side – like when they used to simulate stereo on Beatles records. The vocals would be on one side and the band would be on the other side. It's kind of fixed like that, too."

Released on March 12, 1980, *Glass Houses* would feature a now-iconic cover image. "I think the cover photo of *Glass Houses* was the first house that he bought with [his first wife] Elizabeth," explains Cannata. "That was right on Long Island, in Cove Neck. A great shot. Again, I don't think a lot was given to...there is something meant by 'glass houses.' It was a metaphor: 'People should not throw stones at glass houses,' right? Again, he's brilliant. He came up with these intros and ideas and we all ran with them. I remember once, he had called me to come over [to the house], because he had written 'Until the Night.' I walked into the living room, and he had a big piano in there – and he plays the beginning, and played it and sang it for me. We had many dinners there, he was very gracious – he and Elizabeth. We had gone there time and time again. I was living in Sea Cliff at the time."

Glass Houses would establish Joel once and for all as one of the world's top singer-songwriters, as the album would rocket to #1 on the *Billboard 200* (and hold that spot for six weeks) – thanks to such hit singles as "It's Still Rock and Roll to Me" (#1, his first-ever chart-topping single), "You May Be Right" (#7), "Don't Ask Me Why" (#19), and "Sometimes a Fantasy" (#36). It would also prove to be one of the year's top-selling albums (coming in at #4 on the year-end album charts), and at last count, was certified 7x platinum in the US. Additionally, the singer would be awarded the 1981 Grammy for "Best Male Rock Vocal Performance" due to his work on the album (*Glass Houses* was also nominated for "Album of the Year," but would lose out to Christopher Cross' self-titled debut).

Although Attila's lone self-titled release from 1970 was the *heaviest* release of Billy's career, *Glass Houses* remains the *rockingest.* "We were shooting from our hip and our heart – that's why those records are so good," Cannata adds about the era that gave us *Glass Houses.* "And keep in mind, those records were done on 24-track tape, a Neve console, Studer machines – no automation, no digital set of tools, no metronome, no Auto-Tuning, no beat-detecting. *Just count the song off and play.*"

British Steel
(Judas Priest, 1980)

There are certain years in which an impressive amount of classic hard rock and heavy metal albums arrived all at once. One of those years is 1980, when Judas Priest's metal opus *British Steel* was released along with AC/DC's *Back in Black*, Rush's *Permanent Waves*, Van Halen's *Women and Children First*, Ozzy Osbourne's *Blizzard of Ozz*, Black Sabbath's *Heaven and Hell*, Motörhead's *Ace of Spades*, and Iron Maiden's self-titled debut, among others.

From 1974 through 1979, there were few metal bands on the planet that were as heavy as Priest – *Rocka Rolla, Sad Wings of Destiny, Sin After Sin, Stained Class, Killing Machine* (titled *Hell Bent for Leather* in the US), and *Unleashed in the East* were issued during this span. However, the UK metal act (comprised of singer Rob Halford, guitarists KK Downing and Glenn Tipton, bassist Ian Hill, and a rotating cast of drummers) had yet to score a true global commercial breakthrough by the time the '70s ended. While *Unleashed in the East* did peak at an impressive #10 on the UK charts, it only managed a meagre #70 in the United States.

Satisfied with the sonics of *Unleashed*, the band re-enlisted producer Tom Allom to oversee what would be their sixth studio album overall. Fresh off tours supporting Kiss in the States and AC/DC in Europe, the Birmingham band set up shop in a small British town, Ascot, to record the album. But they didn't choose your average/ordinary recording location – they rented Ringo Starr's mansion, Tittenhurst Park (which had previously belonged to John Lennon and Yoko Ono). Although equipped with a recording studio (called Startling Studios), Priest instead opted to record throughout the house.

Another important happening around this time for the band was welcoming drummer Dave Holland into their ranks. Formerly a member of Trapeze, Holland's straight-ahead drum style fit their more focused direction perfectly, and for quite some time, served as Priest's longest-tenured drummer (as he occupied the drum throne throughout the rest of the decade, until being replaced by Scott Travis in 1990).

The key at the time for hard rock bands to achieve breakthrough commercial success was to offer up a melodic tune that could be played on mainstream radio and would carry over to the charts. Case in point, AC/DC with "Highway to Hell," Van Halen with "Dance the Night Away," Cheap Trick with "I Want You to Want Me," etc. And while *British Steel* (whose title was a tip of the cap to their hometown, known for its steel production) did indeed contain mostly hard rockers aimed straight at headbangers, there were two tracks in particular that remain to this day among Priest's most played radio tunes – "Breaking the Law" and "Living After Midnight."

The US tracklist of the album was slightly different than the UK one, but we will go with the UK version (since that is the listing replicated on subsequent reissues over the years). Kicking things off with one of the band's all-time great openers (perhaps only second to "The Hellion/Electric Eye"), "Rapid Fire," as its title states, is an unrelenting metallic rocker which kicks your keister from beginning to end.

Up next is an anthem that would soon become a live highlight/standard for the band, "Metal Gods," which led to others (and even the man himself!) referring to Halford with the rather fitting nickname "Metal God." And then...one of Priest's most recognizable tunes, "Breaking the Law" – which features lyrics about a down-and-out bloke running amok, an instantly memorable up-and-down chromatic guitar riff, and one of metal's all-time great scream-along choruses.

One of the album's more underrated tunes follows, "Grinder," which includes great guitar bits throughout, before side one of the vinyl version closes with a tune that was obviously intended to be an anthem, "United." However, while most metal anthems are quite lively ("Back in Black," "Running Free," "Detroit Rock City," etc.), "United" is surprisingly glum-sounding – and quite honestly, not one of the album's strongest selections.

The opener of side two, "You Don't Have to Be Old to Be Wise" is the closest thing to a throwaway on the album – but you know you have an incredibly strong album on your hands when even your "B-material" is more inspired and stronger than most other artist's "A-material." And then...another one of the most celebrated tunes of Priest's entire career, the feel-good anthem "Living After Midnight," which along with "Metal Gods" and "Breaking the Law," has probably been included in every single full-length Priest live show since its release.

And while the album's final two songs may not be as well-known as the aforementioned classics, they still pack a mighty wallop – "The Rage" (which kicks off with a surprisingly reggae-ish bassline) and another underrated track, "Steeler," featuring guitar squeal-solo trade-offs between Downing and Tipton.

When released on April 14, 1980, *British Steel* featured a now-classic cover image of a hand gripping an immense razor blade so tightly that it appears to be cutting into the fingers. Certainly one of Priest's strongest and most consistent releases from start to finish, the buying public agreed, too – rocketing to #4 on the UK charts, and reaching a respectable #34 in the States (where it eventually earned platinum certification).

"*British Steel* was a really simple, direct moment of creativity for the band," Halford once told *Heavy Consequence*. "I remember we came off tour, we'd been on tour with AC/DC. Sadly, Bon Scott passed away just as we made that record. We made it practically from scratch. And Tom Allom says we made it in 30 days. We went in the studio and 30 days later, it was done – which is fast, by today's standards."

He added, "That was an important exercise in getting songs down quickly, effectively, precisely, and getting the job done with the minimal amounts of production. Very, very straightforward record. And two of our biggest songs come from that album – 'Breaking the Law' and Living After Midnight'."

Forty years later, *British Steel* remains a heavy metal highpoint.

Iron Maiden
(Iron Maiden, 1980)

When punk rock first hit the scene in the mid to late '70s, it appeared to draw a line in the sand, and longhaired metalheads and spiky-haired punkers had to remain on their respective sides. But eventually, certain bands became bold enough to combine both styles together, including Motörhead, Venom, and early Iron Maiden – especially the latter's classic self-titled debut album from 1980.

Granted, Maiden would soon transform themselves into more of a traditional heavy metal band, and erase most of the "punk" from their sonic equation. But in 1980, punk's attitude was still well on display within the grooves of their debut recording. And one of the most obvious reasons for this was because their singer at the time, Paul Di'Anno, was a shorthaired punk rocker.

Originally formed in London circa 1975 by bassist Steve Harris, Maiden would endure countless line-up changes for the remainder of the decade, but in the process, also built a rabid following, issued a popular self-released recording (1979's *The Soundhouse Tapes*) and aligned themselves with the fast-rising New Wave of British Heavy Metal – which also included the likes of Def Leppard, Saxon, and Diamond Head, among others. But by the time they inked a deal with EMI in the UK and Harvest/Capitol in North America, Maiden's line-up consisted of Di'Anno, Harris, the twin guitar tandem of Dave Murray and Dennis Stratton, and drummer Clive Burr.

If you are only familiar with "the Bruce Dickinson era" of Maiden – especially their studio recordings post-1984 – you could quite possibly be tricked into believing that their debut was by another band entirely. While Dickinson could get quite operatic at times, Di'Anno's vocals sound like a punkier Bon Scott, while lyrically, the "Di'Anno Maiden" seemed to focus more on streetwise lyrics. It was only later on that Maiden would eventually expand their song structures and tackle broader lyrical topics…which admittedly, could border on Spinal Tap territory at times ("Alexander the Great," anyone?). But certain trademark Maiden elements could already be detected at this early stage –

especially their Thin Lizzy-esque twin guitar harmonies and galloping basslines.

To oversee the recording of Iron Maiden, the band enlisted producer Wil Malone, who supposedly was hired due to the fact that he had done an arrangement for Black Sabbath (the song "Spiral Architect," off 1974's *Sabbath Bloody Sabbath*), and set up shop at Kingsway Studios in London. When interviewed for the book *Iron Maiden '80 '81*, Malone recalled that the "street punk" vibe of the material also spilled over into the studio.

"The one thing that sticks in my mind is that when they had a disagreement between themselves, they'd fight each other and roll around on the studio floor, fighting – which is behavior I hadn't seen since I was at school," remembered Malone. "Which is quite eye opening. Apart from that, the sessions were good sessions. They played well. It was a small studio, with a very large underground car park. And the equipment wasn't very good. But we managed to get through it, and we did all the tracks in about ten days – which is very fast for an album."

The album's tracklist would be slightly altered depending on region, but going by the "1998 remastered release," Iron Maiden would kick off with a breathless one-two punch of "Prowler" (which contained a nifty guitar riff drenched in wah) and "Sanctuary" (a tune that deals with being on the run from the law…a theme that "Di'Anno Maiden" would return to several times), before taking the tempo down a bit with "Remember Tomorrow." Although Harris penned the majority of the songs on the album, "Remember Tomorrow" was one of the few tunes to be co-credited to the bassist and Di'Anno.

And it turns out the song's meaning had a special meaning to the singer. "That about my grandfather," explained Di'Anno. "I lost him in 1980, when I was on tour. He was a diabetic and they cut his toe off, and his heel, then he lost his leg from the knee down, and he just sort of gave up. But the lyrics don't sort of relate to it, to be honest with you – just the words 'remember tomorrow.' Because that is what he always used to say – that was his little catch phrase. 'You never know what is going to happen, remember tomorrow, it might be a better day' sort of thing. So I just kept it in, and that was it."

Up next was the album's first single – and the second and final song on the album co-penned by Harris and Di'Anno – "Running Free," which kicks off with a now-classic drum beat by Burr (while only appearing on three Maiden albums, he did compose an impressive amount of classic/instantly recognizable song-opening drumbeats, including "Run to the Hills"), and once more, lyrics about being on the run from the law. Wrapping up side one of the LP version would be the album's mega-epic "Phantom of the Opera," which would serve as a preview of things to come ("Hallowed Be Thy Name," "To Tame a Land," "Rime of the Ancient Mariner," etc.).

Side two continues the metal mayhem with one of Maiden's best instrumentals, the oft-overlooked "Transylvania," before again taking the tempo down a notch, with the ballad "Strange World" – which remains one of Di'Anno's best vocal performances on record. Then finishing off the album are a pair of tunes that are decidedly light-hearted in the lyrical department – "Charlotte the Harlot" (penned by Dave Murray) and "Iron Maiden" (with such oh-so-sunny lyrics as "I just want to see your blood, I just want to stand and stare, See the blood begin to flow, As it falls upon the floor").

And while there is no denying that the debut was pretty bloody brilliant from start to finish (not a dud detected in the bunch), what really put the whole enchilada over the top was the striking album cover artwork by Derek Riggs – which featured a headshot of the band's viciously homicidal/seemingly immortal mascot, Eddie.

"Maiden was so masterful at the way that they were able to really market themselves – right from the get-go – with the album covers and the imaging of Eddie and all that," explained long-time Maiden fan and radio host Eddie Trunk. "You've got to remember; I was a kid at the time. Most of us were kids. And that is a very powerful thing, to see something like that – this drawing of this monster. It starts to conjure up stuff in your head, like, 'Hey, what's the story with these guys? What are these guys about?' There was just a great imagery there. And then of course, this thing came out [on stage] with the mask on and became more elaborate over time. I think that as great as the music is on the record, that's a big part of the Iron Maiden story, that you can't brush under the carpet – there was almost this imagery about the band, right from the get-go, driven by the fact that this character, this mascot, was on the cover of every one of their records."

Upon its release on April 14, 1980, in the UK (a bit later in the US), *Iron Maiden* was a smash hit in their homeland (peaking at #4 on the UK album charts), while the rest of Europe was introduced to the band when they landed the opening spot on Kiss' tour of arenas and large halls later that year – as well as a show-stealing performance at the Reading Festival. But it would turn out to be the only Maiden album to include Stratton (who was fired after the album's tour had wrapped, and replaced by Adrian Smith), while Di'Anno would only stick around for one more album (1981's equally as brilliant *Killers*), before being replaced by Dickinson.

Despite not registering on the US album charts – probably due to the fact that the band did not begin touring the States until album #2 – *Iron Maiden* has aged marvellously, and has served as an obvious influence on what would become known as thrash metal. All you have to do is listen to the early works of the "Big 4" of thrash (that would be Metallica, Anthrax, Slayer, and Megadeth), for all the sonic proof you'll ever need.

Guess Di'Anno wasn't kidding when he sang "Iron Maiden's gonna get ya, no matter how far" – the album continues to inspire this deep into the legendary band's career.

Heaven and Hell
(Black Sabbath, 1980)

Although Black Sabbath is now rightly/widely considered one of the greatest – and most influential – rock bands of all-time, it's easy to forget that around the dawn of the '80s, they seemed dead and buried. Not only had their last two albums floundered both artistically and commercially (1976's *Technical Ecstasy* and 1978's *Never Say Die!*), but their long-time singer, Ozzy Osbourne, had also just flown the coop.

But that all changed when former Rainbow singer, Ronnie James Dio, signed on as Ozzy's replacement – which seemingly instantly reinvigorated the band, and snapped the veteran Sabs (guitarist Tony Iommi, bassist Geezer Butler, and drummer Bill Ward) out of their creative slumber. And the proof was in one of Sabbath's best-ever albums – *Heaven and Hell*.

Since we've already covered the Birmingham band's early history in the *Black Sabbath* and *Paranoid* entries and Dio in Rainbow's *Ritchie Blackmore's Rainbow* and *Rising* entries, let's just pick up from around 1979, shall we? With Sabbath suddenly singer-less and Dio having recently departed Rainbow, the union made perfect sense. And amusingly, it was supposedly Sharon Arden (later *Sharon Osbourne*) who introduced Dio to his soon-to-be new bandmates.

"After Ozzy's departure, we had to do something," Iommi told me during an interview for *Heavy Consequence* in 2021. "It sort of made us get down to it and say, 'Y'know, we've got to prove ourselves again and do something. And work hard at it.' And it was great with Ronnie involved, because Ronnie came in with a lot of enthusiasm, and we sort of hit it off straight away. It really worked. He was a great person to sit down and write with, as well. We could swap ideas, and it was very productive, I thought."

However, while things were clicking musically, behind the scenes, one of Sabbath's members had to step away for a spell. "At that point, Geezer had left because he had personal problems to sort out. And Ronnie played bass before, so he jumped on just to keep the momentum going with Bill Ward and myself. Then, I brought in my friend from England, Geoff Nicholls, to play bass while

Ronnie sang. It worked out that way for a bit and at the end of the day, we kept Geoff – he played keyboards and was on quite a lot of stuff from *Heaven and Hell* onward."

With the Dio-Iommi-Butler-Ward line-up now back firmly in place, the quartet recorded from October 1979 through January 1980 at a pair of studios – Criteria in Miami and Ferber in Gay Paree. And the producer of Rainbow's last few albums, Martin Birch, was hired to oversee the sessions. "Martin was a great help to me, in particular, because I could take it easy a bit with trying to be involved in the production," Iommi explained to *Vintage Guitar* in 2021. "So, I'd have somebody there who was brought in as a producer. And he was good – he got some different ideas for me, and it worked. I had a different sound for those albums than the earlier Sabbath stuff – a bit tighter and a bit more present."

Although the briskly-paced album-opening "Neon Knights" sounded almost punk-ish musically, when it came to its lyrics, Dio had borrowed some of the medieval imagery of his previous band ("Circles and rings, Dragons and kings, Weaving a charm and a spell"). "That was done I think in Jersey," Iommi told *Guitar World* about the track's creation. "We had gone to the Jersey Isles – on the way back from America. I came back to England too early, and I had to get out, quick. Because my accountant said, 'Get out! You're back too early – just go somewhere.' I said, 'Well, where am I going to go?' He said, 'Just go anywhere. Just get out of the country'!"

"So, I got the first flight out to wherever, and it happened to be the Jersey Islands. I went there for two or three weeks or so, and stayed in a hotel. I think I came up with the ideas for 'Neon Knights,' and we ended up going to Paris – because I couldn't come back into England again. And everybody came over to Paris – Ronnie, Bill, and Geezer – and we ended up using a studio in Paris [Studio Ferber], and recorded 'Neon Knights'."

The tempo and volume dips on the next tune, "Children of the Sea," which was one of the first tunes that Dio and Iommi worked on together (during their "tryout period"), and turned out to be one of the album's very best compositions. As Iommi reminisced, "The idea of 'Children of the Sea' was before Ronnie came in. We'd demoed this idea with Oz – and he put a melody line on 'Children of the Sea.' But we never ended up using it, because we'd parted company with Ozzy at that point. So, we only had a bit of it. And then we put a beginning on 'Children of the Sea,' when Ronnie came in and worked on a beginning. And I had the initial heavy riff, but didn't have the beginning. So, we worked on the beginning, and built that song up when Ronnie came in, really. And that was in LA."

"Lady Evil" is another upbeat number (but truth be told, not one of the album's best – although it does include standout soloing from Iommi), before side one of the *H&H* vinyl/cassette closes with the title track. Featuring one of Iommi's best-ever guitar riffs, the epic tune (almost seven minutes in length) also includes exceptional vocals and lyrics from Dio – particularly such phrases as "The less that you give, you're a taker" and "The world is full of kings and queens, Who blind your eyes and steal your dreams." While interviewing Ronnie's manager/widow Wendy Dio for the book *The Other Side of Rainbow*, I asked if the lyrics to the Dio song "Rainbow in the Dark" were about Ritchie Blackmore. But her reply surprisingly brought it back to this tune. "I don't think so, no. 'Heaven and Hell' was – 'The world is full of kings and queens that blind your eyes and steal your dreams, it's heaven and hell'."

And according to Iommi, the "Heaven and Hell" riff was created during the period of Geezer going MIA. "We didn't want to bring a bass player in to join the band, so Ronnie played bass for a bit, and then I brought a friend in from Birmingham [Nicholls], just to stand in, to play anything, really – guitar, bass, whatever. So, that's how we came up with that riff. It's just the initial [sings the repetitive bass part when the vocals first start], then I put a riff to it, and it took form from there – we built it up like we built everything else up. Literally, we came up with that riff, and then it goes into the other riffs. But we left a lot of gaps, so Ronnie could sing. It all depends what you put next to what they're going to sing. And what Ronnie was singing went great, so I knew where to go for the next part of it."

Spotted on side two would be two rockers, "Wishing Well" and "Walk Away," which as it turns out, Iommi does not particularly fancy. "I just came up with a riff [for 'Wishing Well'] in LA when we were in a rehearsal and we just put it together as a song. 'Wishing Well' and 'Walk Away' were probably my least favorites of what we'd done with that lineup. It was done just the same as the others: play a riff and get on from there." But the undisputed standout of the second side would be "Die Young," a tune that switches gears tempo and volume-wise throughout.

"We adjusted in the way that Ronnie would sing more on chords. He hadn't sung on riffs, as such, that much. So, it was a learning curve for both, really. It made me play differently, and it made him sing in a different way, as well. One particular song, when we were writing, 'Die Young,' I put a part in the middle that drops down to a quieter section. And Ronnie went, 'Oh, you can't do that.' And I said, 'You can! This is what Sabbath is about – we change tempos, we drop down into different parts.' And he went, '*Oh.*' And he liked the idea after we'd done it. And it worked for him and it worked for us. Again, it was a learning curve." And closing the first Dio-led Sab LP would be "Lonely Is the Word" – a mid-paced tune that features another great Iommi solo in the middle.

Released on April 25, 1980, *Heaven and Hell* – featuring an infamous illustration of three angels smoking cigarettes and playing cards – was the band's best-selling release in years. Peaking at #8 in the UK and #28 in the US (in comparison, their last two LP's peaked at #51 and #69 Stateside), it would eventually be certified gold and platinum in the aforementioned countries, and re-established Sabbath as one of the world's top metal bands. And other musicians were impressed with what they heard, too.

"I was trying to make amends with my family, I'm standing in the kitchen, and they have the radio on, and I hear 'Heaven and Hell'," recalled eventual Dio guitarist Craig Goldy, in the book *The Other Side of Rainbow*. "I'm like, *"Oooo.* OK, I get it. Wow...this is amazing.' And that song, 'Lonely Is the Word,' man, that is the perfect example of the true merge of strengths of Ronnie James Dio and Tony Iommi. That song nails it."

"Those two Sabbath records with Dio [*Heaven and Hell* and 1981's *Mob Rules*] are classics," Anthrax's Charlie Benante said in the book *Survival of the Fittest: Heavy Metal in the 1990s.* "I'll never forget leading up to that first record, I just didn't know what to expect. I only knew that Dio was killer with Rainbow. I loved those records that he did with Rainbow – he was just awesome. I knew anything that he was going to do was going to be great. And of course, I had faith in Sabbath. But when that *Heaven and Hell* record came out, I was just *blown away*. Because it was a totally different approach. It was a new band, basically. I don't even know if they should have called it 'Black Sabbath,' but it just had legs. It could have been called anything and it just would have blew up just as big."

"He could sing *anything*," added Blue Öyster Cult's Eric Bloom about Dio's vocal talent circa the time of *Heaven and Hell.* "He could sing the phonebook. He had that 'big voice.' He was a little guy, but he had that big voice. God only knew where it came from. He had a God-given talent. I saw a whole tour with Black Sabbath [with Ronnie] – *the Black & Blue Tour* – and got to see them play on a nightly basis. And the guy could shake the walls with this voice."

The Dio-led Sabbath line-up – with drummer Vinny Appice eventually taking Ward's spot – would last for one more album (*Mob Rules*) and live set (*Live Evil*), before the singer departed to form his own band, Dio, and enjoy success with such subsequent metal classics as *Holy Diver* and *The Last in Line*. Dio and the Sabs would reunite again in 1992 with *Dehumanizer* before splitting, and then uniting under the name Heaven & Hell (rather than "Black Sabbath") for 2009's *The Devil You Know* – and remaining in business until Dio's passing in 2010.

And one last observation – besides being a supreme riff lord, Iommi is one of the few musicians who can say he played alongside two of heavy metal's all-time great singers for long durations of time. So…how about a comparison? "Ozzy was more of a 'showman,' I'd say really. Ozzy would jump about and sing. But Ronnie was different in that way – he was more a 'perfectionist.' He liked to be more concentrating on his singing than what he did [physically], really. So, they were both very different, and it worked both ways. Ozzy was great at what he did and great with the band, and then Ronnie came along and he made his thing with Black Sabbath – he became accepted for what he did."

Freedom of Choice
(Devo, 1980)

Some found it difficult to look past the highly visual aspects of Devo (the biohazard suits, the "energy dome hats," their obsession with potatoes, etc.). Which is unfortunate, as they were responsible for creating some truly amazing rock n' roll – particularly their stellar 1978-1982 period, which included their biggest hit album and single in 1980, *Freedom of Choice* and "Whip It," respectively.

Originally formed in 1973 in Akron, Ohio, the group took its name from a concept called "devolution" (i.e., mankind's backwards evolution behavior-wise), and played their highly robotic form of music to baffled local crowds – also combining thought-provoking concepts with a video accompaniment. By 1976, the classic Devo line-up was formed – singer/keyboardist Mark Mothersbaugh, singer/bassist Gerald Casale, guitarists Bob Mothersbaugh and Bob Casale, and drummer Alan Myers. And soon after traveling east to perform at CBGB's in NYC, the quintet were awarded a recording contract with Warner Bros.

A now-classic debut followed in 1978 (produced by Brian Eno), *Q: Are We Not Men? A: We Are Devo!*, which spawned a popular cover of the Rolling Stones' "Satisfaction," followed by a solid sophomore effort, *Duty Now for the Future*. But despite mucho press coverage (and even a memorable appearance on *Saturday Night Live* during the show's immensely popular Aykroyd-Belushi-Murray era), it did not translate into strong sales nor leaving much of an impression on the US charts – peaking at #78 and #73, respectively.

Their third LP would be co-produced by Devo and Robert Margouleff (a gentleman who had served as associate producer, engineer, and synthesizer programmer on Stevie Wonder's string of classic synth-heavy albums from 1972-1974), with sessions running from late '79 through early '80 at the Record Plant in Hollywood. And it just happened to turn out that the resulting material would be incredibly hooky and concise (twelve tracks clocking in at a tight 32 minutes and 33 seconds).

Case in point, the album opener, "Girl U Want," which as the title suggests, deals lyrically about unobtainable love (and includes one of the more imaginative descriptions in a song lyric concerning hanky panky – "pleasure burn"). Musically, although the group is thought of primarily for their synth work, there have been a few memorable guitar riffs spotted in their discography. And "Girl U Want" certainly contains one of them – proven as fact a little more than a decade later, when Soundgarden covered it exceptionally, at a much slower tempo (and totally bypassed the synths and put the emphasis solely on the guitar riff). However, guitar was to take a backseat on the remainder of the material, including the next tune, the herky jerky "It's Not Right."

And next…the tune that would put Devo over the hump commercially, "Whip It." Think "classic new wave," and most people would automatically name this speedy little number – which contains several different memorable synthesizer bits, the memorable phrase "Break your mama's back," as well as a repeated single-note synth solo. Another tune that easily could have been another hit is the melodic "Snowball," which lyrically seems to be a tune about "love gone bad" (a recurring topic on several tunes here…perhaps one or two of the Spud Boys were experiencing troubles in the romance department around this time?). Side one of the vinyl/cassette version closes with quite possibly/probably your humble narrator's favorite tune of the entire LP – the title track, which lyrically deals with the cons of consumerism (a message which has proven to ring even truer over the years, particularly in the modern day/Internet age).

While side one was chock full of goodies, side two would admittedly prove to be padded with a bit of filler and/or forgotten tunes – including "Cold War," "Don't You Know," "That's Pep!", and "Mr. B's Ballroom." However, a pair of gems open and close the second half – the uptempo ditties "Gates of Steel" (which contains the standout lyric, "A man is real, not made of steel!") and "Planet Earth" (not to be confused with the popular Duran Duran tune of the same name).

Released on May 16, 1980, *Freedom of Choice* featured a now-iconic front cover shot of the five band members standing side-by-side, sporting their soon-to-be trademark red energy domes. But it was not a big seller straight out of the gate – that all changed once "Whip It" was issued as a single on August 13th. "The way ['Whip It'] happened was Warners had never focused on that song, and frankly, neither had we," Casale told me in the book *MTV Ruled the World: The Early Years of Music Video*. "We weren't sitting down going, 'Let's write a hit.' We just wrote songs we liked and only put the songs on the record we liked. The record company said, "Girl U Want' – *that's your hit!'* And, of course, it went nowhere. So they had us make a video for 'Girl U Want,' and then somebody at the label said, "Freedom of Choice!" So we made these two videos. They released 'Freedom of Choice' when 'Girl U Want' tanked, and 'Freedom of Choice' went nowhere."

"We were on tour for like three months, and while we're out there, 'Whip It' starts being played by Kal Rudman, who was a major programmer/radio mogul in the Southeast. Back when people could start things regionally. He did, and it grew out of there and went up to New York City, and the *Rudman Report* had it on fire, so all these other stations started picking it up. So in the middle of our tour, they had to keep changing venues, canceling shows and putting them in other places, because suddenly, we were playing to twice as many people...and sometimes even more than that. And when we got back off that leg of the tour, they go, 'You've got to make a video for 'Whip It'."

"We were rather burned out and really on a schedule, and Chuck Statler, the cinematographer that had been my college friend that we shot everything with, was busy. He was working with Elvis Costello. So I planned the whole video with my friend, John Zabrucky, who is a prop designer and an artist. We planned the whole thing out, and Mark and I storyboarded it, and we cast it and built a set out of a rehearsal space we had in a warehouse outside of Beverly Hills. Chuck flew in with just a four-man crew, and we started shooting at something like 7:00 in the morning, and we ended at like 1:00 in the morning. We shot the whole thing in like 16 hours. And then the editor, Dale Cooper, followed the storyboard, we tweaked it a bit, and it went out. It was one of the quickest videos we ever made. Other than 'Beautiful World,' it's the most favorite Devo video I ever directed."

As a result of the popularity of the "Whip It" single (peaking at #14 on the *Billboard Hot 100*) and video, *Freedom of Choice* would go on to become Devo's highest-charting album in the US (#22), and best seller – certified platinum by the RIAA, and even coming in at #61 on the *Billboard 200* year-end charts. The band would keep their winning streak going with two more stellar releases, 1981's *New Traditionalists* and 1982's *Oh, No! It's Devo*, and would be introduced to a whole new audience in the early '90s, when two of the leading grunge bands would cover *Freedom of Choice*-era material – Soundgarden with the aforementioned "Girl U Want" and Nirvana tackling "Turnaround" (the non-LP b-side of "Whip It"). And let's not forget Pearl Jam covering "Whip It" on Halloween 2009 in Philly...*while dressed as Devo*.

Back in Black
(AC/DC, 1980)

Going into 1980, it most certainly seemed like it would be smooth sailing across the finish line for AC/DC. After several years of slowly climbing up the ladder of success Stateside and in Europe (they were already gigantic in their homeland of Australia), 1979 had perfectly set the stage for a bona fide worldwide breakthrough in the new decade.

Their last album, *Highway to Hell*, had peaked at #17 in the US and went gold (while the album's anthemic title track reached #47 on the singles chart), and the band – then comprised of singer Bon Scott, guitarists Angus and Malcolm Young, bassist Cliff Williams, and drummer Phil Rudd – were about to make the transition from opener to arena headliner. And then…tragedy struck.

Well-known for his fondness for partying and in particular, for alcohol, Scott was found dead on February 19, 1980, at the age of 33 in the backseat of a car in London (his death certificate lists the cause as "death by misadventure" – for many years it was assumed caused by alcohol, but in recent times, the possibility of a heroin overdose has come to light).

A decision was eventually made by the surviving members to carry on, with former Geordie singer, Brian Johnson, officially being named Scott's successor on April 1st. Soon after, Johnson and his new bandmates (and the producer behind *Highway to Hell*, Mutt Lange), congregated at Compass Point Studios in the Bahamas to get to work on AC/DC's next studio LP. By May, the sessions had wrapped up, and on July 25th, the world was given one of rock's all-time classic (and largest-selling) recordings, *Back in Black*.

"They're night and day," Testament singer Chuck Billy explained concerning the differences between crooner Bon and shouter Brian in the book *A Rockin' Rollin' Man: Bon Scott Remembered*. "And I think especially lyric-wise for sure, I totally see the difference. But, something about Brian's technique and his style of vocals – because he's unique – really made him fit in there with a unique band. I think if they had someone ordinary, I don't know if it would be the same AC/DC – they had to have that unique thing as the lead person out there. And I think Brian Johnson was that guy."

With all ten of the album's tracks crediting both the Young brothers and Johnson as the sole composers, it later surfaced that Scott had some sort of involvement in the genesis of the material (at the very least, playing drums on a few demos – with others going so far as to allege he may have contributed a bit lyrically). But either way, the end result was simply stunning, as *Back in Black* (whose title was an obvious nod to their recently deceased bandmate) rocked hard from front to back – one of the rare albums where not a single weak track was included.

It's not to say that every single track is regularly aired on the radio or has gone on to receive regular renditions on the concert stage – for instance, such solid selections as "Given the Dog a Bone," "Let Me Put My Love into You," and "Shake a Leg" have gone overlooked at times. But probably more so than on any other AC/DC album, the classics outweigh the lesser compositions, including four songs that have never left their setlists (nor rock radio playlists) since their initial unveiling: "Hells Bells," the title track, "You Shook Me All Night Long," and "Rock and Roll Ain't Noise Pollution." And then there are tunes that would probably be most other bands' A-listers – "Shoot to Thrill," "What Do You Do for Money Honey," and "Have a Drink on Me" – but here, are just a step below the aforementioned "Big 4."

While Johnson's vocals were probably the thing most eager listeners were focusing on around this time, the amount of exceptional guitar riffs and chord progressions that the Young brothers bashed out throughout *Back in Black* is another ingredient that makes the album such a timeless classic. And while seemingly most hard rock/heavy metal guitarists of the era were favoring Eddie Van Halen-like high-tech shredding, Angus refused to stray far from his Chuck Berry boogie approach.

And this was not lost on Racer X/Mr. Big guitarist Paul Gilbert, as he recounted in the book *Shredders! The Oral History of Speed Guitar (and More)*. "At the time in the late '70s, early

'80s, the virtuoso thing was just starting to take off. In a way, if you were into the virtuoso culture at the time, Angus, people would put him down. Like, 'Oh, that's so simple,' or 'All they play are blues licks.' And I don't think I ever fell into that."

"I remember as a guitar player, I was more into Van Halen," Gilbert continues, "but I still loved what AC/DC did, and I still spent time with that music. I learned all the songs and played those songs a ton when I was in a band. Just loved them. And when you listen to Angus, you wouldn't want to put an Yngwie solo in an AC/DC song. It would just be wrong. Angus is playing the perfect guitar for the style, and you wouldn't want to change a note."

And AC/DC was immediately rewarded for their efforts. *Back in Black* rocketed as high as #4 on the *Billboard 200* while going all the way to #1 on the UK, France, Australia, and Canada charts. And a total of four singles were issued from the album (you guessed it, it was once again the aforementioned "Big 4"), with "You Shook Me All Night Long" and the title track cracking the top 40 on the *Billboard Hot 100* (#35 and #37, respectively).

But unlike certain rock albums that storm the charts and then become largely forgotten over time (or sound increasingly dated as the years progress), *Back in Black* has possessed incredible staying power in the consciousness of rock fans. So much so that at last count (December 2019) the album has sold a staggering 25 million copies…in the US alone.

Looking back on *Back in Black* 40 years after its original release, it remains impressive both how the band was able to assemble and record the album so soon after the death of Scott and also how they happened to locate the perfect replacement behind the mic (something that is quite difficult to do in most cases – all you have to do is take a gander at how many rock bands have failed after trying to replace an already established singer).

"For me, I was the hugest AC/DC fan, and I was so ready to be disappointed," Chuck Billy adds. "And I wasn't. That record was always my go-to record at a certain point in my life. It always makes me smile or think of good times – *Back in Black*. Just that point in my life, that record means a lot to me. I was so happy for them to continue on with such great records with him. Not many bands can do that – and sell 200 million records."

Fresh Fruit for Rotting Vegetables
(Dead Kennedys, 1980)

By the late '70s/early '80s, punk rock had become largely a bunch of copycats – mimicking such trailblazers as the Stooges, Ramones, and/or Sex Pistols, and not really putting their own unique spin on things. But there were certainly some most-welcomed exceptions – particularly the debut full-length by the Dead Kennedys, *Fresh Fruit for Rotting Vegetables.*

Originally formed in 1978 in San Francisco, the DK's core included singer Jello Biafra (real name: Eric Boucher), guitarist East Bay Ray (Raymond Pepperell), and bassist Klaus Fluoride (Geoffrey Lyall) – with original drummer Ted (Bruce Slesinger). Although using punk rock as the basis of their sound, the group refused to be one-dimensional nor predictable, as heard by their original melding of surf music, jazz, psychedelia (largely due to Ray's use of an Echoplex), rockabilly, and even spaghetti western soundtrack sounds – plus Biafra's lyrics that seemed evenly split between politically-charged, thought-provoking, and humorous.

"That was a really golden age – at least for us here in California, and particularly in San Francisco," East Bay Ray reminisced to *Guitar World* in 2022. "We had a club called the Mabuhay Gardens – which was basically the 'CBGB's of San Francisco.' And the promoter, Dirk Dirksen, he would book a punk band, an art band, and a new wave band all in one night. So, for a period of time, you had this mix of people and this mix of music that I think made everybody more interesting."

"Basically, the history of rock music in America is this cross-fertilization – country, gospel, R&B and all that mushing together. So to me, it's really a golden age. We'd play and there were some independent halls. We'd do shows at the San Francisco Art Institute, we did a few shows in high schools under assumed names – one of the high schools had the chess club sponsor us! *A very cool chess club.* And we used the name 'Pink Twinkies,' and then at another high school we were 'The Creamsickles.' We played with some great bands – the Zeros, the Avengers."

And it was during this era that the group penned the material that would eventually comprise *Fresh Fruit.* "The writing process, there were basically two processes," said Ray in the same *Guitar World* interview. "One, like 'Holiday in Cambodia,' came out of a jam session – that was literally in my garage. Our first rehearsal studio was my garage – until the neighbors complained and we had to move. And we would tape it, and Biafra would go through his lyrics and find lyrics to fit the music. The other way we would do it is we would sit on the sofa at Klaus' with an acoustic guitar. So, it would be Klaus, Biafra, and myself, going over the songs, finding keys, finding arrangements, finding chord changes. One of the interesting things I'd do is I'm from the East Bay, so I'd go across the bridge and I'd be listening to Merle Haggard on my car stereo. It helps with your songwriting structure – he's kind of a master songwriter."

After building a following on the strength of their unpredictable/high-energy live shows and a handful of singles, the lads congregated at San Francisco's Möbius Music from May through June 1980, to work on their full-length debut. The producers on the LP would be listed as Ray plus a mysterious gentleman by the name of "Norm." "Norm was not a gentleman!," Ray clarified. "Norm is the cat that lived in Möbius Music Studios when we were working there. To be blunt, some people have taken credit for work that I've done, and a lot of 'punk Taliban' don't recognize Klaus and my contribution to the band. I did the producing, organized the sessions, a lot of the sheets are all in my handwriting, and I did a lot of the mixing – along with Oliver DiCicco."

Song for song, the album would turn out to be the DK's strongest – as it included such classics as "Kill the Poor," "Let's Lynch the Landlord," "Drug Me," "California Über Alles," and "Holiday in Cambodia." And let's not forget selections that while lesser-known, were just as ferocious – "Forward to Death," "When Ya Get Drafted," "Your Emotions," "Chemical Warfare," "I Kill Children," "Stealing People's Mail," "Funland at the Beach," "Ill in the Head," and a cover of a tune Elvis made famous, "Viva Las Vegas."

"Biafra did most of it [the lyric writing], but I'd have lyrics – 'Dead End,' 'Your Emotions Make You a Monster,' Klaus did 'Dog Bite.' And also, we adjusted some lyrics – like, I think in 'I Kill Children,' the original lyric was, 'The Ayatollah told me to skin you alive.' And I suggested to change that to 'God,' because in 10/20 years, people won't know who the Ayatollah was. One of the things is you're turning journalism into poetry. Y'know, journalism doesn't really keep up with the times...while poetry can."

"We had another guitar player, 6025 [Carlos Cadona, who had exited the band a year before *Fresh Fruit*], and he actually wrote whole songs...or at least brought in the idea for whole songs. Because like I said, everything got changed in the garage – people added their two cents. He did 'Forward to Death' and 'Ill in the Head'." But at least one song on the album featured lyrics penned by Ray, "Your Emotions." "We had a person involved in the band – kind of a booking-type person. But they were friends. And they would just go off. I guess the phrase now is 'trigger.' They would get easily triggered and just go off, and they were very hard to deal with."

Possibly the best-known tune of the DK's entire career resides here, "Holiday in Cambodia," which Biafra discussed the creation of with *Songfacts* in 2013. "Some Dead Kennedys songs had more than one writer – a lot of the best ones did. 'Holiday in Cambodia' was one of the few that actually was group-written – or at least group-constructed. The original 'Holiday in Cambodia' is more a straight punk song. We called them 'chainsaws' back then, 'chainsaw punk' after the Ramones song ['Chainsaw']."

"The other guys didn't like it. They didn't want to play it. I was heartbroken, I was crestfallen, they'd never done that to me before. And then Klaus began noodling around on what became that signature bass line. I thought, 'Hey, wait a minute. That's cool. What would happen if we swiped everything from my 'Holiday in Cambodia' song – verse, chorus, bridge – but used that as the original root rhythm'?"

"Actually, we had a three-chord chorus and bridge that came from the original, and then the verse we swapped out. Eventually, Ray came up with that signature guitar part when he enters the song. It was taking a while; we didn't even play it at our first show, although we knew we had it under our belt. It was a pretty chief song for making me decide I ought to stick with these guys and it might turn into something really unusual, because I was playing around with some other people, too."

"Before we played, I came back out of the bathroom and back to Ray's garage and heard that lick, and I was like, 'Yow!' And Ray told me he'd seen Pink Floyd with Syd Barrett at Winterland when he was a kid, and I took note of that. So when I was trying to get something to put on top of Klaus' riff, I kept trying to get it to fit there, and fit there, and fit there, and finally, it appeared."

Released on September 2, 1980 via the band's Alternative Tentacles label (although it would be reissued several times over the years, including a remixed version by Chris Lord-Alge in 2022, via Manifesto Records), the album's front cover would include a black and white photo of police cars on fire – snapped during the White Night riots, on May 21, 1979. *Fresh Fruit for Rotting Vegetables* would immediately become an underground hit (eventually being certified gold in the UK) and is widely/rightly considered one of the greatest punk rock recordings of all-time.

But it turns out that it took many years for Ray to recognize that the album was special and/or a classic. "Way later. We kind of stopped playing in 1986 and I figured, 'I'll have to get a day job in about two years.' Everybody in the band kind of did. We all tried solo projects, but the Dead Kennedys was a collaboration of we were '2+2=5.' We were still selling pretty well, so we were like, 'OK. People are still interested in us.' We didn't really think it was a classic at the time. We were just playing the best we can and writing the best we can – and working hard on it. And we liked it. Then Nirvana came out and punk rock got kind of rediscovered. And it's been kind of building since then."

Blizzard of Ozz
(Ozzy Osbourne, 1980)

Ozzy Osbourne is one of the few examples of an established rock artist whose solo career was as commercially successful (and creatively on par) with the work of his previous band – in this case, the legendary Black Sabbath. And especially, his now-classic solo debut, *Blizzard of Ozz*. However, just prior to the album's arrival, it looked as if Ozzy was finished. As previously described in the entry for Sabbath's *Heaven and Hell*, Ozzy had been fired from the Sabs in 1979, while their last few albums featuring Oz (1976's *Technical Ecstasy* and 1978's *Never Say Die!*) fell flagrantly flat when compared to their untouchable 1970-1975 efforts.

And as we learned from his 2011 autobiography, *I Am Ozzy*, he was holed up at the time in a Los Angeles hotel, supposedly drinking and drugging his way to oblivion. But eventually, he began searching for potential players for his next band, to be called Blizzard of Ozz (but ultimately, would just go by the good ol' "Ozzy Osbourne" name). Which in turn, led to the discovery of soon-to-be guitar icon Randy Rhoads in Los Angeles, plus hooking up with a killer rhythm section of rock vets back home in Britain – Bob Daisley (bass, ex-Rainbow) and Lee Kerslake (drums, ex-Uriah Heep).

"Ozzy was fairly easy to work with," Daisley recalled to *Songfacts* in 2014. "He was a bit down at first, because he'd just been fired from Black Sabbath and he was depressed and he was unsure of himself. It really damaged his confidence, being fired from Black Sabbath. But Randy and I used to encourage him and try to bring him up out of the doldrums. Writing with Ozzy was fairly easy because we had a little songwriting machine going. Randy and I would work on music together just sitting on chairs opposite each other, and then we'd put parts together and then we'd knock it off and Ozzy would sing a melody over it."

"His melodies were always good. Ozzy's good for melodies. Usually the music came first, Ozzy would sing a melody, and then I would take a tape away into my room and write lyrics by myself to Ozzy's phrasing and melodies that would fit with what he was comfortable with. He wasn't a lyricist and neither was

Randy, so I had to wear the lyricist hat. But I enjoyed it. I like writing the lyrics. That's how we wrote together."

And just how much of the lyrics did Daisley pen on Ozzy's first two LP's post-Sabbath? "Oh, more than 95 percent. Some songs 100 percent, some songs 95 percent. Ozzy used to just sing whatever came into his head, and it was usually nonsense. But I got the idea of his phrasing and his melodies from that. Every once in a while he might sing a line and I'd think, 'Actually, that's not a bad line. I'll use that.' It might be one line or he might have come up with a title like he did with 'Mr. Crowley.' But yeah, the majority, I'd say 95 percent plus."

Although Rhoads was a virtual unknown at the time (his previous band, Quiet Riot, had only played LA clubs and issued two obscure Japan-only releases, 1977's *Quiet Riot* and 1978's *Quiet Riot II*), the bassist instantly recognized that not only was he a gifted guitarist, but also, a songwriter. "Well, Randy as a songwriter, he had lots of influences. There was the definite sort of 'basic rock thing,' there were the guitarists that he'd listen to like Ritchie Blackmore and Hendrix and Clapton and the blues influence, Jeff Beck, for sure. And I know he listened a lot to Uriah Heep, the *Demons and Wizards* album in particular. And he had his classical thing, too. He was very into classical music and came from that background. His mother had the music school [Musonia School of Music] and he grew up in that environment, so he had that classical ingredient, and he wanted to pursue that even more so."

Recorded from March 22nd through April 19th, 1980 at Ridge Farm Studio in Rusper, England, the four band members would serve as the subsequent album's producers. And the material – which mostly listed Osbourne, Rhoads, and Daisley as its writers – bore little resemblance to the dark and oft-plodding style of Ozzy's former band…yet, still managed to rock hard. And this was apparent right from the get-go with the opening riff-heavy rocker, "I Don't Know," which lyrically seems to deal with the fact that although Oz is often put on a pedestal by many, he's just a normal bloke ("Don't look at me for answers, Don't ask me I don't know").

And then…the album's best-known tune, the classic "Crazy Train," which includes one of rock's most instantly identifiable guitar riffs – courtesy of Rhoads. "Well, Randy had the basic riff, the signature riff," recalled Daisley in the aforementioned *Songfacts* chat. "Then we worked on music together. He needed something to solo on so I came up with a chord pattern and the section for him to solo over. Before it was called 'Crazy Train,' before we even had a title, Randy and I were working on the music."

"He had his effects pedals, and coming through his amp was a weird kind of chugging sound. It was a phase-y kind of psychedelic effect, this chugging sound that was coming through his amp from his effects pedal. Randy was into trains – he used to collect model trains and so did I. I've always been a train buff and so was Randy. So I said, 'Randy, that sounds like a train. But it sounds nuts.' And I said, '*A crazy train.*' Well, that's when the title first was born. And then Ozzy was singing melodies and he was phrasing exactly how it ended up. And I started writing lyrics to it."

"When we demoed that song in the demo studio in Birmingham, before we'd done the album, before we had Lee Kerslake, we had another drummer with us named Dixie Lee. Dixie Lee was on the demos. We demoed four songs for the record company, Jet Records, so that they could hear what we were doing and what material we were going to be writing. The demo was 'Crazy Train,' 'I Don't Know,' 'You Looking at Me, Looking at You,' and 'Goodbye To Romance.' We didn't have the last verse in 'Crazy Train' written at that stage, so Ozzy just sang whatever it was he sang, so that demo version has a different last verse. But I wrote the last verse for 'Crazy Train' when we were at Ridge Farm recording. So that's how all that came about. I've still got the lyrics sheet that I wrote the lyrics on."

As Daisley just explained, Kerslake was not a member of the new band from the get-go. And when I spoke with the drummer for BraveWords in 2020 (sadly, just a few months before his passing from cancer at the age of 73), he recalled getting involved just before – or quite possibly, even after – recording sessions for the album began. "They'd started recording, and they were using any drummers they could get their hands on – and they were bloody awful. Believe me, they were awful. So, I phoned Bob, and said, 'What songs are you using?' And over the phone he told me the idea and he played me the idea of 'Crazy Train' and 'I Don't Know.' And I went, 'OK. I got it.' So, the day came that I went into the studio rehearsal, and I went, 'One, two, three, four...' [sings beginning of 'Crazy Train']. We did all of that, I started playing heavy, and Randy Rhoads jumped up in the air, and said, 'WE'VE GOT OURSELVES A FUCKING DRUMMER!' And that was it – I was in. And I co-wrote the second album. But I did a lot of work with the drums to get it right with the style of the first one, *Blizzard of Ozz*."

Not all of *Blizzard of Ozz* was metallic rock, however – as evidenced by the ballad "Goodbye to Romance," as well as a sweet classical guitar interlude, "Dee," penned and played entirely by Rhoads in tribute to his mother, Delores. But the first side's closing number, "Suicide Solution" (which lyrically deals with an alcoholic drinking themself to death – and has been rumored to have been inspired by AC/DC's Bon Scott), returned to headbanging rock.

Up next...the second best-known tune on the album, the goth metal masterpiece, "Mr. Crowley" (featuring some nifty synth noodling courtesy of Don Airey at the beginning). "Ozzy had that title, 'Mr. Crowley,' remembers Daisley. "And obviously what he meant was it was supposed to be about Aleister Crowley, the black magician. But I wanted to look at the darkness and question Aleister Crowley. 'Aleister, what were you thinking?' You know. All this darkness and negativity. So that was a snag that I put on it. In the 'Was it polemically sent?' line, 'polemic' means controversial, and Aleister Crowley was very controversial in his day. He used to sign books or his autograph 'Polemically Yours, Aleister Crowley.' So that's why that word's at the end of the song."

The only throw-away tune on the album, "No Bone Movies" (and its only other tune not credited solely to the aforementioned trio – as Kerslake was granted a writing nod) follows, before a pair of tunes arrive that would be combined together on stage to create one long epic, the mid-paced "Revelation (Mother Earth)" and the more uptempo "Steal Away (The Night)."

Released on September 20, 1980 in the UK (but not until March 27, 1981 in the US), *Blizzard of Ozz* – which features a photo of Ozzy lounging on a wooden floor, while clutching a cross – was an immediate hit, peaking at #7 in the UK and #21 in the US (eventually selling five million copies Stateside). As a result, a bit of a "chart battle" broke out between the singer and his former band (who had issued *Heaven and Hell* with Ronnie James Dio on vocals several months before *BoO*), as both had unveiled surprisingly strong albums around the same time.

However, the Osbourne-Rhoads-Daisley-Kerslake line-up would remain together for only one more album, 1981's *Diary of Madman*, before Daisley and Kerslake were excused from their duties, and Rhoads tragically perished in a plane crash on March 19, 1982, at the age of 25. Despite only playing on two albums with Osbourne, Rhoads' playing on both has served as a major influence and inspiration on countless subsequent guitarists.

"Randy was very much a pioneer of the classical feel in hard rock," said Testament's Alex Skolnick in the book *Shredders! The Oral History of Speed Guitar (and More)*. "Taking a classical melodicism and combining that with virtuosity. I guess you could say Ritchie Blackmore had done it, but Randy Rhoads did it in a sort of 'post-Van Halen' way. And he was admittedly inspired by Van Halen – as far as tone and some of the two-handed technique. But he definitely did his own thing with it. I think he had a big impact for a lot of us at that time."

"I think that original line-up was phenomenal," modern-day Ozzy guitarist Zakk Wylde once told me about the *Blizzard of Ozz* line-up. "You can't even argue that. Just listen to the records. They're timeless, classic albums. Hands down, that line-up was fuckin' sick. When they were making the record, they didn't know. Randy didn't know any of the guys. Randy never met Bob Daisley or Lee Kerslake before. I mean, if me and you took four complete strangers, stuck 'em in a room, and then they ended up coming out with two amazing records – what are the chances of that happening?"

Zenyatta Mondatta
(The Police, 1980)

By the dawn of the '80s, the Police were already ginormous in the UK (where two of their three members hailed from). But in the US, they had yet to break big. That all changed by the time of their third full-length studio offering, the rather peculiarly-titled *Zenyatta Mondatta* – thanks to the success of their first two top-10 hit singles Stateside, "Don't Stand So Close to Me" and "De Do Do, De Da Da Da."

Several months after forming in the UK in 1977, the definitive Police line-up was properly positioned – singer/bassist Sting (real name: Gordon Sumner), guitarist Andy Summers, and drummer Stewart Copeland (the latter of whom was the lone American). Despite its members having backgrounds in either jazz or prog rock, the trio streamlined (some wisenheimers could even say "dumbed down") their approach – combining punk and reggae on their debut, 1978's *Outlandos d'Amour*. And soon after, dialing down the punk part of the equation and replacing it with rock and pop for 1979's *Regatta de Blanc*. But as mentioned earlier, while they had already conquered the UK charts (*Outlandos* peaked at #6, while *Regatta* topped the charts – in addition to already scoring two #1 singles with "Message in a Bottle" and "Walking on the Moon"), substantial US chart success still hadn't materialized.

Recording sessions for album #3 would run precisely for one month (July 7 through August 7, 1980) at Wisseloord Studio in Hilversum, Netherlands, with the same production team in place as their last album – the band plus Nigel Gray. But as Summers recalled in a *Vintage Guitar* interview in 2017, it turned out to be not exactly a full month spent in the studio. "We were supposed to have a month to make it, and we went to Holland to record. Then, in the middle of it we were told, 'You've got to go to England now for a week, to do this giant gig at Milton Keynes Festival. It's a big deal.' So, in the middle of the album, we stopped and went to London for a few days, did this big show, then came back to finish. But when we listened to it, we didn't like the mixes. So, we remixed the whole album in one night, then left for tour the next morning!"

However, the unexpectedly reduced time spent in the studio did not affect the quality of the album – starting off with one of the band's best-ever tunes, "Don't Stand So Close to Me," which tells the tale of a male teacher who lusts after one of his female students (and vice versa). Also, it is undoubtedly the only tune in rock history to namecheck author Vladimir Nabokov (and hint at his 1955 novel, *Lolita*) – in the memorable line, "Just like the old man in that book by Nabokov." And as similarly stated in the earlier entry for Devo, the Police at the time were a band wise enough to see the value in making videos for their singles – something that would definitely benefit them big-time with the launch of MTV in 1981. And one of the fledgling channel's most-spun clips early on was the one for "DSSCTM," which sees Sting play the role of the tormented teacher.

In the book *MTV Ruled the World: The Early Years of Music Video*, Copeland discussed a memorable scene in the song's video. "Sting pulled his shirt off – unrehearsed. I'm sure he had it planned in his mind. But as I said, he would have been mortified to have discussed such a brazen tactic, and he would have pretended that it was spontaneous. Although he's very calculated about that sort of thing. I mean, to his credit, he's a professional. When we would tease him about this sort of thing, he would say, 'Look guys, *we're professionals.* I'm doing my job...how about you guys start thinking about it, too?' We'd catch him teasing his hair or something like that. He was right. It was his job, and it was our job, too."

"I think the Police brought a lot of class to the place," added original MTV VJ Alan Hunter in the same book. "They seemed to be 'the real thing.' I loved their stripped-down, three-man sound – that stuff from *Zenyatta Mondatta*, and somewhat *Ghost in the Machine*, although it started to become more produced at that point. It was kind of like Rush – three guys make a lot of noise. A good, full sound. I thought it was amazing how you only had three instruments playing and Sting's voice – in those early days."

One of rock's finest lyricists, the following two tunes feature Sting touching upon such topics as becoming numb to atrocities going on around us ("Driven to Tears") and detailing a lifestyle that sounds akin to the Bill Murray film *Groundhog Day* ("When the World Is Running Down, You Make the Best of What's Still Around"). And as Hunter alluded to earlier, it really was quite something how a trio could create such a large yet expansive sound as the Policemen. Several tunes of varying tempos proceed, including the hurried "Canary in a Coalmine," the more leisurely-paced "Voices Inside My Head" (which if listened to on headphones, airy/swirly sound effects are discovered at the beginning), and the somewhere-in-between "Bombs Away."

Side two commenced with the album's other best-known tune, "De Do Do Do, De Da Da Da," which lyrically seems to deal with not taking everything so bloody seriously in life, or also, as the famous saying goes, "When life gives you lemons, make lemonade." Additionally, the tune would be used in a key scene in one of the best teen comedy-drama films of the '80s, *The Last American Virgin.* The tune also features Summer's trademark chorus pedal – which by this point had become the main ingredient of the Police's sound. And just how did the guitarist come to use this effect?

"I created it sort of out of necessity; my mission was 'We're going to play for two hours each night as a trio,' so I wanted to have this fantastic, colored guitar sound that was different for every song," he recalled in the same *Vintage Guitar* interview. "So, I used the Echoplex, then a chorus, and a few other pedals...envelope filters. As we went on, I acquired more stuff and got a Pete Cornish board. But what was driving it was to invade and push the edge of what the guitar was supposed to sound like, and make it really interesting over a show. So, it wasn't just one straight sound all the time. I could move it around. And it was appreciated by many millions of people. [Laughs] Of course, it's very tired and a bit 'retro' now; I'm not very keen on it anymore. But in those days it was new, fresh, and exciting."

Up next is the instrumental "Behind My Camel," which would showcase then-cutting edge technology – the guitar synthesizer. "I was thinking about something that was sort of edgy," Summers recollected to *Songfacts* about penning the tune. "Like a horror movie. [Laughs] I wanted something with a lot of atmosphere. But it wasn't jazz, it was almost like movie music. I wrote a lot of music like that. It was almost like a blues in a way. A Middle Eastern blues." The song would also give the Police their second Grammy Award, when it won "Best Rock Instrumental Performance" at the 1982 Grammys. Why an '80 song wins in '82? *No clue.*

A tune that sounds like a not-so-distant cousin of "Canary in a Coalmine" is next, the lyrically self-explanatory "Man in a Suitcase," before the mood-shifting "Shadows in the Rain," and then *Zenyatta* wraps up with another instrumental, the uptempo "The Other Way of Stopping." "You start with just music or sound in the beginning, but I think you're trying to find a place you're going to connect where the music is, or an identity," is how Summers explains writing instrumental tunes. "It's like finding an active role."

Released on October 3, 1980 (and featuring a rather colorful front cover, with the three members' faces together in a triangle), *Zenyatta Mondatta* finally served as the album that broke the Police in the US – peaking at #5 on the *Billboard 200* and earning double platinum certification, while becoming their second LP in a row to top the UK charts. As for its head-scratching album title, Copeland explained to *Musician's Only* in 1980, "It's not an attempt to be mysterious, just syllables that sound good together, like the sound of a melody that has no words at all has a meaning."

The Police would last for only two more blockbuster albums, 1981's *Ghost in the Machine* and 1983's *Synchronicity*, which led to them becoming unquestionably one of the world's top rock bands on the planet (they sold out Shea Stadium in '83, fer cryin' out loud!), before quietly splitting. But listening back today, *Zenyatta Mondatta* remains the sound of the Police becoming…*the Police.*

Double Fantasy
(John Lennon and Yoko Ono, 1980)

There must have been a time during the late '70s where most rock fans wondered if they'd heard the last from John Lennon – as the former Beatle had completely disappeared from the public eye, and seemed to have transformed into a "house husband" (married to Yoko Ono, and looking after their infant son, Sean). But at some point in 1979, Lennon had a change of heart, and his desire to rock had returned. Over the years, there was talk that it was being inspired by some of the era's now-classic rock tunes – namely, Queen's "Crazy Little Thing Called Love" and the B-52's "Rock Lobster."

"The B-52's, yes," explained Yoko Ono in a 2013 *Songfacts* interview. "Listening to the B-52's, John said he realized that my time had come. So he could record an album by making me an equal partner and we won't get flack like we used to up to then. I have not heard about Queen [inspiring John]. But we both loved Queen. So it's possible that we got some energy from them."

With an album's worth of tunes penned by Lennon and Ono (seven compositions each), the pair enlisted producer Jack Douglas, who was coming off chart success with the likes of Aerosmith and Cheap Trick, to oversee the album – although Lennon, Ono, and Douglas would each be listed as the resulting album's producers. Recorded from August 7 through October 19, 1980 at the Hit Factory in New York City, several ace session musicians were utilized – including guitarist Earl Slick, bassist Tony Levin, and drummer Andy Newmark, among others.

Speaking to *Long Island Pulse* in 2017, Levin recalled his memories of the recording. "It was only two weeks of sessions. I was of course honored and thrilled to be asked to be a part of that album. Working with John and Yoko was fun and relaxed and also musically very creative. It was very special. It wasn't technically difficult. When you're asked to play a bass part and John Lennon is playing guitar and singing songs while sitting right in front of you, playing the bass parts is about the easiest thing in the world because it's what you dream about doing."

"The song is there and the bassline is there for you. It's just a matter of getting it down and recording it. So, in that sense, I was just honored to be the one of the many bass players who could have done a very good job on the album. And John was very nice to me. His first words when he met me were, 'They tell me you're good. Just don't play too many notes.' I smiled and felt good – I'm not a guy who plays too many notes."

Utopia bassist Kasim Sulton also remembered his friend Earl Slick's experience playing on the album, in the book *John Winston Ono Lennon*. "I know when Earl Slick first met him – when he got the call to go play guitar on *Double Fantasy* – he walked into the studio, and he was the first musician in the studio that day. It was just him and John in the studio. And John couldn't have been nicer to him. I guess it just depends on the time of day and what he was doing and who you were and you were to him. Like anybody."

And it turned out that two members of Cheap Trick were present for the sessions as well, guitarist Rick Nielsen and drummer Bun E. Carlos – at the suggestion of Douglas. "We met John and I noticed he was as tall as all the other English guys I met – he wasn't like, nine feet tall," remembered Carlos in the aforementioned *John Winston Ono Lennon* book. "But he played me and Rick a cassette of him doing it acoustic. John had gone somewhere to the Virgin Islands or the British West Indies the winter before that – he had two ghetto blasters and he'd play acoustic guitar and sing into one, and then he'd aim the other one and record it again, and do little overdubs. So, he had a cassette tape of all his songs. He played this acoustic version of 'Losing You,' and then Jack said, 'Can you guys come up with an idea for this? An arrangement or something?" Me and Rick said, 'Yeah. Give us a few minutes'."

"We went into the studio, and to me and Rick, it seemed like it had a 'Cold Turkey' type of feel to it. Rick's like, 'I got a riff that might work' – a little riff that starts it off. Somebody came in, and they had sheet music for the thing. I walked over to Tony and said, 'Can you tell me what this says? Does the bridge come after two verses?' And he was like, 'What? You've never done a session before?' I was like, 'Not really. I'm in a band – I'm not a session cat.' So, we ran it down a few times with John – he was playing live on guitar with a vocal track, and Tony on bass, George Small on piano, Rick on guitar, and me on drums. We ran it down a few times, did a couple of takes, and got a take. Then Rick started doubling the guitar solo on it."

Once the Trick duo finished "Losing You," work immediately began on "Moving On" – a Yoko composition. "John didn't play guitar on it – he sat in the booth and we got out there and Rick basically came up with the riff on the thing," recalls Carlos. "We were trying to figure out how to get the song rolling and get into it. And the reason I got the call in the first place was this was a real cool song and they were going to cross-feed it with 'I'm Losing You.' They were both almost the same tempo. But I had a drum part for a Cheap Trick song that worked real good, and Jack was like, 'Play that drum part.' So, I did."

"Then we were doing the arrangement, and Yoko was on the mic in the studio, and we were trying to figure out what to do on the first verse before the chorus. And Tony Levin goes, 'Well, I've got this bass riff' – a fancy, involved eight-beat pattern. He goes, 'I do this every day at soundcheck. It's my favorite riff I ever came up with...but I've never been able to get it into a song.' We're like, 'You can start the song like this, and when the chorus comes in, we come crashing in and do our arrangement that we came up with'."

Song-wise, *Double Fantasy* recalled the set-up of *Some Time in New York City*, in that it was comprised 50/50 between John and Yoko compositions. And this time, the tracklist alternated between a tune from each from start to finish (although the very end had two Yoko tunes back-to-back). Musically a bit reminiscent of the new wave and melodic rock of the day, most of John's tunes lyrically reflect where he was at, at that point of his life (as a 40-year old husband/father) – especially on such standouts as "(Just Like) Starting Over," "Beautiful Boy (Darling Boy)," "Watching the Wheels," and "Woman."

And as far as the Yoko tunes, they sounded perfectly at home with the then-current crop of new wave artists (the B-52s, Nina Hagen, Lene Lovich, etc.). And in particular, the tune "Kiss Kiss Kiss," which in the same aforementioned *Songfacts* interview, she described as "This song was created when I was withdrawing from a bad drug. I kept breathing in pain. All that time, I realized that there was a crack in my beautiful art deco mirror. At the recording studio, I sung in total darkness, which gave the right mood to it."

However, a decision was made at some point to axe the contributions by Nielsen and Carlos. "We didn't hear anything after the session – whether if the track was going to be on the record or not. And then of course, *Double Fantasy* came out and it wasn't. We thought, 'Well, our version probably didn't fit in real good with that kind of MOR feel that the rest of the record has.' It's more pop or middle of the road. Our version of 'Losing You' was pretty rocking. So, we thought, 'They just re-cut it with the other guys.' Jack later told us – and I've heard it on a bootleg – he said, 'I made the session guys, Andy Newmark and Earl Slick, play along with your guys' track to do another take. That didn't work very good – they still couldn't get the feel.' And then they came up with a slightly different arrangement which ended up on the record."

"So, we thought that was kind of funny that the top session dogs didn't have a feel for it. I'm not slamming Andy Newmark – who is one of the greatest drummers in the world. And Earl's a great guy – we've known Earl and he gets up on stage and jams with us. We'd seen him with David Bowie, so we thought he was just the cat's pajamas, too. I don't mean to slight the guys we stepped in for. Then in '97 or '98, Yoko got ahold of us, and said, 'We are going to put this thing on a box set for John [1998's *John Lennon Anthology*]. Would you do a video?' Me, Rick, and Tony Levin went out to LA and did a video for it, too – 18 years later."

Released on November 17, 1980 (and featuring a black and white cover photograph by Kishin Shinoyama, of John and Yoko smooching), *Double Fantasy* – which was Lennon's first studio release since 1975's *Rock n' Roll* – was an expected hit. But it was only after Lennon's tragic murder on December 8th that its sales skyrocketed – resulting in it topping the album charts in numerous countries (including the US and UK), while the singles "(Just Like) Starting Over" and "Woman" would reach #1 and #2 respectively, on the *Billboard Hot 100*. The album would also win the 1981 Grammy Award for "Album of the Year" at the 24th Annual Grammy Awards, and upon its last certification in 1984, it had gone triple platinum in the US (which leads one to believe its sales figure would be substantially higher if re-certified today). And sadly, according to Levin, the bassist was told of an idea Lennon had in mind to promote his latest album. "There was a rough plan to do a world tour in the following January. But of course, that never happened."

Double Fantasy also proved that up to the very end, Lennon was penning music that deeply affected others. "When he came out with *Double Fantasy* just before he passed away, that was the ultimate comeback album," said original Dream Theater drummer Mike Portnoy. "When he gets to *Double Fantasy*, I think some of his best solo songwriting happens on that album," adds Jellyfish multi-instrumentalist/singer Roger Joseph Manning Jr.

And former Nirvana drummer, Chad Channing, also offered praise. "I always liked 'Watching the Wheels' off *Double Fantasy*. And stuff like '(Just Like) Starting Over' is really good, but to me, 'Watching the Wheels' is probably my favorite of the individual songs he did. *Double Fantasy* might be my favorite. I liked the production of it, and where he was going – it's sad that he didn't get a chance to do more. It's one of these records that made me curious to hear more of the direction that he was going. And I think at that point, he was living in New York, and he seemed to be in a very good space during that time. The dust had sort of settled, and it seemed like he was in a very happy place when he was doing that record."

But sadly, we will never know what the next musical step would have been for one of rock's all-time greats. "It would have been fascinating even if he'd have lasted another year," adds the co-author of the book *Recording the Beatles,* Brian Kehew. "To see how he would have done with *Double Fantasy*, and maybe getting on stage again, and maybe doing a couple of TV shows, putting a band together and having fun with it."

Moving Pictures
(Rush, 1981)

By the dawn of the '80s, it was clear that prog metal trailblazers Rush had become intrigued by new wave sounds – starting with 1980's *Permanent Waves*, and perfecting the approach on what many consider to be their tour de force, 1981's *Moving Pictures*. Since we already touched a bit upon Rush's backstory in the aforementioned *Permanent Waves* entry, let's just skip all that mumbo jumbo and get down to the real nitty gritty, comprendo?

As with all of Rush's LP's since 1975's *Fly by Night*, *Moving Pictures* was once again produced by Terry Brown and the band (and served as the seventh studio effort by the line-up consisting of singer/bassist/keyboardist Geddy Lee, guitarist Alex Lifeson, and drummer Neil Peart). "It was wintertime, and we were holed up in a small studio in Quebec," Lee told me during a *Rolling Stone* interview back in 2010. "Really, that studio became our home for a few years, Le Studio, just outside of Montreal. A beautiful environment, and a great working relationship that we had with people at the studio, and our producer, Terry Brown. Got a lot of fond memories of making that record."

The album opens with Rush's best-known tune, "Tom Sawyer," which is probably being played somewhere in the world right this second on a classic rock radio station, or, at a sporting event. One of Peart's finest lyrics (co-penned with Pye Dubois, and featuring the memorable repeated phrase, "The world is, the world is..."), the track also features some of his best drum fills – beginning around the 2:32 mark. By far, the greatest melding of the worlds of Mark Twain and hard rock, or as Peart explained in the 1981 home video, *Exit...Stage Left,* "A very modern urban setting for that 'Tom Sawyer mentality,' of having a very carefree stride and a very self-possessed kind of air. The stance of it does definitely have a modern day rocker's persona about it."

"'Tom Sawyer' was in many ways the most difficult song to record on that record," Lee recalled in the same chat for *Rolling Stone*. "I remember even though the writing of the song came together pretty quickly, putting it down on tape was a little difficult. We were trying different sounds, and going with a whole different approach to lyrics – the kind of spoken word thing, getting the right sound for Alex's guitar, and so on. It was kind of a dark horse. And then in the mixing, it all came together. When we finished it, we were so pleased with what happened, because we kind of had the least expectations of it, because of the difficulty we had. I think a lot of musicians probably go through a similar thing, where they have this one song that they beat themselves up over, and then the next thing you know, it's their biggest song."

Besides Peart's extraordinary drumming on the tune (in a way, almost serving as a declaration that Neil was hereby now the top rock drummer on the planet…with the passing of John Bonham just several months earlier), the other two Rushers add their special sauce, as well. First off, Lee's use of Moog synths to open the tune – that create a surprisingly sinister-sounding vibe. "In the late 70s/early 80s, he would write this stuff, and then would have to incorporate in this new Moog, and then put his vocals on at the end of it," explained Pantera bassist Rex Brown in the book, *Survival of the Fittest*. "After they had done these extremely experimental things, and made 'pop sense' out of it. The way he did it was just huge."

But Lee was also not only providing exceptional bass on the tune (he would play both bass and synth in concert by utilizing Moog Taurus foot pedals), but also, creating an outstanding bass tone that many other players would subsequently copy. In fact, ten years later, Primus' Les Claypool even consulted Lee directly. "Back then [in the early '90s], Geddy was playing those Wal basses, which I really didn't like the sound of. And I'm like, 'What is the bass you played on *Moving Pictures*?' And he was like, 'That was my old [Fender] Jazz bass.' I go, *'That's the bass you've got to play!'* And if you notice, that's the bass Geddy plays now. I can pat myself on the back a little bit for getting him to stop playing those Wal basses."

Also contained in "Tom Sawyer" was one of Lifeson's most expressive and best guitar solos. "Alex has this ability to really 'bite' into music," Triumph's Rik Emmett explained in the book *Shredders*. "He's a very physical kind of guy when he plays, and he plays hard when he's getting excited. I can't think of it in any other way except you know the way he makes that face, like his teeth are gritted and his eyes are squeezing closed? He just looks like he's using every fiber of his body to squeeze notes out. Whereas Clapton always has this very calm, placid, 'British gentleman' kind of approach to playing. Whereas Alex looks like, '*This hurts*' – which I love, because I totally come from that school, where you make all the stupid faces, that you're not even aware that you're making."

And lastly concerning "Tom Sawyer" (I know, this is a bit of a "data dump" concerning one song, but come on…this is *"Tom Sawyer"* we're talking about here!), there were two videos released for the tune. "The first 'Tom Sawyer' video we did was just filming us recording at Morin Heights, and you can see us playing in the studio with the big glass window surrounding us," Lee said in the book *MTV Ruled the World*. "You can see the winter outside. So that was kind of a 'let the camera into the session' kind of thing. And then when we were on tour, we filmed another version of it, and that became another thing that got a lot of airplay [on MTV]. Again, because we were unsure of any kind of image to attach to us, we just went with us playing. 'When in doubt, *just play*'."

OK, *now* we can explore the rest of the album. Up next was another of the band's all-time great tunes, "Red Barchetta." Lyrically inspired by a short story entitled *A Nice Morning Drive* by Richard Foster (originally appearing in the November 1973 issue of *Road & Track*…just a few short months before Peart would join forces with Lee and Lifeson), the tune tells the story of an uncle telling his nephew a tale about his cherished, speedy car, and ultimately, going for a death-defying spin in it. And while some assumed a "Barchetta" was a make or model of a car, this proved to be hogwash – it's actually an Italian word, that when translated to English, means "small boat." Featuring another standout Lifeson guitar solo, we find out by the song's conclusion that the uncle was merely telling a tall tale, while situated "fireside" on a farm.

One of the best-ever rock instrumentals follows next, "YYZ" (pronounced by Canadians as "Why-Why-Zed"), and serves as the IATA airport identification code of Toronto Pearson International Airport. And once more, Lifeson takes center stage with a terrific extended guitar solo (which judging from sound effects in the middle of it, required cracks of a whip to be tamed…or is that glass shattering?). "The thing I like about Alex is that in many ways, he humanized what Rush was doing," Rik Emmett also stated in *Shredders*. "He made it so that the punters were going, 'Oh yeah, that's rock.' Which is not to say that Geddy doesn't have bass lines that are fantastic lines, but I think Alex was kind of the guy that would say to the band, 'Yeah, but let's make this *heavier*. Let's not keep it so esoteric, let's have a moment where all hell breaks loose and I'll turn my amp up to eleven and we'll see what happens.' I always liked that about his playing."

And the tune also certainly left its mark on Primus, as the lads would open their sets with a snippet of it early on, before going directly into their own composition, "John the Fisherman" (as heard on their 1989 release, *Suck On This*). And many years later, Primus' Les Claypool got the lowdown on the song's basslines – straight from the lips of the master himself. "He *did* teach me a few things recently though," Claypool said in the book *The 100 Greatest Rock Bassists*. "He was interviewing me for some book that he's working on. And I said, 'OK. Part of the deal is you have to show me the proper way to play 'YYZ'.' He showed me, and I had been playing it wrong all these years!"

Another great tune closes side one, "Limelight" (which begs the question…does *Moving Pictures* contain the greatest side one of an LP in rock n' roll history?!). Driven by one of Lifeson's best guitar riffs, lyrically, the tune deals with the downside of celebrity, and in particular, such lines as "I can't pretend a stranger is a long awaited friend" prove to be standouts. Side two opens with the near 11-minute epic, "The Camera Eye" (split into two different parts: "New York" and "London"), which showed that the group had not turned their back entirely on penning extended compositions.

"Witch Hunt" was probably the album's underrated gem, as it seems to lyrically deal with the McCarthy hearings of the '50s (during which Senator Joseph McCarthy "hunted" for supposed Stateside communists) – particularly in such lyrics as "They say there are strangers who threaten us, Our immigrants and infidels" and "They say there is strangeness too dangerous, In our theatres and bookstore shelves." And in a sad twist, the lyrics in the tune reflect what society had regressed to at the time of this book's release (reflected in views by both the radical right and Cancel Culture). And closing the album would be "Vital Signs," a tune that musically was obviously heavily influenced by the Police's "white reggae" (*Reggatta de Blanc*...geddit?) stylings, and lyrically, encourages to shun conformity – most obviously in the lyric, "Everybody got to elevate from the norm."

Released on February 12, 1981, *Moving Pictures* featured a cover image of movers dressed in red jumpsuits "moving" several pictures housed in frames (also in the front cover image is a group of onlookers including a woman crying, and on the back cover, a photo that shows film cameras filming the proceedings...resulting in a three-time pun on the album's title) – outside the Ontario Legislative Building in Queen's Park, Toronto. And the LP dominated both the US and UK album charts upon arrival – peaking at #3 in both countries (and topping the charts in their homeland of Canada) and coming in at an impressive #18 on *Billboard's Year-End Album Chart.* Additionally, the album spawned the trio's first near honest-to-goodness US hit single, with "Tom Sawyer," which narrowly missed the top-40 (#44). And over the years, *Moving Pictures* moved units – certified 5x platinum in the US, and on February 11, 2022, a 40th anniversary box set of the album was issued (even though it was really a *41st* anniversary box set...but who's keeping count, right?).

Lastly, does Lee agree that *Moving Pictures* is Rush's best album? "It's certainly our most universally accepted, most popular album. If that means best, then I guess so. But obviously, Rush fans and different members of the band have different favorites. It's certainly our most popular record, and it's also the one that I think has aged very well."

Discipline
(King Crimson, 1981)

By the dawn of the 80s, punk had returned rock music to its foundations. So much so, that even one-time prog rockers were streamlining their sound/approach. [Note: I know, this point has been driven home by now…but stick with it!] King Crimson were one such band, as evidenced by 1981's exceptional *Discipline*.

When leader/guitarist Robert Fripp decided to form a "new Crimson," overindulgences were trimmed and replaced with a sound heavy on rhythm and experimentation. A chance meeting would shape the rest of the line-up. "I met Robert Fripp one night in New York, at a club called the Bottom Line," remembers singer/guitarist Adrian Belew. "I was playing with David Bowie at the time [1979/1980] and [we] went to see Steve Reich. When the lights came up, Robert was at the table next to us. So I went over, and he wrote his hotel number on my arm. We had coffee, and got to know each other. In 1980, I started with the Talking Heads, and when they arrived in England I got a call from Robert saying: 'I'm starting a new band with [drummer] Bill Bruford and myself. Would you like to be a part of it?' I jumped at the chance."

New York auditions landed studio-veteran bassist Tony Levin (Lou Reed, Peter Gabriel, et al), which solidified the new Crimson. "I don't think any of us knew we were creating something so unusual," Belew says. "But now that I look back, it's easy to see – every one of us had new technology. I was the first to have a guitar synthesiser, and Robert was probably the second. Tony had the Chapman Stick, which no one had used before, and Bill was fooling with electronic drums. So you had these four monkeys in a cage together with new toys. Something was bound to happen."

Something did indeed happen. With funky workout "Elephant Talk," ambient soundscapes ("Sheltering Sky"), tranquil moments ("Matte Kudasai") and controlled freak-outs ("Thela Hun Ginjeet," "Indiscipline"), 1981's *Discipline* sounded like nothing before it. An interesting occurrence developed during sessions for "Thela Hun Ginjeet" [whose title is an anagram for the song's original title, "Heat in the Jungle"]. Belew remembers it vividly: "John Lennon had been killed, and he was my hero. So I tried to write a lyric about being molested with a gun on the streets of a city. I tried to think of phrases, as though it was an interview on the street after the occurrence."

"We were in a part of London that was a dangerous area, but I didn't know that. I had a tape recorder, and Robert said: 'If you want to get realistic sounds, why don't you walk around on the street and say your lines?' I walked down one of the streets, and there was illegal gambling going on by a group of Rastafarian guys – pretty tough-looking. And they'd gathered around me. They thought I was an undercover policeman. They were about to kill me! At one point the 'leader' grabbed my tape recorder and played back what I had just been saying: 'He had a gun!' [Laughs] The guy freaked out. 'What gun?!' They finally let me go, I'm not sure why. I went back to the studio. I was so shook up, and I ran into the control room and was telling Robert the story. Meanwhile, he had whispered to the engineer to record it, and that's what you hear on the record."

Although *Discipline* wasn't a big hit, it re-established King Crimson, and touched a legion of young musicians. Says Belew: "It certainly wasn't a record that your average person would know, but it had an effect on Primus, Tool, Trent Reznor and so many people. That record affected the way they saw music. And for me, that's even better than saying we had a big hit record."

Bad Brains
(Bad Brains, 1982)

Looking back through rock history, there are certain punk albums that you can make a valid argument were game changers. Case in point, Ramones' *Ramones*, Sex Pistols' *Never Mind the Bollocks, Here's the Sex Pistols*, the Clash's *London Calling*, etc. And you can most certainly add the Bad Brains' 1982 full-length debut, *Bad Brains* [aka *The ROIR Cassette*, or *The ROIR Sessions*, or *The Yellow Tape*], to the list. Heck, if you aren't willing to take my word for it, how about late/great Beastie Boy Adam Yauch, who on a sticker stuck on a CD reissue of the album years later, was quoted as declaring it as "the best punk/hardcore album of all time."

Comprised of singer HR (real name: Paul D. Hudson), guitarist Dr. Know (real name: Gary Miller), bassist Darryl Jenifer, and drummer Earl Hudson (yes, HR's brother), the band originally hailed from Washington, DC, and began life as a jazz-fusion band, Mind Power. But shortly before the close of the '70s, the quartet had discovered punk rock and Rastafarianism, changed their name to the Bad Brains (quite possibly after the Ramones song title, "Bad Brain"), and had elevated the intensity and sped things up a few notches – resulting in the creation of hardcore. But by the early '80s, the Bad Brains had relocated to New York – building a following by regularly playing such venues as Max's Kansas City, CBGB's, and A7.

Back in the pre-Internet days, in most cases, to truly establish yourself if you were a rock band, you needed to find a record company to back you (which was probably a major reason why the Bad Brains had a few sessions that would go unreleased for decades – *no record label involvement*). And in the BB's case, they eventually grabbed the attention of the NYC-based label, ROIR (short for "Reach Out International Records"). Founded by a gentleman by the name of Neil Cooper in 1979, what set ROIR apart from the rest of the labels at the time was that they initially only issued their releases in the cassette format (keep in mind, this was during the era that the popularity of the Walkman was skyrocketing). Additionally, the label specialized in signing artists aligned to either one of two genres – punk or reggae. And with the

Bad Brains devoted to both styles by this point, ROIR was a perfect fit.

The recording would be produced by Jerry Williams (aka "Jay Dublee") and released in February of 1982, while the album's original 15 tracks certainly fit a popular phrase often linked to standout albums – "all killer/no filler." At the top of the "must hear" song list is the album opening "Sailin' On" (which would become an instant classic) and what your humble narrator feels is the definitive version of "Pay to Cum" (which was at least the third time the Brains had attempted to record the tune), as well as such adrenaline-soaked ragers as "Attitude," "The Regulator," "Banned in DC," "Supertouch/Shitfit," "Fearless Vampire Killers," "Big Take Over," "Right Brigade," and "I" (the latter of which Henry Rollins declared as his all-time fave BB tune in his 1994 book, *Get in the Van*). And to give the listener a much-needed breather in certain spots, the Brains offer up some calming reggae detours – "Jah Calling," "Leaving Babylon," and "I Luv I Jah."

It turns out that the sessions were recorded at good ol' 171A. A sorta Off-Broadway theater, 171A was located above a glass shop, and consisted of one long room that included a stage on one end, and back near the entrance was an elevated soundbooth for recording. Williams' rates were $10 an hour for recordings (the cheapest in town at the time!), while the décor inside consisted of couches dragged in off the street.

But as Darryl recalls, the sessions didn't exactly run smoothly. "[The recording] was a pain in the ass – none of this stuff is like, 'Let's go do this and be that,' it's just like HR pushing things this-a-way and that-a-way. It was kind of labor intensive to be in Bad Brains at times – emotionally and physically." Also, Earl remembers that the band followed a golden rule during the recording – "We put 110% into what we did back then. It was totally from the heart, so I guess you could say the intentions were there to do our best." The majority of the album's songs would be recorded during August, September, and October 1981, while the tracks "Pay to Cum," "I Luv I Jah," and "Jah Calling" were recorded live (also at the same location) on May 16, 1981.

And although Dr. Know didn't own a real guitar at the time, producer Williams supplied him with an instrument that he recorded the entire album with. "I was playing a white SG – that was Jerry's guitar. That's what I used, because I didn't have shit – nobody had anything. It was a real vintage, whatever year [model]. Whatever SG that was, that was like the baddest shit they made. It had gold pickups on it – three of them – and I think it had a whammy on it, too." Unsure of which amplifier he used for the recording, the only guitar effect utilized for the recording was an Echoplex.

Besides supplying his six string skills, Dr. Know also offered a suggestion regarding the artwork of the initially cassette-only release (which would be reissued on both vinyl and CD subsequently). "My direct influence on that cassette was the artwork, because when cassettes first came out, you got your cover and the little flip thing with the names of the songs. And we were like, 'Yo, we got to have our lyrics, we got to have pictures.' Y'know, like how a record would have. And Neil [Cooper] was like, 'Oh man, it's going to be so expensive.' Hence, you have that foldout eight section, and front and back of a cassette format."

"We also wanted red, yellow, and green cassettes. I wish I had one of each – whoever has them, I'm sure they're worth a lot of money. If you have original ones, not opened, in all three colors, good God. *You'll get paid.* I don't think anybody has one." And the cover has gone on to become absolutely iconic – a thunderbolt coming down from the heavens, striking the Capitol Building in DC. It turns out the cover concept was provided by Cooper, with the actual artwork done by a chap simply named Mir (who also went by the names David Lee Parsons and Dave Ratcage).

Almost immediately, *Bad Brains* began connecting with local music fans, and soon, throughout the world. Case in point, eventual Living Colour guitarist, Vernon Reid. "The whole album rocks from 'Sailin' On' to 'I Luv I Jah.' It's hard to pick out one track above another, but 'Banned in DC' is the band war cry and gets me every time – HR's vocal is outstanding and Dr. Know's Eddie Hazel-esque lead is the icing on that 'Chocolate City' cake. I heard the song 'I' and my life changed. The reggae numbers are wonderful too – strictly roots. Bad Brains are one of the greatest rock bands. *Ever."*

Brief Red Hot Chili Peppers guitarist Arik Marshall was also affected by the album. "It sounds better now than it did then. I think most music is so terrible now that the Osmonds' 'One Bad Apple' would sound revolutionary today! That Bad Brains album is definitely a timeless classic. I really dig that intro to 'FVK' and then how it just blasts into the first verse. 'Banned in DC' has that great juxtaposition of the first fast punk thing, then the slowed down groovin' type thang behind the guitar solo. And 'The Regulator' just makes me wanna destroy somethin' – always the mark of a great punk rock song. And since Dr. Know's guitar playing was so integral to the sound of the album, I would say his axe work is influential as well. He influenced me – made me realize it's not so much what you play, but how you play it."

Anthrax guitarist Scott Ian also offers praise – "The Bad Brains invented hardcore, not Black Flag or Fear. Those bands ruled as well, but they didn't have the intensity of the Bad Brains. [It's] one of the most influential albums ever because like I said, they invented hardcore – aggressive and tight. No one sounded like this in 1982."

Lastly, Nirvana drummer and Foo Fighters singer/guitarist Dave Grohl pays his respects – "I was living in DC in the early '80s and got into the hardcore scene, but nobody else blew me away as much as Bad Brains. I'll say it now, I have never ever, ever, ever, ever seen a band do anything even close to what Bad Brains used to do live. Seeing Bad Brains live was, without a doubt, always one of the most intense, powerful experiences you could ever have. They were just, oh God, words fail me, incredible. They were connected in a way I'd never seen before. They made me absolutely determined to become a musician, they basically changed my life, and changed the lives of everyone who saw them."

"Rage Against The Machine are about the only band who get near to them, but even they aren't in the same league. Bad Brains are one of those bands that everyone who's ever heard them has come away with a real extreme reaction, either love or hate. I loved 'em. The fact that there were four black guys, coming on to a predominately white scene that they then just surpassed and destroyed with everything they did, just staggered you. The studio albums are great, but for me, *ROIR*, this unofficial bootleg, comes closest to capturing their live sound on tape. Awesome."

Lastly, Doc offers a final thought as to what makes *Bad Brains* so darn classic. "That's when we made 'our sound.' That record, all of the songs I love. We were playing that shit from the heart – there wasn't no filler material."

The Number of the Beast
(Iron Maiden, 1982)

Certain years have seen the release of an overabundance of classic metal albums. And 1982 was undoubtedly one of them. Case in point, the arrival of Judas Priest's *Screaming for Vengeance*, Venom's *Black Metal*, Scorpions' *Blackout*, Kiss' *Creatures of the Night*, and Accept's *Restless and Wild* all within that particular calendar year. However, most metalheads would probably agree that the top metal release of '82 was Iron Maiden's tour de force *The Number of the Beast* – which celebrated its 40-year anniversary on March 22nd, 2022.

Lead singer switches in already established rock bands seem to not work out far more times than they do. But Maiden were one of the fortunate ones – when Paul Di'Anno (who provided vocals for Maiden's first two albums, 1980's self-titled debut and 1981's *Killers*) was replaced by former Samson singer Bruce Dickinson in late 1981.

With their new vocalist singing in a more operatic style than his predecessor, Maiden – whose line-up at that point consisted of Dickinson, guitarists Dave Murray and Adrian Smith, bassist Steve Harris, and drummer Clive Burr – began working up new material shortly after their new bandmate's arrival. "We had most of the songs and we were rehearsing them," Dickinson told *Heavy Consequence* while discussing the 40th anniversary of *The Number of the Beast*. "So, we thought we had a fairly good idea of what they should sound like. [Producer] Martin Birch showed up for a couple of days of rehearsals, nodded his head, and went, 'Yep, yep. OK. Fine.' And then we started recording it."

The band eventually started recording early in 1982 in a section of Morgan Studios in London, called Battery Studios. But it's not to say that the sessions were all business. "There was kind of a big party atmosphere throughout the whole thing," recalls Dickinson. "In fact, we actually made a wall of those 7-pint beer cans – the entire wall of the control room was a pyramid of kegs of beer that we had drunk during the proceedings. We would be up until 4 or 5 in the morning, after we had finished recording, listening back to what we had recorded, until basically the producer said,

'Right. You need to go to bed, because you're going to come back and do this all again tomorrow.' There was a really great vibe."

The singer also recalled unexpected surroundings. "I did most of my vocals in a dilapidated kitchen. It had been stripped out, and there was nothing in there, except a lot of wet plaster on the walls...and me. So, to say there was a natural echo would be an understatement!"

At this stage of Maiden's career, the band was still young and hungry, as Dickinson recalls "Maiden was a different animal – we were so fierce and snarling and snapping at everybody." Maiden's aggression was definitely captured on such tunes as "Invaders," "22 Acacia Avenue," "Gangland," and especially a tune that would go on to become an all-time classic, "Run to the Hills." The group also showed they possessed a melodic side on "The Prisoner," and hinted at their future specialty of penning epics, with the seven minutes-plus album-closer, "Hallowed Be Thy Name."

However, with such song titles as "Children of the Damned" and the title track — plus the album's awesome eye-popping artwork by Derek Riggs (which saw the band's mascot Eddie working Beelzebub like a puppet amidst an Armageddon-like setting) Maiden were erroneously labeled "Satanists" by certain overzealous religious groups in the US at the time.

The unexpected press coverage and hoopla along with *Beast* being such a strong album, MTV airing the videos for "Run to the Hills" and the title track, landing spots on arena tours (opening for the likes of Scorpions, Rainbow, 38 Special, and Judas Priest), plus appearing on such high profile festivals as the Day on the Green in the US and headlining a night on the Reading Festival in the UK made Maiden one of the world's top metal bands. As a result, *The Number of the Beast* topped the UK charts, and peaked at #33 in the US (eventually obtaining platinum certification in both countries). "We had no idea how big it was going to be," Dickinson admits. "How big the influence was."

In the book *Iron Maiden '80 '81*, Anthrax's Scott Ian recalled what it was like seeing Maiden on the album's supporting tour (dubbed "The Beast on the Road"). "Initially, it wasn't that much different when Maiden came back with Bruce on *The Number of the Beast* and were still playing theaters, because we saw them in the city at the Palladium [in 1981 with Di'Anno], and also saw them at this place called the North Stage Theater out on Long Island [in 1982 with Dickinson] – a small place. So it wasn't that much different at that point, because it was still on that level."

"Obviously, it was way different a few months later, when they became an arena band. But when they were still playing the same sized places from *Killers* to *The Number of the Beast*, yeah, obviously Bruce's vocals were completely different than Paul's. But as far as the energy and all that of the band, it was still very similar to me. They did become much more polished on *The Number of the Beast*, that's for sure."

Despite the success, once "The Beast on the Road" tour wrapped in late '82, Maiden would experience another line-up hiccup, when Burr exited (and was eventually replaced by Nicko McBrain). "I don't think I appreciated Clive until years later," ex-Dream Theater drummer Mike Portnoy explained in the *Iron Maiden '80 '81* book. "And Dream Theater covered the entire *The Number of the Beast* album back in 2002, I think it was. So obviously, I had to sit there and really study Clive's playing, and it gave me a whole new appreciation for...he had an incredible 'swing' to him. He gave all the songs a real swing."

Portnoy continued, "He also had incredibly fast hands – like if you listen to the hi-hat work on 'Run to the Hills' or 'Gangland' – I think a lot of that I took for granted until I actually sat down and learned all of his parts. Now, I have a tremendous amount of respect for what he did on those first three albums." Sadly, Burr would pass away on March 13, 2013 at the age of 56 from complications related to multiple sclerosis.

Maiden kept climbing the ladder of success throughout the '80s, continuing their winning streak with such subsequent classic releases as 1983's *Piece of Mind*, 1984's *Powerslave*, 1986's *Somewhere in Time*, and 1988's *Seventh Son of a Seventh Son*. But *The Number of the Beast* will forever be considered one of Maiden's most enduring and crucial albums – to both their own career and to the heavy metal genre as a whole.

SPECIAL/SECRET/HIDDEN BONUS ENTRIES!

You Don't Mess Around with Jim
(Jim Croce, 1972)

Few singer/songwriters were able to tell the stories of characters as expertly as Jim Croce could. Case in point, "Rapid Roy," "Speedball Tucker," "Bad Leroy Brown," "Roller Derby Queen," and especially "Big" Jim Walker and Willie "Slim" McCoy – the last two of which are the stars of the title track from Croce's first hit album, *You Don't Mess Around with Jim.*

And although he is often classified as a "folk artist" (which is understandable, as he chose to play acoustic guitar during his brief recording career), there were other styles of music detected in Croce's tunes. And his son, AJ Croce, explained to me in 2018 (for *Long Island Pulse*) how his father pulled influences from other styles of music – and made them his own.

"I think of there being three kinds of songs that he wrote. There's the character songs, which are very inspired by Leiber and Stoller – 'Leroy Brown,' 'Car Wash Blues' or 'Rapid Roy.' They're kind of like R&B songs that the Coasters would have played. And they were about people he met; it's not really about himself. Then, you have songs that are very personal, like 'Time in a Bottle,' 'These Dreams' or 'Lover's Cross.' And then, you have something like 'Operator,' which is more him stepping back from his perspective and looking at it from another person's story."

Born on January 10, 1943 in Philadelphia, Pennsylvania, James Joseph Croce issued his first album in 1966, *Facets* (which was self-released), before signing with Capitol and teaming with his wife, for 1969's *Jim & Ingrid Croce.* Both albums proved unsuccessful commercially however, but by 1972, the singer/guitarist had signed as a solo artist with ABC – which resulted in the release of *You Don't Mess Around with Jim.*

And while it was solely Jim's name featured on his album covers from here on out, by this point, he was joined in the studio and on the stage by another singer/guitarist, Maury Muehleisen. "Maury was one of the most unusually talented human beings I've ever met," Ingrid recounted to *Rolling Stone* in 2012. "He could sing anything and play any instrument. He was a classically trained pianist, and he'd only been playing a couple of years before he got a record deal. There was a period where Jim was backing Maury, and then because things changed, Maury started to back Jim."

Although in live video footage from this era it is either Jim by himself or being accompanied by Muehleisen, there are instances on *You Don't Mess Around with Jim* (which was co-produced by Terry Cashman and Tommy West) where Croce is backed by a full band and back-up singers – perhaps the most obvious example being the aforementioned album-opening title track. Certainly one of Croce's most rocking tunes, the tune tells the tale of two pool players – which results in one killing the other, after being swindled out of money. And the chorus is one of Croce's most sing-along best – "You don't tug on Superman's cape, You don't spit into the wind, You don't pull the mask off the old Lone Ranger, And you don't mess around with Jim" (with later in the song, "Jim" being replaced with "Slim"). And it also became known years later that the tune was a favorite of Hawkins, Indiana police chief Jim Hopper – especially when cleaning his country home.

And while the album contains three other of Croce's best-known tunes (more on those in a bit), it also includes several of his most underrated – particularly "Tomorrow's Gonna Be a Brighter Day" (which as you can gather simply from the title, carries quite a positive message lyrically) and "Walking Back to Georgia" (one of Croce's best love songs). Why neither of these two tunes were issued as singles – or at the very least included on subsequent compilations, such as *Photographs & Memories: His Greatest Hits* – makes no bloody sense at all. Other lesser-known standouts include "New York's Not My Home" (which sounds like it may have been lyrically autobiographical), the surprisingly Chuck Berry-ish "Rapid Roy (The Stock Car Boy)," the uptempo "Hard Time Losin' Man," and the more reflective/instrumentally stripped down "A Long Time Ago" and "Hey Tomorrow."

But it is another overlooked tune on the album, "Box #10," that AJ picked as one of his favorites of his father's compositions, when I interviewed him for *The Yacht Rock Book*. "I like 'Box #10' because it was written at a time when after my mother and father recorded a record on Capitol, and like most records in the world, it didn't do well. And he was still trying to play music, and they moved to New York City. And if you listen to the lyrics, it's really very poignant and it's heartbreaking, because although my father became very famous after he died – and even was famous a short period while he was alive – he never had more money than he did when he was as broke as he was when he wrote that song. To me, there's something tragic and beautiful about it."

Concerning the earlier claim of there being three other Croce classics, I won't mess around with Jim – those tunes include the blue ballad "Photographs and Memories," one of his best-ever sets of storytelling lyrics in "Operator (That's Not the Way It Feels)," and "Time in a Bottle." And in the same *Yacht Rock Book* (in case you were wondering how come Jim was featured in such a book, it was because there was a section spotlighting artists of the era that specialized in smooth sounds...but weren't *quite* yacht rock), AJ discussed "Time in a Bottle" at length.

"As far as the hits go, 'Time in a Bottle' was written for me, so I of course have a special place in my heart for it. And it was also really the breakthrough song for him – not because it was the first hit, in fact, it was on the first record and didn't become popular until after the third record came out and was in a movie. All of a sudden, he found his identity. I was once listening to a tape, and he was just doing covers. He was practicing songs he was going to play at the Riddle Paddock, at the Main Point – places that he was playing in and around Philadelphia. We lived in the country outside of Philly. So there was all kinds of stuff – he was playing old blues songs, great old country songs, and all of a sudden, out of nowhere really, came *this* song."

"And there was pressure – my mom was pregnant with me, he was educated, had gotten a degree at Villanova and was able to get a job in a lot of different fields. He had two majors and a master, and he chose to do other things – he did teach, but he also drove a truck. Out of the blue, this song on the tape...it was like one of those really unusual moments – regardless of whether you like the song or hate the song or have any feeling at all about it, where you see a songwriter or artist of any kind, all of a sudden, *they found themselves.*"

"He had been doing covers and originals for many years. He had been playing folk clubs and coffee shops – and doing that kind of 'folk circuit' – for ten years by that time, or more. But for whatever reason, this song came out, and it was completely original. And I think every artist that seems to last will find a place, or a time when they find their voice. Like my father, I found mine kind of late in a lot of ways. He was twenty-eight when he found that. Whereas the Beatles found it at seventeen, eighteen, and they found themselves, and that was who they were. There are a lot of artists like that. People find themselves at different times, and find their identity as an artist. Even if it's just a jumping-off point."

"My feelings [for the song now] are of just true sincerity. He was a sincere person, and his lyrics really represent that, but I think he hid some of that. Although I think they're great songs, like 'Rapid Roy' are amazing lyrics, and 'Speedball Tucker' has great lyrics, you can say, 'Oh yeah, that comes from Chuck Berry, or that is reminiscent of this or that.' The thing about the lyrics to 'Time In a Bottle,' I think, is that they are universally sincere. I think most people who don't take their music with pure cynicism will find that it's just that – it's a sincere desire to save a moment."

"In all honesty, it's not my favorite song – maybe I've heard it too many times, like 'Satisfaction,' that I'll never have to hear it again. Y'know, I like 'Pretty Woman,' but I never have to hear it again. 'Baby Love,' I don't need to hear that again. But for the last couple of years, I do a half a dozen shows of two generations of Croce music. And I really dug deep in this in the process of doing it. I play mostly his music and my stuff that I've written over the last twenty-five years, and then the stuff that we really have in common. And there is a lot that we have in common. Well, I sort of went toward jazz and New Orleans and that stuff, when he went toward folk – the Kingston Trio kind of folk. I think otherwise, we had a lot in common – early jazz, early blues, Pink Anderson, Fats Waller. And the R&B stuff that made a huge impact for him in the

50s, like Chuck Berry, Sam Cooke, Otis Redding, or anything like that."

"So, while for me it's an amazing thing, and when it comes to the point where I sing that song, it is extremely emotional for me. And I think the audience feels the same way. I think that's the whole point of it. A lot of people danced their dance at their wedding to it, or it was at their wife's funeral...it was at these very powerful times in people's lives when that song got played. I didn't even touch any of his stuff for most of my life. I didn't even play guitar until the mid 2000s. But once I did and once I got a handle on it and got decent at playing the fingerstyle stuff, it was like a natural thing to dig into it – because it's really complicated."

The last bit of business was the album's cover photo. And photographer Paul Wilson snapped a classic non-color shot of a mustachioed Jim enjoying a smoke, while staring out from behind a glass-less window frame within a small structure on the property of his family's farmhouse just outside Philadelphia, in Lyndell, Pennsylvania (it was later discovered that the structure was used to house pigs, and later, chickens!).

Released in April 1972 (the exact day could not be located), *You Don't Mess Around with Jim* sold well during Croce's life – thanks to the success of the singles "You Don't Mess Around with Jim" (#8 on the *Billboard Hot 100*) and "Operator" (#17). But it was after his tragic death in a plane crash at the age of 30 (on September 20, 1973 in Natchitoches, Louisiana – with Muehleisen also perishing in the crash) that the album would go on to top the US charts, while "Time in a Bottle" would also reach #1 on the singles charts. And judging from the high quality of the material on the two albums after *You Don't Mess Around with Jim* (which would be *Life and Times* and *I Got a Name*), it leaves you wondering how many more classics this talented singer/songwriter could have gone on to pen had he not boarded that Beechcraft E18S on that fateful night.

"Jim was prolific beyond prolific," Ingrid also recalled in the aforementioned *Rolling Stone* article. "There was never a time when we weren't doing music – 12 hours a day, minimum. But I think that Jim was really getting into writing, and he wanted to do movies. He could have been a stand-up comic. When he opened for Woody Allen or George Carlin, they were a little afraid to get on stage [after Jim], because his humor was so unique. He was asked to be the summer replacement for Johnny Carson [on *The Tonight Show*] – that's why we moved out to San Diego. He would have done an enormous amount of things."

Crazy Horses
(The Osmonds, 1972)

What the heck is one of the era's most family-friendly pop bands doing on this list? Let me explain. In one of the most dramatic stylistic shifts in pop history, the Osmonds suddenly transformed into a true hard rockin' band for their fourth studio release overall, *Crazy Horses*.

Although some of the brothers had been performing music as far back as the late '50s, it was with the release of the group's self-titled debut in 1970 that the five-piece line-up of Alan, Wayne, Jay, Merrill, and Donny Osmond became solidified (it's difficult to ascertain which instruments each member played exactly...more on that later). And thanks to such smash pop hits as "One Bad Apple," "Yo-Yo," and "Down by the Lazy River," the Osmonds were one of the top pin-up/teeny bopper bands of the era.

But by the time the band began sessions at MGM Recording Studios in Hollywood on March 17, 1972 (with Alan Osmond and Michael Lloyd co-producing, and lasting until June 23), the band had apparently tired of their "boy band" sound, *and wanted to rock*. "We were headed in that direction as a band," Donny told me for *Songfacts* in 2021. "Here's the problem...I was recording and we were writing all of this progressive rock n' roll music in a studio, and then I'd go into another studio and record bubblegum music. So I was living a double life musically...actually triple, because I'd go home and listen to Tower of Power and P-Funk. That was the stuff I was into at home. So I was into funk, recording bubblegum, and writing rock n' roll with the brothers."

Despite Donny's musical conundrum, there are several tracks here that would certainly fall under the "hard rock" category – the album-opening "Hold Her Tight" (which is propelled by an airtight bass-drum groove), the mid-paced "Life Is Hard Without Goodbyes" (which musically sounds surprisingly similar to the future Rainbow composition, "Love's No Friend"), the prog-meets-Vegas "We All Fall Down," and the screamed vocal showcase "Hey, Mr. Taxi."

But unquestionably, the hardest rocker of the entire album is the title track – a tune which contains a Zep-like guitar riff whose title and lyrics have been misconstrued over the years (supposedly, it's a pro-environment tune, not a drug tune – which some misinterpreted via the lyric "What a show, there they go smokin' up the sky"). And although many assume it is a theremin at the song's beginning that replicates the sound of a squealing horse, Donny cleared up this misconception in the same *Songfacts* interview.

"No, it wasn't theremin – it was a YP-30 Yamaha organ with a portamento slide. We had a wall of Marshalls in the studio. It was so loud that you couldn't even walk in the studio. So, we had to play the organ from the control room. And my brother Alan actually played it on the record. I played it live. But the secret to it was a wah-wah pedal. We opened the wah-wah just enough to get that really harsh kind of a piercing sound. But it was the loudness of the Marshalls that got us that sound. And then we doubled it. That was the secret to that sound."

As mentioned earlier concerning who played what in this era of the Osmonds, if you were to view footage on YouTube of the group performing "Crazy Horses" around the time of its release, it appears as though it would be: Alan on lead vocals, Wayne and Jay on guitar, Merrill on bass and vocals, and Donny on keys (with the other instruments being played by studio musicians). But then there are other times on Osmond recordings where Alan is listed as rhythm guitarist and Jay as drummer, so, who the heck knows for sure? Admittedly, there are moments that the band slips back into slightly shlocky territory ("Girl," "What Could It Be?", "That's My Girl," etc.), but it remains impressive how the Osmonds could hold their own with some of the era's best-known rock acts with the aforementioned harder selections.

Released on October 14, 1972, *Crazy Horses* would feature a cover shot of the band standing atop jalopies in a junkyard – with factory smoke stacks in the distance spewing smog into the sky (with the album's title superimposed on top of the nasty cloud). And it turns out that their audience was willing to accept the group's new sound – in a strange twist, *Crazy Horses* the album and both its singles (the title track and "Hold Her Tight") would all reach the same spot on the *Billboard* album and singles chart...#14.

However, Donny recalls that the group tried to continue in the same rock direction as *Crazy Horses* for their next release, 1973's *The Plan*, but were met with resistance by a certain faction of the music biz. "*The Plan* album, my brother Alan – seeing what was going on with the dynamics of the Osmonds' career, with the juxtaposition of my career – took the album into I think it was KLOS in Los Angeles, it was a heavy rock n' roll station. But he white labeled it – the same thing I did with 'Soldier of Love.' So, his name was 'Alan from a band,' and he had the program director and the music director there. He played the album for them, and they said, 'This is unbelievable! This is like the Stones, this is like the Who. It's got all these Zeppelin type of influences. What's the name of the band?' And he said, 'It's the Osmonds.' No lie, they turned to him and said, 'I'm sorry. We can't play it'."

Regardless, *Crazy Horses* – and in particular, its title track – left its mark on quite a few rockers, including praise from one of heavy metal's all-time great artists, according to Donny – "Ozzy Osbourne actually told me one time that 'Crazy Horses' is one of his favorite rock n' roll songs." Additionally, such varied artists as the Sensational Alex Harvey Band, the Mission, KMFDM, Butcher Babies, and Mike Portnoy have all covered the tune at various points.

But as Donny reiterated, the Osmonds' transformation as hard rockers proved to be short-lived, because as he explained, "The problem is my teenybopper career was selling like crazy – and it overshadowed anything we did as a rock n' roll band. But that's the direction we were headed – *Crazy Horses*. That's where the band was headed. But history changed and didn't allow it because of Donny Osmond's career."

Bang
(James Gang, 1973)

Led by guitarist/singer Joe Walsh, the James Gang was the Stateside answer to Cream – a hard rockin' outfit who had no problem filling the spaces with only three players. But when Walsh exited the group at the height of their popularity (after scoring hits with "Funk #49" and "Walk Away"), the rhythm section of bassist Dale Peters and drummer Jim Fox decided to soldier on – expanding to a quartet with singer Roy Kenner and guitarist Domenic Troiano. After a pair of spotty releases, Troiano left, and at the suggestion of their old pal Walsh, Tommy Bolin (who was previously a member of Colorado-based blues rockers, Zephyr, and was previously mentioned in this book in the Billy Cobham: *Spectrum* entry) was welcomed aboard.

"We had signed with Atlantic Records, and they wanted a record," Fox recounted in the book, *Touched by Magic: The Tommy Bolin Story*. "In order for Atlantic to wish to continue [working with the band], they wanted to know who the guitar player was we had in mind. When we told them it was Tommy, they were delighted, because they had a distant eye on Tommy. They thought, 'That oughta work real good. How soon can you get a record to us?' Our attitude was, 'Let's get together and play some.' I don't believe we played any gigs in front of audiences before we recorded. We may have done some playing, and then a whole bunch of practicing, and prepared to work on the tunes that were available."

Immediately, Peters could hear the difference between Bolin and Walsh's playing. "Joe is a much more methodical, very deliberate kind of player. Absolutely phenomenal. But Tommy was just *wild*. Just this crazy, wild guitar player. Completely different. He seemed like the right guy, played the right way. He was a spectacular guitar player. He was incredible – he didn't sound like anybody else. He had this frantic, great style of playing rock guitar. He could play anything, he had a great sound."

And according to Fox, Bolin's arrival couldn't have come at a better time, as the group's songwriting well had run dry. "As Dale and I not being major writers by any means, it's a little different situation. Here we have this band and we didn't really have writing capabilities – or at least not the kind that we felt we needed for success. So when we were looking for a guitar player, writing was important – or at least the ability to 'write with' was important. And here comes Tommy, and he has half an album's worth of tunes ready, and we liked most of them. So we took what we liked, and I think we maybe left a couple behind. The rest of them came together as we were getting ourselves together. The result is pretty much stuff that Tommy had written ready to go or came in time for the sessions."

Bolin's brother, Johnnie Bolin, also confirms that Tommy had material raring to go. "The James Gang *Bang* album was pretty much already written with Energy [another former band of Tommy's]. So when he got with the band, he'd already had the songs written – most of them." And it turned out that Bolin had been penning this original material with a pair of songwriter pals, John Tesar and Jeff Cook.

"He and I were almost never in the same city at that point," remembers Tesar. "He was in Los Angeles and I was in Arizona, the Dakotas, or Chicago. All of the stuff on *Bang*, we did those long distance – by mail and by telephone. I did go to Denver at one time and watched him play around the James Gang time frame. There were too many drugs – I got spooked by that. I liked it too much, and he liked it too much. I couldn't afford to run with that crowd. I liked it and knew I had to stay away from it. It was mostly marijuana and cocaine. That was not the worst times for him – it got much worse later on. Those were sort of 'recreational times.' As I recall, during those times, he was pretty professional. It was later that it got the better of him. Around the middle of '74, it just got dingier and harder. I suspected there was smack and stuff like that."

Despite Bolin's drug use, it seemed/sounded like a match made in heaven musically, as the album's sessions – which saw the group producing themselves – went smoothly. Fox: "We recorded the basics here in Cleveland [at the Cleveland Recording Company]. So it was a very comfortable situation for Dale and myself – it was a studio we knew well. He just fit right in. I don't have that much in the way of specific recollections. It was really easy to work with Tommy. The stuff we set out to do, we seemed to be very much on the same page with. It was very easy to communicate ideas back and forth, to create arrangements, and to have the dialogue. It was a pleasure. Tommy was just a superior musician. Very flexible, very willing – not hung up about things. It was a great collaboration. He had a lot of stuff ready to go, and we were able to mold it very quickly and easily into stuff that we were all comfortable with."

From front to back, *Bang* is chockful of strong material. Kicking things off was the album opening rocker, "Standing in the Rain" (which begins with the sound of Bolin's trademark Echoplex), before things get taken down a notch with the slightly spooky-sounding "The Devil Is Singing Our Song," and the fun bluesy tune, "Must Be Love." And then…the album's undisputed best track, "Alexis." A gorgeous tune about lost young love set in the south of the US, "Alexis" features one of Tommy's best vocal performances (his first-ever on record), while the music slowly builds before erupting into a smoldering solo. Although the song made its official debut on *Bang*, it was written and demoed earlier in Colorado. "I think it's one of the best songs he ever did," praises co-writer Cook. "It had sensitivity, strong lyric imagery, and the music fit the mood of the song very well."

Interestingly, years later, the song's lyrics came true for Cook. "I wrote the lyrics to that. The song was just a piece of fiction. When I wrote the song, I'd never been to Atlanta, I'd never been to New Orleans, and the lyrics were all just imagination. But what's very interesting, is that whole song came true in my life. Ten years later, I ended up moving to Atlanta, meeting a woman younger than myself, marrying her, and having a daughter – so we named her Alexis. And her whole family was actually from New Orleans. So the song actually came true."

It remains a wonder why this standout track was never issued as a single, as it had "hit" written all over it. Cook: "I live in the constant hope that someday, somebody will cover that song. Because I still believe it could be a hit song." And although Bolin possessed a fine singing voice, Fox recalled his new band mate "Agonizing over singing ['Alexis']. Tommy went through a whole lot of changes over, 'How am I going to sing this?' I don't think that where he ended is very far from where he began. It was right in his head to begin with. I remember being very pleased with his vocal performance – 'This is just what we need'."

Another one of the album's standouts is next, the slightly Zeppelin-ish rocker, "Ride the Wind," before once again, things get taken down a notch, with the reflective "Got No Time for Trouble" and a tune comprised solely of vocals and handclaps, "Rather Be Alone with You." Finally, *Bang* wraps up with a Santana-esque Latin rocker, "From Another Time," and another one of the album's very best selections – the haunting, acoustic-tinged epic (which also included strings), "Mystery."

The last piece of business would be the album cover – a photo of all four members on a bed with a young lady (if you read the band's name and the album title together, you'll be able to piece together what the band was going for…in this "un-PC" era). Johnnie Bolin also offered up an interesting factoid about the cover photo. "That's Tommy's head on Domenic's body! Domenic's hands were a lot bigger, plus he had rings on all his fingers. Tommy never wore rings, and his hands were fatter. So other than the hands, you can't tell it's Domenic's body – but it is. They didn't want to shoot the picture again, so they just took his head off and put Tommy's on there."

Released on September 1, 1973, *Bang* was a disappointment chart-wise (peaking at only #122 on the *Billboard 200*), despite it being an incredibly consistent listen and the band touring steadily behind it – and even performing a spirited mini-set on *Don Kirshner's Rock Concert* (which can nowadays be viewed/heard on YouTube). However, after only one more album, 1974's *Miami*, Bolin would boogie from the James Gang (replacing Ritchie Blackmore in Deep Purple for the underrated 1975 release, *Come Taste the Band*).

"Tommy was great," recalls Peters. "He just seemed like the right guy, played the right way – a spectacular guitar player. Very nice guy. Tommy was actually relatively quiet, just the drug thing was hideous. He'd get up in the morning and take like a zillion aspirins. I mean, like 20, just to get going. When he was high, he was great – happy, showed up on time, played great. You could tell immediately when he couldn't find anything, because man, he was just miserable. Just a massively addictive personality." Sadly, Bolin would die under mysterious drug-related circumstances (read all about it in *Touched by Magic*) a little over three years after the release of *Miami* – on December 4, 1976, at the age of 25.

Blank Generation
(Richard Hell & the Voidoids, 1977)

For many, song lyrics that leaned toward the poetic side of things is not what automatically comes to mind when you think about the punk bands to emerge from CBGB's in the mid-late '70s (Ramones, Heartbreakers, Dead Boys, etc.). But in the case of at least two artists, expressive lyrics played a major part – most notably Patti Smith, but also, Richard Hell. And concerning the latter (who listed such poets as Rainer Maria Rilke, William Shakespeare, Bill Knott, Charles Baudelaire, and Lou Reed as influences), this was especially evident throughout *Blank Generation* – the debut LP by his band, Richard Hell & the Voidoids.

Hell (real name: Richard Meyers) was an original member of two renowned CBGB's bands – Television and the Heartbreakers – before forming the Voidoids (a name that Hell nicked from a novel he was working on at the time) in 1976. With Hell handling vocals and bass duties, he was joined in the group by guitarists Robert Quine and Ivan Julian, plus drummer Marc Bell (who later became...Marky Ramone).

Not long after their formation, the band signed with the Ramones and Talking Heads' label, Sire, and on March 14, 1977, began recording their debut at Electric Lady, with Hell and Brill Building songwriter Richard Gottehrer co-producing. However, the band was not pleased with the results, and opted to re-record the entire album at Plaza Sound (the same studio that the Ramones recorded their self-titled debut, located in Radio City Music Hall) – although a handful of tracks from the Electric Lady sessions would ultimately make the final cut.

When all was said and done, the album kicks off with a pair of hyperactive rockers – the delightedly double-entendre-titled "Love Comes in Spurts" and "Liars Beware" (the latter of which manages to fit possibly the most "ohs" in a single song – right at the end). Sonically, it was clear from the get-go that the Voidoids' guitarists did not reproduce the distorted power chords of the Ramones, Pistols, or Clash, but rather, offered much more clean, Strat-y tones. And although he was not the most skilled of bassists,

Hell's playing could get surprisingly busy at certain points, and he also favored playing with his fingers instead of a pick (the latter of which the majority of punk bassists utilized).

"The bass playing I never took seriously," Hell admitted to *Songfacts* in 2013. "And that's probably the main thing that is a weakness of my bands. I feel like I recognize good bass playing and I would have been capable of it, but that I just didn't care. The songs would have benefited from better bass playing, so it's not something I'm proud of. It's not like I have horrible regrets or anything, either. It's just the way things went down. But it sure isn't something that I'm affirming as being good." Despite his low opinion of his bass skills, Hell would prove influential on quite a few subsequent bassists – most notably Mike Watt (of Minutemen, fIREHOSE, and Stooges fame).

Up next is one of my personal favorite Hell ditties, "New Pleasure," which features a very Television-esque sounding guitar opening, and also, a surprisingly Chuck Berry-esque solo. And when speaking with Bell/Ramone for *Long Island Pulse* in 2015, he still held the guitar talents of Quine in high regard. "Unbelievable. He was very influenced by the early jazz guys. He especially loved Miles Davis, and he liked Roland Kirk – he liked all these jazz greats, and he just put it into his guitar playing. But he knew rock, too, and that was important. So he just integrated the two, and that was the style Bob Quine was known for."

The album's slowest tune follows, "Betrayal Takes Two," before the hyperactivity returns with "Down at the Rock and Roll Club" (which obviously alluded to CBGB's, without naming names) and "Who Says?" And then…Hell's best-known tune, the title track – which became an anthem for the CBGB's scene, and contains some of his best lyrics ("I was sayin' let me out of here before I was even born, It's such a gamble when you get a face" and "I belong to the blank generation, And I can take it or leave it each time").

"Well, that was a really early song for me," Hell recalled in the same *Songfacts* chat. "I think it was maybe the second song I ever wrote, in 1973. I really liked the stuff I was writing really early like that. I don't feel like I ever really got stale or anything. I feel like my lyrics and my songwriting sort of held up, that I kept trying new things. But there's something about when you first start where you don't have many habits yet in how you go about writing songs, and you're really ambitious, you want to get everything you can into a song. I'm thinking of the lyrics, really. You want to make the lyrics as effective and interesting as possible. What benefited the writing of that song was that I hadn't written many songs yet and I was really ambitious, I really wanted to make the lyrics do everything I could make words do. So that's how I remember it. It was really exciting to write it."

"Walking on the Water" features slashing guitar lines played in unison by Quine and Julian, while the surprisingly gentle "The Plan" contains music that brings to mind '50s rock n' roll, before the album wraps up with the its longest tune, "Another World," which twists, turns, wiggles, and warbles for over eight minutes – and again features the jagged lead guitar work of Quine, who sounded quite unlike any other rock guitarist at the time.

When I later mentioned to Hell that I felt Quine was one of rock's more underrated guitarists, he replied, "Well, I think by now Quine is really pretty widely acknowledged. It can never be enough, really, because to my mind he's in a class of his own. But we had a fairly long history. We actually recorded for the last time together just a couple of years before he died in I think it was 2004 [May 31, 2004, at the age of 61]. We'd been working on and off, now and then for five or six years steadily at the beginning since 1976. So it was near 30 years. It went through many stages. It wasn't like any one thing."

"I always knew that he was really exceptional and how interesting and inspired his guitar playing was. But I kind of took it for granted at the very beginning. It was also because he was a little bit more inhibited at the very beginning, because it was my group and my songs and he wanted to do what I wanted for them. He wanted to do what was appropriate for the songs, so he was a little bit reserved, because he was worried about finding what worked without us having the familiarity with each other that we eventually had and without him having quite the confidence that he eventually had."

"So at the beginning the way it usually worked is that he would be holding back too much, and I would have to really get him pissed off to play great. [Laughs] Because I just wanted him to break free and go crazy, just have an intensity that he was too nervous to arrive at on his own. So I would really provoke him. That's how a lot of his playing on *Blank Generation* came about – he played really pissed off. He can play really sweet and beautifully, too, though. There are plenty instances of that. But on *Blank Generation*, the material was generally pretty aggressive."

I also once had the opportunity to ask Bell/Ramone, "How different was it writing and recording in the Ramones compared to the Voidoids?" He replied, "Well, the Voidoids is a different kind of band altogether. We were very influenced by say, Miles Davis, John Coltrane – especially our guitar player, Bob Quine. We were into the Velvet Underground, we were into all that stuff. And then we put out the *Blank Generation* album, which [the album's title track] was a major anthem in New York City on the punk scene in '76."

"The difference between the Voidoids and the Ramones is that in the Voidoids, there was different time changes, the songs were longer, the subject matter was different, and there were a lot of stops, a lot of different things that the Ramones couldn't even do. So that's why the Ramones always stuck to the 4/4, 2/4. But that was really the difference. The Voidoids were a lot more intricate."

Released in September 1977, the album featured a photo (taken by Roberta Bayley) of a spikey-haired Hell all by his lonesome, exposing his bare chest, which displays the message, "YOU MAKE ME ___". And like all punk releases issued in the US that year, was *not* a commercial success. Additionally, due to Hell's addiction to substances, the band would prove unable to sustain a steady record-tour-record-tour schedule, and members would begin to come and go. "Unfortunately, he succumbed to heroin, and it definitely got him off the path," explains Bell/Ramone. "It's like me with the alcohol – the booze. I said, 'I had enough,' so I straightened out at an early age. But I just wish he would have stopped and continued, because he could have been somebody. Definitely."

Still, *Blank Generation* is often credited as contributing to getting the initial punk movement moving, has been reissued several times over the years, and has proven quite influential on a wide range of subsequent rockers – including Soundgarden's Kim Thayil, who in 2022, selected Quine and Julian as one of his "11 guitar players who shaped my sound" in *Guitar World*, and said, "Robert Quine from the Voidoids was also a big influence for me. That album, *Blank Generation*, which had Ivan Julian and Robert Quine, was just amazing stuff."

Tokyo Tapes
(Scorpions, 1978)

As mentioned earlier in the entry for *Rock n' Roll Animal*, for some unexplained reason, the '70s gave us more classic live rock albums than any other decade. Case in point, Kiss' *Alive!*, Cheap Trick's *At Budokan*, UFO's *Strangers in the Night*, Thin Lizzy's *Live and Dangerous*, and certainly, the Scorpions' *Tokyo Tapes*, among countless others. But just as it appeared as though the German band was finally going to "go global" commercially (and this assumption soon proved to be correct), one of the most important members of the band was about to exit.

Originally formed during the '60s in Hanover, the Scorpions saw many members come and go for the first few years of their existence. But by 1974, a semi-stable line-up was finally solidified – singer Klaus Meine, lead guitarist Uli Jon Roth, rhythm guitarist Rudolf Schenker, and bassist Francis Buchholz (although just like Spinal Tap, they went through various drummers...until Herman Rarebell brought stability to the position in 1977). With five studio albums to their credit by '77 (*Lonesome Crow, Fly to the Rainbow, In Trance, Virgin Killer*, and *Taken by Force*), the time was right to put together their first concert recording – recorded over two nights during their first-ever Japanese tour (on April 24 and 27, 1978, at Nakano Sun Plaza, in Tokyo).

"I finally said, 'I'll do one more tour' – and that was Japan – 'And then I really need to leave, because I want to do the other thing'," recalled Roth in the book, *German Metal Machine: Scorpions in the '70s*, about wanting to skedaddle and launch a solo career. "And that was that. So we did *Tokyo Tapes*, and that was the final thing." And as Buchholz added in the same book, "We had security people, screaming girls everywhere. So, it was totally different from what we had experienced in Europe before. And the recordings went very well."

"I remember [producer] Dieter Dierks was in the mobile studio, which was parked outside of the hall, and I was so happy that I did not have to repair one single note. Everything I played – with drums together – is what is on the record. I'm very happy about those recordings." And Rarebell backed up the bassist's claim. "This is a real live album. I can't do overdubs as a drummer. What I play is what you get, because you always have the 'room sound.' You can – if you fuck up in the solo – repair that. That's easy. But as far as I remember, there was hardly any repairs on that album. It is a real live album."

As with the aforementioned classic live recordings of the '70s, the double LP *Tokyo Tapes* features renditions of many of the Scorps' best tracks up this point – "Pictured Life," the Uli-sung "Polar Nights," "In Trance," "We'll Burn the Sky" (a tune that Uli's girlfriend, Monika Dannemann, wrote about her previous boyfriend, James Marshall Hendrix), "In Search of the Peace of Mind," "Fly to the Rainbow," "Speedy's Coming," "Dark Lady," etc. However two top tunes were noticeably absent from the album's original 18-song tracklisting – "Hell Cat" and "The Sails of Charon" – while almost-unlistenable back-to-back covers of "Hound Dog" and "Long Tall Sally" were befuddlingly included instead.

Concerning "Hell Cat," it was just a matter of running out of room (as it was indeed included on the album's expanded 2015 remastered version, along with other previously unreleased selections). But as Roth told me in the October 2017 issue of *Vintage Guitar*, it was for an entirely different reason why "Charon" was nowhere to be found. "We weren't really able to play it convincingly. We tried a few times in rehearsal, but it fell short of my expectations. It was one of those things I had recorded myself except for drums and vocals. When it came to the stage, we didn't get it together, so I never thought it fit our live set. In the early 2000's, I did an orchestral version, then later I started integrating it in various guises. It went through some metamorphosis along the way, but the theme always remained even if the arrangement changed."

And while *Tokyo Tapes* did not set the charts alight Stateside upon its release in January 1979, it *did* succeed in creating a buzz about the band worldwide – resulting in the group signing on with the US-based Q Prime Management, switching record labels (from RCA to Mercury), and soon, touring North America for the first time ever. However, even with massive success on the horizon, Roth had

had enough. "But even *Tokyo Tapes*, my heart wasn't in it. I mean, while we played the concerts, my heart was in it. It was very exciting to play in Japan for the first time, and we did our best shows there – certainly the best ones that I had ever done with them. And some of that was captured on the album. But afterwards, I didn't take any interest in the mix."

"And with hindsight, I think that was a big mistake, because I was very, very unhappy with the final mix when I heard it. I felt the guitars were mixed all wrong, and the overall sound I wasn't so happy with. And then afterwards, I was very surprised about the great success that this album had over the years. And still has. It became something iconic. But those were pretty much the best shows we did – from the entire period of the Scorpions. It was a very definitive kind of statement."

Tokyo Tapes also proved to be incredibly influential and inspirational to a wide range of subsequent renowned rock musicians, including Exodus' Steve "Zetro" Souza ("Every single song on that album kicks ass"), Anvil's Lips ("For guitar players, it's Bible pages"), and Smashing Pumpkins' Billy Corgan ("You listen to *Tokyo Tapes*, far better live band than just about everybody"). But according to Eddie Trunk, there is a reason why *Tokyo Tapes* seems to get lost in the shuffle whenever the "great live rock albums of all-time" discussion arises.

"I think it's a great live record and there's great stuff on there. I think the reason why it's overlooked – it's overlooked in America, for sure – is because in reality, everything that the band did in the '70s is overlooked in America. To this day. So, it's never going to get any sort of real acclaim in this country, because people to this day do not know that material. They don't know the Scorpions from that period of time. There's no point of reference for them for it. So, I think that is the reason why the landmark records of the '70s that get a lot of acclaim are records that had a great deal of success in America."

Lastly, Rarebell will get the final word – as he attempts to solve the mystery of why so many now-classic live rock albums were issued during the '70s. "Because the bands were great in those times! The secret is everybody could play their instruments. You didn't have to fiddle about. And the '70s produced really all of the great guitar players, when you think about it. So I think people were proud to show how good they can play live. And the strength of the Scorpions was always the live performance. We could deliver live – like on the album. Everybody who heard the Scorpions live told us this afterwards – 'You guys play like the record.' This was the strength of the Scorpions – to be a great live band."

Deface the Music
(Utopia, 1980)

Usually when a rock band is on the cusp of major breakthrough commercial success, they continue on in the same stylistic direction that got them to this highly desired point. But there have been instances in rock history where artists opted to take unexpected sharp left turns, rather than playing it safe – case in point, Neil Young with *Time Fades Away*, Lou Reed with *Metal Machine Music*, Beastie Boys with *Paul's Boutique*, Faith No More with *Angel Dust*, and certainly, Utopia with *Deface the Music.*

Although beginning life as a Todd Rundgren-led band (who had already established himself as a pop star and highly-sought after producer), Utopia started as an artsy-fartsy prog band, before finding their definitive line-up in 1977 and fine-tuning their sound/approach – Todd on guitar, Kasim Sulton on bass, Roger Powell on keyboards, and Willie Wilcox on drums…with all four taking turns behind the mic.

"Because Todd is such a creative force, and Utopia was really Todd's band, he always kind of had a good idea of what the next record was going to be," Sulton explained in the book, *John Winston Ono Lennon.* "What *he* thought the next record should be for the band. So, when we did *Adventures in Utopia* – which I believe was 1980 [actually, the very end of 1979, and possessed a Cars-meets-Queen, radio-friendly sound] – that record was pretty successful for us. Todd – being Todd – does not want to do the same record again. And I think that he went out of his way to try and figure out, 'What can we possibly do that's *nothing* like the last record we did'?"

"Both myself, Roger, and Willie said, 'I think we found something that worked. Why don't we capitalize on it and do another record exactly like it? We sold almost half a million records with *Adventures in Utopia*…maybe we'll crack that half a million on the next one if we make a similar record?' And Todd didn't want to have *anything* to do with that. So, I think he being the type of artist that Todd is, he would rather have done something completely different – something completely left field…which is how we wound up with *Deface the Music*. It couldn't be more of a departure. Now, why that album? Why a Beatles parody album? I have no idea what Todd was thinking when he came up with that idea."

"All I know is that when we got up to the studio in Bearsville to start recording our next record – which ultimately became *Deface the Music* – Todd had already written three or four songs for the record. So, pretty much almost half the record was already done before we got there. And he just said, 'This is what we're doing.' You didn't really want to argue with Todd. You just said, 'OK...I guess this is what we're doing'."

And despite an assumption by some that the cult success of the Rutles (another Beatle-parody spoof around that time) may have inspired Utopia to also pay tribute to the Fab Four in a light-hearted manner, Sulton explained this was simply not the case. "I don't think so. I think Todd is a big Beatles fan, and he appreciates their contribution to popular music. It was just something that seemed like a good idea to him at the time. I think there was a time when we were like, 'Well, we can't do that because it's just *too* similar.' So, there were a couple of points where we had to make slight little changes in the music – to avoid being sued!"

Listening to *Deface the Music* today, it is quite uncanny how close the Utopia lads replicated the sound and vibe of everyone's favorite Liverpudlians from start to finish. In fact, the inspiration behind each of the album's thirteen tracks can be traced back to specific Beatles tunes – several of which Sulton was willing to discuss. "'I Just Want to Touch You' was the opening track for that record, and that was our attempt at re-writing 'I Want to Hold Your Hand.' So, we wanted to open the record with something that was extremely catchy and recognizable, and reminiscent of 'I Want to Hold Your Hand' – which is how we came up with 'I Just Want to Touch You.' I did not have a hand in writing that – I think that was one of the ones that Todd initially wrote and said, 'This is what the album is going to be like'."

"I think Todd and Roger wrote 'Hoi Poloi' – it's just a really catchy melody and lyric. I think what song that came from...probably 'Penny Lane.' Because every song on the record is reminiscent of a Beatles song that is similar to that. And if you listen to the bassline in 'Penny Lane,' it is similar to 'Hoi Poloi.' 'Silly Boy' was one of mine – I just recall coming up with a basic idea for a chord change, and a little bit of a melody, bringing it to the band, and Todd saying, 'OK, I know what to do with this one,' and finishing the song for me! [Laughs] 'Alone' was one of mine – it was supposed to be like 'Michelle.' 'All Smiles' was one of mine also, but I don't remember anything about it – other than just coming up with the chord changes and bringing it to the band."

"Everybody had little ideas of songs that they were doing, that they would bring in, and then we would finish them as a band. So, somebody would come in with a chorus, somebody would come in with a verse, somebody would come in with a bridge, and we'd jumble everything together – until we had an album's worth of material." Additionally, other standouts on the album included "Take It Home" (perhaps the best tune on the entire LP, and bearing a resemblance to "Day Tripper"), "Feel Too Good" (a la "Getting Better"), and "That's Not Right" (an obvious nod to "Eight Days a Week").

Released on September 24, 1980, *Deface the Music* failed to build on the chart success of its predecessor – reaching only #67, with no charting singles (by comparison, *Adventures* peaked at #32 on the *Billboard 200,* and one of its singles, the Sulton-sung "Set Me Free," reached #27 on the *Billboard Hot 100*). But that's not to say the band did not properly promote the release in an attempt to bring it to a wide audience.

"We did a whole tour like that [dressed like the Beatles circa their first *Ed Sullivan* appearance]," adds Sulton. "We had to do a video to promote the first single from the record ['I Just Want to Touch You'], and we wanted it to be reminiscent of a '60s video. This guy was a local artist in the Woodstock area, and he introduces the band at the beginning of that video, and we just tried to make it like...if you go back and look at these early '60s videos of bands and the little vignettes that they made for whatever single they had at that time, you'll see they're a lot like what we did for 'I Just Want to Touch You'."

Another obvious blow to *Deface the Music* enjoying any significant chart success – not only was it issued shortly before the tragic assassination of John Lennon [on December 8, 1980], but it later came to light that Lennon's murderer, Mark David Chapman, was a major Utopia fan, and allegedly, an 8-track tape of *Deface the Music* was found amongst his belongings in a hotel room he was staying at when he committed the heinous crime.

Listening to *Deface the Music* today, the album certainly is a fun, witty, and curious listen, and when compared to the band's best albums of that era (particularly 1982's self-titled release and the aforementioned *Adventures*) – still sticks out like a glorious sore thumb. Which leads to the question…*was this Rundgren's goal all along?*

Business as Usual
(Men at Work, 1981)

1981? *Business as Usual* is not an album from '81! It hit big in the summer/fall of '82, well into '83, right? Well…*yes and no*. It turns out that one of the first albums that MTV put their muscle behind and clearly made a difference in its success – and gave us the classic singles/videos "Who Can It Be Now?", "Down Under," and "Be Good Johnny" – was indeed issued some time earlier than when it arrived Stateside.

Originally formed in Melbourne, Australia during 1978, the classic Men at Work line-up consisted of singer/guitarist (and primary songwriter) Colin Hay, flautist/keyboardist Greg Ham, guitarist Ron Strykert, bassist John Rees, and drummer Jerry Speiser. By 1981, the quintet had obtained a recording contract with CBS Records. But according to Hay in the book *MTV Ruled the World: The Early Years of Music Video*, one of the world's best-known and most successful labels pulled a fast one.

"The record label that we signed to was CBS, which then became Sony-CBS in Australia. I supposed we had a mistrust of record companies, and we were very suspicious of their motivations. We were given reason for that, too. I mean, we had almost a criminally bad record deal, even for then. It wasn't as bad as the acts would have gotten in the '50s and '60s, but our deal was horrible. But it was the only game in town. It was the only label that was interested in us, and it was really one of the only labels that we were interested in."

Recorded from March through September 1981 at Richmond Recorders in Melbourne, and produced by a chap by the name of Peter McIan, Men at Work specialized in a sound that was subsequently often described as sounding quite Police-like, due to MaW's fondness for combining reggae, new wave, and pop hooks all together. But while the Police could get a bit experimental ("Behind My Camel") or just downright odd ("Mother"), on *Business as Usual*, Men at Work played it much more straight.

Opening up the album was one of the best pop-rock tunes to be driven by an instantly memorable sax line, "Who Can It Be Now?" (and also creatively features a kick drum replicating the knocking on a door). And by this point, it's impossible to think of the tune without immediately picturing its accompanying music video – which includes Hay playing the role of a rather paranoid chap inside an apartment.

"The videos that we did were very inexpensive," Hay explained in the same *MTV Ruled the World* book. "I think 'Who Can It Be Now?' cost $5,000. It was shot by two guys, primarily John Whitteron and Tony Stevens. They were two guys who were responsible for a lot of the other videos that we did. It was a case really of finding a good location and coming up with a couple of ideas that would be interesting. Primarily, Greg Ham and myself came up with what we would shoot, in collaboration with John and Tony. We never went to the cops and got permission or anything like that. We just went in, shot, and got out of there as quickly as we could, if we weren't supposed to be somewhere."

"I Can See It in Your Eyes" was an upbeat new wave ditty, before what has become probably the group's best-known tune, "Down Under" (as in "the land down under"- in reference to the group's homeland). And similar to the album's opener, it is a musical motif supplied by Ham that propelled the tune (but this time, performed on flute), while the tune contains much more of an obvious reggae-ish vibe. And as original MTV VJ Alan Hunter remembers, the most memorable part of the song's lyrics was food-based. "I think I did interview them, because I remember asking about Vegemite. That was the only pertinent question, 'What is Vegemite?' I think all of America learned a little bit more about them and how nasty Vegemite was." In case you were wondering, according to dictonary.com, Vegemite is "an Australian vegetable extract used as a flavoring or spread."

And once again, it was the song's imaginative video (which saw the group trapsing across what appears to be a desert, plus a restaurant and…an opium den!) that provided a memorable visual accompaniment. "'Down Under,' we had to fight for another $1,000 from the record label. That one cost $6,000. The great thing about that I think was just finding the sand mine at Cronulla, which was a suburb of Sydney, that great location at the end of the video, that we use to come over the top of the hill. I think that was a beautiful shot, that clip, which is a strong visual and really worth doing. It was kind of an inspired location to find, that sand mine." Also, it should be noted that Men at Work and their record label would be sued in 2009 by Larrikin Music, when the music publisher felt that the flute riff in "Down Under" was a tad too reminiscent of a nursery rhyme they owned the rights to, "Kookaburra" (the Federal Court of Australia eventually ruled in favor of Larrikin, who were awarded 5% of the song's royalties going back to 2002).

Up next was another tune that opens with some Ham sax, "Underground," before "Helpless Automaton" closes the first side of the vinyl/cassette version, and features the aforementioned chap on lead vocals (the first – and only – time on the LP that a member other than Hay was the primary singer). The second side/half begins with admittedly one of the album's least memorable tunes, "People Just Love to Play with Words," but everything quickly gets back on track with another of the album's best ditties, "Be Good Johnny" (whose title is an obvious play on the Chuck Berry classic, "Johnny B. Goode"). And like "Who Can It Be Now?" and "Down Under," had a memorable music video filmed for it, which included a young actor playing the role of Johnny.

Hay: "The young kid we found to play 'Johnny' was great. I think more than anything, our videos had our personality to them. Because, as I said, we didn't have any money for effects or fancy locations or extra stuff. It was just very much, 'OK, here's the band, and here's a few ideas.' It was pretty much just do everything ourselves, because that's all we really had at our disposal. It was an enormous amount of fun doing them. We really enjoyed putting them together." And while there were no other hits to be found throughout the remainder of the album, the material still proves to be quite worthwhile – "Touching the Untouchables," "Catch a Star," and the outstanding album closer (and one of MaW's more underrated tunes), "Down by the Sea."

Business as Usual (whose front cover featured a plugged-in guitar amp, with mountains atop) would be released on

November 9, 1981 in their homeland, but would not appear in the States until April 22, 1982. Why? Let's let Hay take it away. "We had supporters from CBS affiliates in different parts of the world. There was a convention around that particular time, and they played 'Who Can It Be Now?' at that convention. And there was the CBS label in Switzerland, the CBS label in Israel, different countries around the world that saw the potential of our band and released the album, and it did very well. But the country that really was the hardest country to crack was the United States, because our album was actually rejected twice. The A&R department didn't want to release our album, because they didn't think there was a hit on it. Even though it was gaining all this success in different parts of the world, they couldn't see it."

"We were amazed at the level of idiocy that we struck with record company executives, who were in strong positions of power. We just thought, more than anything, the music business was like an obstacle course. It had nothing to do with what we were interested in, which was to be as creative as possible and get to as many people as possible. This was an obstacle course that had to be maneuvered and negotiated."

And it turns out that Men at Work were experts at maneuvering and negotiating the treacherous music biz, as *Business as Usual* quickly became a global blockbuster – topping the album charts in the US, UK, Australia, Canada, New Zealand, and Norway. And singles-wise, both "Who Can It Be Now?" and "Down Under" topped the *Billboard Hot 100* (with the latter holding that spot for an impressive four weeks). And the album proved to be a steady seller – coming in at the #2 spot on Billboard's year-end album list for 1983 (yes, a full year after the album's initial release), and at last count, has been certified 6x platinum in the US.

And while the group would enjoy further success (but admittedly not as massive as their debut) with a sophomore effort, *Cargo*, in 1983, Men at Work would soon be out of work, only remaining together for one more album – the forgettable *Two Hearts*, in 1985. As of this book's writing, Men at Work are back in business, but Hay is the sole remaining member from the group's glory days (with Ham passing away in 2012, at the age of 58).

Looking back on the success of *Business as Usual* years later, Hay described it as "I think that radio was still the thing that really created the success with the band, certainly the initial success. And then MTV 'rammed it home,' if you like. It reinforced that and gave a really strong visual to the band, that really did help. Because I think our videos had some sort of personality that people responded to." And for a spell, the record buying masses certainly responded to *Business as Usual*.

Sources

Black Sabbath (Black Sabbath) - Heavy Consequence: February 13, 2020

Paranoid (Black Sabbath) - Heavy Consequence: September 18, 2020

Harvest (Neil Young) - Best Classic Bands: 2020

Thick as a Brick (Jethro Tull) - Classic Rock: 1970s Special, issue 1

The Rise and Fall of Ziggy Stardust and the Spiders from Mars (David Bowie) - Best Classic Bands: 2020

Raw Power (Iggy & the Stooges) - Vintage Guitar: December 2019

Spectrum (Billy Cobham) - Vintage Guitar: July 2020

Kiss (Kiss) - Heavy Consequence: February 18, 2019

Ritchie Blackmore's Rainbow (Rainbow) - Best Classic Bands: 2020

Rising (Rainbow) - Vintage Guitar

Never Mind the Bollocks…Here's the Sex Pistols (Sex Pistols) - Vintage Guitar: November 2018

Highway to Hell (AC/DC) - Heavy Consequence: July 26, 2019

Permanent Waves (Rush) - Best Classic Bands: 2020

British Steel (Judas Priest) - Heavy Consequence: April 14, 2020

Iron Maiden (Iron Maiden) - Heavy Consequence: April 14, 2019

Back in Black (AC/DC) - Heavy Consequence: July 21, 2020

Discipline (King Crimson) - Classic Rock: September 28, 2021

Bad Brains (Bad Brains) - *Punk! Hardcore! Reggae! PMA! Bad Brains!* book, 2014

The Number of the Beast (Iron Maiden) - Heavy Consequence: March 22, 2022

All other entries were penned exclusively for this book.

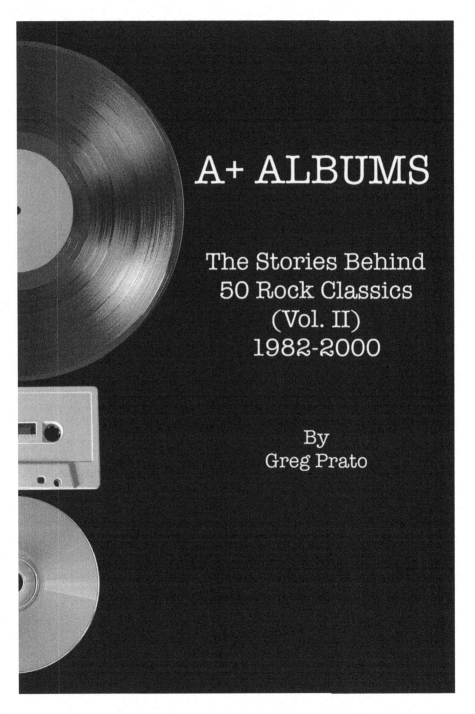

A+ ALBUMS

The Stories Behind 50 Rock Classics (Vol. II) 1982-2000

By
Greg Prato

If you enjoyed *Vol. I*, be sure to check out *Vol. II!*

Other Books by Greg Prato

Music:

A Devil on One Shoulder and an Angel on the Other: The Story of Shannon Hoon and Blind Melon

Touched by Magic: The Tommy Bolin Story

Grunge Is Dead: The Oral History of Seattle Rock Music

No Schlock...Just Rock! (A Journalistic Journey: 2003-2008)

MTV Ruled the World: The Early Years of Music Video

The Eric Carr Story

Too High to Die: Meet the Meat Puppets

The Faith No More & Mr. Bungle Companion

Overlooked/Underappreciated: 354 Recordings That Demand Your Attention

Over the Electric Grapevine: Insight into Primus and the World of Les Claypool

Punk! Hardcore! Reggae! PMA! Bad Brains!

Iron Maiden: '80 '81

Survival of the Fittest: Heavy Metal in the 1990s

Scott Weiland: Memories of a Rock Star

German Metal Machine: Scorpions in the '70s

The Other Side of Rainbow

Shredders!: The Oral History of Speed Guitar (And More)

The Yacht Rock Book: The Oral History of the Soft, Smooth Sounds of the 60s, 70s, and 80s

100 Things Pearl Jam Fans Should Know & Do Before They Die

The 100 Greatest Rock Bassists

Long Live Queen: Rock Royalty Discuss Freddie, Brian, John & Roger

King's X: The Oral History

Facts on Tracks: Stories Behind 100 Rock Classics

Dark Black and Blue: The Soundgarden Story

Take It Off: Kiss Truly Unmasked

A Rockin' Rollin' Man: Bon Scott Remembered

Avatar of the Electric Guitar: The Genius of Jimi Hendrix

BONZO: 30 Rock Drummers Remember the Legendary John Bonham

John Winston Ono Lennon

Shannon

Iconic Guitar Gear

Sports:

Sack Exchange: The Definitive Oral History of the 1980s New York Jets

Dynasty: The Oral History of the New York Islanders, 1972-1984

Just Out of Reach: The 1980s New York Yankees

The Seventh Year Stretch: New York Mets, 1977-1983

Butt Fumbles, Fake Spikes, Mud Bowls & Heidi Games: The Top 100 Debacles of the New York Jets

Made in United States
North Haven, CT
22 November 2022

27072152R00157